THE WINSLOW BOY

and two other plays by

TERENCE RATTIGAN

D0676386

For a description of this book
and some information about
the author, see back of cover.

THE WINSLOW BOY

with two other plays

FRENCH WITHOUT TEARS
FLARE PATH

TERENCE RATTIGAN

PAN BOOKS LTD : LONDON

First published by Hamish Hamilton Ltd.
("The Winslow Boy," 1946; "French Without Tears," 1937;
"Flare Path," 1942)

This edition published 1950 by Pan Books Ltd.,
8 Headfort Place, London, S.W.1

Printed in Great Britain by
Wyman & Sons, Ltd., London, Fakenham and Reading

CONTENTS

THE WINSLOW BOY

For
MASTER PAUL CHANNON
in the hope that he will live to see a world
in which this play will point no moral

THE CHARACTERS
(in order of their appearance)

RONNIE WINSLOW
VIOLET
ARTHUR WINSLOW
GRACE WINSLOW
DICKIE WINSLOW
CATHERINE WINSLOW
JOHN WATHERSTONE
DESMOND CURRY
MISS BARNES
FRED
SIR ROBERT MORTON

The action of the play takes place in Arthur Winslow's house in Kensington, London, and extends over two years of a period preceding the war of 1914–1918.

ACT I
A Sunday morning in July

ACT II
An evening in April (nine months later).

ACT III
An evening in January (nine months later).

ACT IV
An afternoon in June (five months later).

The Winslow Boy was first produced at the Lyric Theatre, London, on May 23rd, 1946, with the following cast:

RONNIE WINSLOW	Michael Newell
VIOLET	Kathleen Harrison
ARTHUR WINSLOW	Frank Cellier
GRACE WINSLOW	Madge Compton
DICKIE WINSLOW	Jack Watling
CATHERINE WINSLOW	Angela Baddeley
JOHN WATHERSTONE	Alastair Bannerman
DESMOND CURRY	Clive Morton
MISS BARNES	Mona Washbourne
FRED	Brian Harding
SIR ROBERT MORTON	Emlyn Williams

The play directed by Glen Byam Shaw

ACT I

SCENE: *The drawing-room of a house in Courtfield Gardens, South Ken-*
sington, on a morning in July, at some period not long before the war
of 1914–1918.

The furnishings betoken solid but not undecorative upper middle-
class comfort.

On the rise of the curtain A BOY *of about fourteen, dressed in the*
uniform of an Osborne naval cadet, is discovered. There is something
rigid and tense in his attitude, and his face is blank and without
expression.

There is the sound of someone in the hall. As the sound comes
nearer, he looks despairingly round, as if contemplating flight. An
elderly maid [VIOLET] *comes in, and stops in astonishment at sight*
of him.

VIOLET: Master Ronnie!

RONNIE (*with ill-managed sang-froid*): Hello, Violet.

VIOLET: Why, good gracious! We weren't expecting you back
till Tuesday.

RONNIE: Yes, I know.

VIOLET: Why ever didn't you let us know you were coming,
you silly boy? Your mother should have been at the station to
meet you. The idea of a child like you wandering all over London
by yourself. I never did. However did you get in? By the
garden, I suppose.

RONNIE: No. The front door. I rang and Cook opened it.

VIOLET: And where's your trunk and your tuck-box?

RONNIE: Upstairs. The taximan carried them up——

VIOLET: Taximan? You took a taxi?

RONNIE *nods.*

All by yourself? Well, I don't know what little boys are coming to, I'm sure. What your father and mother will say, I don't
know——

RONNIE: Where are they, Violet?

VIOLET: Church, of course.

RONNIE (*vacantly*): Oh, yes. It's Sunday, isn't it?

II

VIOLET: What's the matter with you? What have they been doing to you at Osborne?

RONNIE (*sharply*): What do you mean?

VIOLET: They seem to have made you a bit soft in the head, or something. Well—I suppose I'd better get your unpacking done— Mr. Dickie's been using your chest of drawers for all his dress clothes and things. I'll just clear 'em out and put 'em on his bed—that's what I'll do. He can find room for 'em somewhere else.

RONNIE: Shall I help you?

VIOLET (*scornfully*): I know *your* help. With *your* help I'll be at it all day. No, you just wait down here for your mother and father. They'll be back in a minute.

> RONNIE *nods and turns hopelessly away.* VIOLET *looks at his retreating back, puzzled.*

Well?

RONNIE (*turning*): Yes?

VIOLET: Don't I get a kiss or are you too grown up for that now?

RONNIE: Sorry, Violet.

> *He goes up and is enveloped in her ample bosom.*

VIOLET: That's better. My, what a big boy you're getting!

> *She holds him at arm's length and inspects him.*

Quite the little naval officer, aren't you?

RONNIE (*smiling forlornly*): Yes. That's right.

VIOLET: Well, well—I must be getting on——

> *She goes out.* RONNIE, *left alone, resumes his attitude of utter dejection. He takes out of his pocket a letter in a sealed envelope. After a second's hesitation, he opens it, and reads the contents. The perusal appears to increase his misery.*
>
> *He makes for a moment as if to tear it up; then changes his mind again, and puts it back in his pocket. He gets up and takes two or three quick steps towards the hall door. Then he stops, uncertainly.*
>
> *There is the sound of voices in the hall.* RONNIE *jumps to his feet; then, with a strangled sob runs to the garden door, and down the iron steps into the garden.*
>
> *The hall door opens and the rest of the Winslow family file in. They are* ARTHUR *and* GRACE—*Ronnie's father and mother—and* DICKIE *and* CATHERINE—*his brother and sister. All are carrying prayer-books, and wear that faintly unctuous after-church air.*
>
> ARTHUR *leans heavily on a stick. He is a man of about sixty, with a rather deliberately cultured patriarchal air.* GRACE *is about*

ten years younger, with the faded remnants of prettiness. DICKIE *is an Oxford undergraduate, large, noisy and cheerful.* CATHERINE, *approaching thirty, has an air of masculinity about her which is at odd variance with her mother's intense feminity.*

GRACE (*as she enters*): But he's so old, dear. From the back of the church you really can't hear a word he says——

ARTHUR: He's a good man, Grace.

GRACE: But what's the use of being good, if you're inaudible?

CATHERINE: A problem in ethics for you, Father.

> ARTHUR *is standing with his back to the fireplace. He looks round at the open garden door.*

ARTHUR: There's a draught, Grace.

> GRACE *goes to the door and closes it.*

GRACE: Oh, dear—it's coming on to rain.

DICKIE: I'm on Mother's side. The old boy's so doddery now he can hardly finish the course at all. I timed him to-day. It took him seventy-five seconds dead from a flying start to reach the pulpit, and then he needed the whip coming round the bend. I call that pretty bad going.

ARTHUR: I don't think that's very funny, Richard.

DICKIE: Oh, don't you, Father?

ARTHUR: Doddery though Mr. Jackson may seem now, I very much doubt if he failed in his pass mods, when he was at Oxford.

DICKIE (*aggrieved*): Dash it—Father—you promised not to mention that again this vac——

GRACE: You did, you know, Arthur.

ARTHUR: There was a condition to my promise—if you remember —that Dickie should provide me with reasonable evidence of his intentions to work.

DICKIE: Well, haven't I, Father? Didn't I stay in all last night— a Saturday night—and work?

ARTHUR: You stayed in, Dickie. I would be the last to deny that.

GRACE: You *were* making rather a noise, dear, with that old gramophone of yours. I really can't believe you could have been doing much work with that going on all the time——

DICKIE: Funnily enough, Mother, it helps me to concentrate——

ARTHUR: Concentrate on what?

DICKIE: Work, of course.

ARTHUR: That was not what you appeared to be concentrating

on when I came down to fetch a book—sleep, may I say, having been rendered out of the question by the hideous sounds emanating from this room.

DICKIE: Edwina and her father had just looked in on their way to the Graham's dance—they only stayed a minute.

GRACE: What an idiotic girl that is! Oh, sorry, Dickie—I was forgetting. You're rather keen on her, aren't you?

ARTHUR: You would have had ample proof of that fact, Grace, if you had seen them in the attitude I caught them in last night.

DICKIE: We were practising the Bunny Hug.

GRACE: The what, dear?

DICKIE: The Bunny Hug. It's the new dance.

CATHERINE (*helpfully*): It's like the Turkey Trot—only more dignified.

GRACE: Oh, I thought that was the tango.

DICKIE: No. More like a Fox-trot, really. Something between a Boston Glide and a Kangaroo Hop.

ARTHUR: We appear to be straying from the point. Whatever animal was responsible for the posture I found you in does not alter the fact that you have not done one single stroke of work this vacation.

DICKIE: Oh. Well, I do work awfully fast, you know—once I get down to it.

ARTHUR: That assumption can hardly be based on experience, I take it.

DICKIE: Dash it, Father! You are laying in to me this morning.

ARTHUR: It's time you found out, Dickie, that I'm not spending two hundred pounds a year keeping you at Oxford, merely to learn to dance the Bunny Hop.

DICKIE: Hug, Father.

ARTHUR: The exact description of the obscenity is immaterial.

GRACE: Father's quite right, you know, dear. You really have been going the pace a bit, this vac.

DICKIE: Yes, I know, Mother—but the season's nearly over now——

GRACE (*with a sigh*): I wish you were as good about work as Ronnie.

DICKIE (*hotly*): I like that. That's a bit thick, I must say. All Ronnie ever has to do with his footling little homework is to add two and two.

ARTHUR: Ronnie is at least proving a good deal more successful in adding two and two than you were at his age.

DICKIE (*now furious*): Oh, yes. *I* know. *I* know. *He* got into Osborne and *I* failed. That's going to be brought up again——

GRACE: Nobody's bringing it up, dear——

DICKIE: Oh, yes they are. It's going to be brought up against me all my life. Ronnie's the good little boy, I'm the bad little boy. You've just stuck a couple of labels on us that nothing on earth is ever going to change.

GRACE: Don't be so absurd, dear——

DICKIE: It's not absurd. It's quite true. Isn't it, Kate?

　　　CATHERINE *looks up from a book she has been reading in the corner.*

CATHERINE: I'm sorry, Dickie. I haven't been listening. Isn't what quite true?

DICKIE: That in the eyes of Mother and Father nothing that Ronnie does is ever wrong, and nothing I do is ever right?

CATHERINE (*after a pause*): If I were you, Dickie, dear, I'd go and have a nice lie down before lunch.

DICKIE (*after a further pause*): Perhaps you're right.

　　　He goes towards the hall door.

ARTHUR: If you're going to your room I suggest you take that object with you.

　　　He points to a gramophone—1912 model, with horn—lying on a table.

It's out of place in a drawing-room.

　　　DICKIE, *with an air of hauteur, picks up the gramophone and carries it to the door.*

It might help you to concentrate on the work you're going to do this afternoon.

　　　DICKIE *stops at the door, and then turns slowly.*

DICKIE (*with dignity*): That is out of the question, I'm afraid.

ARTHUR: Indeed? Why?

DICKIE: I have an engagement with Miss Gunn.

ARTHUR: On a Sunday afternoon? Escorting her to the National Gallery, no doubt?

DICKIE: No. The Victoria and Albert Museum.

　　　He goes out with as much dignity as is consistent with the carrying of a very bulky gramophone.

GRACE: How stupid of him to say that about labels. There's no truth in it at all—is there, Kate?

CATHERINE (*deep in her book*): No, Mother.

GRACE: Oh, dear, it's simply pelting. What are you reading, Kate?

CATHERINE: Len Rogers's Memoirs.

GRACE: Who's Len Rogers?

CATHERINE: A Trades Union Leader.

GRACE: Does John know you're a Radical?

CATHERINE: Oh, yes.

GRACE: And a Suffragette?

CATHERINE: Certainly.

GRACE (*with a smile*): And he stills wants to marry you?

CATHERINE: He seems to.

GRACE: Oh, by the way, I've asked him to come early for lunch—so that he can have a few words with Father first.

CATHERINE: Good idea. I hope you've been primed, have you, Father?

ARTHUR (*who has been nearly asleep*): What's that?

CATHERINE: You know what you're going to say to John, don't you? You're not going to let me down and forbid the match, or anything, are you? Because I warn you, if you do, I shall elope——

ARTHUR (*taking her hand*): Never fear, my dear. I'm far too delighted at the prospect of getting you off our hands at last.

CATHERINE (*smiling*): I'm not sure I like that "at last."

GRACE: Do you love him, dear?

CATHERINE: John? Yes, I do.

GRACE: You're such a funny girl. You never show your feelings much, do you? You don't behave as if you were in love.

CATHERINE: How does one behave as if one is in love?

ARTHUR: One doesn't read Len Rogers. One reads Byron.

CATHERINE: I do both.

ARTHUR: An odd combination.

CATHERINE: A satisfying one.

GRACE: I meant—you don't talk about him much, do you?

CATHERINE: No. I suppose I don't.

GRACE (*sighing*): I don't think you modern girls have the feelings our generation did. It's this New Woman attitude.

CATHERINE: Very well, Mother. I love John in every way that a woman can love a man, and far, far more than he loves me. Does that satisfy you?

GRACE (*embarrassed*): Well, really, Kate darling—I didn't ask for anything quite like that—— (*To* ARTHUR) What are you laughing at, Arthur?

ARTHUR (*chuckling*): One up to the New Woman.

GRACE: Nonsense. She misunderstood me, that's all. (*At the window.*) Just look at the rain! (*Turning to* CATHERINE.) Kate, darling, does Desmond know about you and John?

CATHERINE: I haven't told him. On the other hand, if he hasn't guessed, he must be very dense.

ARTHUR: He *is* very dense.

GRACE: Oh, no. He's quite clever, if you really get under his skin.

ARTHUR: Oddly enough, I've never had that inclination.

GRACE: I think he's a dear. Kate darling, you *will* be kind to him, won't you?

CATHERINE (*patiently*): Yes, Mother. Of course, I will.

GRACE: He's really a very good sort——

> *She breaks off suddenly and stares out of the window.*

Hullo! There's someone in our garden.

CATHERINE (*coming to look*): Where?

GRACE (*pointing*): Over there, do you see?

CATHERINE: No.

GRACE: He's just gone behind that bush. It was a boy, I think. Probably Mrs. Williamson's awful little Dennis.

CATHERINE (*leaving the window*): Well, whoever it is must be getting terribly wet.

GRACE: Why can't he stick to his own garden?

> *There is a sound of voices outside in the hall.*

GRACE: Was that John.

CATHERINE: It sounded like it.

GRACE (*after listening*): Yes. It's John. (*To* CATHERINE) Quick! In the dining-room!

CATHERINE: All right.

> *She dashes across to the dining-room door.*

GRACE: Here! You've forgotten your bag.

> *She darts to the table and picks it up.*

ARTHUR (*startled*): What on earth is going on?

GRACE (*in a stage whisper*): We're leaving you alone with John. When you've finished, cough or something.

ARTHUR (*testily*): What do you mean, or something?

GRACE: I know. Knock on the floor with your stick—three times. Then we'll come in.

ARTHUR: You don't think that might look a trifle coincidental?

GRACE: Sh!

She disappears from view as the hall door opens and VIOLET *comes in.*

VIOLET (*announcing*): Mr. Watherstone.

JOHN WATHERSTONE *comes in. He is a man of about thirty, dressed in an extremely well-cut morning coat and striped trousers, an attire which, though excused by church parade, we may well feel has been donned for this occasion.*

ARTHUR: How are you, John? I'm very glad to see you.

JOHN: How do you do, sir?

ARTHUR: Will you forgive me not getting up? My arthritis has been troubling me rather a lot, lately.

JOHN: I'm very sorry to hear that, sir. Catherine told me it was better.

ARTHUR: It was for a time. Now it's worse again. Do you smoke? (*He indicates a cigarette box.*)

JOHN: Yes, sir. I do. Thank you. (*He takes a cigarette, adding hastily.*) In moderation, of course.

ARTHUR (*with a faint smile*): Of course.

Pause, while JOHN *lights his cigarette and* ARTHUR *watches him.* Well, now. I understand you wish to marry my daughter.

JOHN: Yes, sir. That's to say, I've proposed to her and she's done me the honour of accepting me.

ARTHUR: I see. I trust when you corrected yourself, your second statement wasn't a denial of your first? (JOHN *looks puzzled.*) I mean, you do *really* wish to marry her?

JOHN: Of course, sir.

ARTHUR: Why, of course? There are plenty of people about who don't wish to marry her.

JOHN: I mean, of course, because I proposed to her.

ARTHUR: That, too, doesn't necessarily follow. However, we don't need to quibble. We'll take the sentimental side of the project for granted. As regards the more practical aspect, perhaps you won't mind if I ask you a few rather personal questions.

JOHN: Naturally not, sir. It's your duty.

ARTHUR: Quite so. Now, your income. Are you able to live on it?

JOHN: No, sir. I'm in the regular army.

ARTHUR: Yes, of course.

JOHN: But my army pay is supplemented by an allowance from my father.

ARTHUR: So I understand. Now, your father's would be, I take it, about twenty-four pounds a month.

JOHN: Yes, sir, that's exactly right.

ARTHUR: So that your total income—with your subaltern's pay and allowances plus the allowance from your father, would be, I take it, about four hundred and twenty pounds a year.

JOHN: Again, exactly the figure.

ARTHUR: Well, well. It all seems perfectly satisfactory. I really don't think I need delay my congratulations any longer. (*He extends his hand, which* JOHN, *gratefully, takes.*)

JOHN: Thank you, sir, very much.

ARTHUR: I must say, it was very good of you to be so frank and informative.

JOHN: Not at all.

ARTHUR: Your answers to my questions deserve an equal frankness from me about Catherine's own affairs. I'm afraid she's not—just in case you thought otherwise—the daughter of a rich man.

JOHN: I didn't think otherwise, sir.

ARTHUR: Good. Well, now——

> *He suddenly cocks his head on one side and listens. There is the sound of a gramophone playing "Hitchy-koo" from somewhere upstairs.*

Would you be so good as to touch the bell?

> JOHN *does so.*

Thank you. Well, now, continuing about my own financial affairs. The Westminster Bank pay me a small pension—three hundred and fifty to be precise—and my wife has about two hundred a year of her own. Apart from that we have nothing, except such savings as I've been able to make during my career at the bank. The interest from which raises my total income to approximately eight hundred pounds per annum.

> VIOLET *comes in.*

VIOLET: You rang, sir?

ARTHUR: Yes, Violet. My compliments to Mr. Dickie and if he doesn't stop that cacophonous hullaballoo at once, I'll throw him and his infernal machine into the street.

VIOLET: Yes, sir. What was that word again? Cac—— something——

ARTHUR: Never mind.   Say anything you like, only stop him.

VIOLET: Well, sir, I'll do my best, but you know what Master Dickie's like with his blessed old ragtime.

ARTHUR: Yes, Violet, I do.

VIOLET: I could say you don't think it's quite right on a Sunday.

ARTHUR (*roaring*): You can say I don't think it's quite right on any day.   Just stop him making that confounded din, that's all.

VIOLET: Yes, sir.

She goes out.

ARTHUR (*apologetically*): Our Violet has no doubt already been explained to you?

JOHN: I don't think so, sir.   Is any explanation necessary?

ARTHUR: I fear it is.   She came to us direct from an orphanage when she was fourteen, as a sort of under-between-maid on probation, and in that capacity she was quite satisfactory; but I am afraid, as parlourmaid, she has developed certain marked eccentricities in the performance of her duties, due, no doubt, to the fact that she has never fully known what those duties were.   Well, now, where were we?   Ah, yes.   I was telling you about my sources of income, was I not?

JOHN: Yes, sir.

ARTHUR: Now, in addition to the ordinary expenses of life, I have to maintain two sons—one at Osborne, and the other at Oxford—neither of whom, I'm afraid, will be in a position to support themselves for some time to come—one because of his extreme youth and the other because of—er—other reasons.

The gramophone stops suddenly.

So, you see, I am not in a position to be very lavish as regards Catherine's dowry.

JOHN: No, sir.   I quite see that.

ARTHUR: I propose to settle on her one sixth of my total capital, which, worked out to the final fraction, is exactly eight hundred and thirty-three pounds six shillings and eightpence.   But let us deal in round figures and say eight hundred and fifty pounds.

JOHN: I call that very generous, sir.

ARTHUR: Not as generous as I would have liked, I'm afraid. However—as my wife would say—beggars can't be choosers.

JOHN: Exactly, sir.

ARTHUR: Well, then, if you're agreeable to that arrangement, I don't think there's anything more we need discuss.

JOHN: No, sir.

ARTHUR: Splendid.

*Pause. ARTHUR takes his stick, and raps it, with an air of studied
unconcern, three times on the floor. Nothing happens.*

JOHN: Pretty rotten weather, isn't it?

ARTHUR: Yes. Vile.

He raps again. Again nothing happens.

Would you care for another cigarette?

JOHN: No, thank you, sir. I'm still smoking.

*ARTHUR takes up his stick to rap again, and then thinks better of
it. He goes slowly but firmly to the dining-room door, which he
throws open.*

ARTHUR (*in apparent surprise*): Well, imagine that! My wife and
daughter are in here of all places. Come in, Grace. Come in,
Catherine. John's here.

GRACE comes in, with CATHERINE behind.

GRACE: Why, John—how nice! (*She shakes hands.*) My, you
do look a swell! Doesn't he, Kate, darling?

CATHERINE: Quite one of the Knuts.

Pause. GRACE is unable to repress herself.

GRACE (*coyly*): Well?

ARTHUR: Well, what?

GRACE: How did your little talk go?

ARTHUR (*testily*): I understood you weren't supposed to know
we were having a little talk.

GRACE: Oh, you are infuriating! Is everything all right, John?

JOHN nods, smiling.

Oh, I'm so glad. I really am.

JOHN: Thank you, Mrs. Winslow.

GRACE: May I kiss you? After all, I'm practically your mother
now.

JOHN: Yes. Of course.

He allows himself to be kissed.

ARTHUR: While I, by the same token, am practically your father,
but if you will forgive me——

JOHN (*smiling*): Certainly, sir.

ARTHUR: Grace, I think we might allow ourselves a little modest
celebration at luncheon. Will you find me the key of the
cellars?

He goes out through the hall door.

GRACE: Yes, dear. (*She turns at the door. Coyly.*) I don't suppose you two will mind being left alone for a few minutes, will you?

> *She follows her husband out.* JOHN *goes to* CATHERINE *and kisses her.*

CATHERINE: Was it an ordeal?

JOHN: I was scared to death.

CATHERINE: My poor darling——

JOHN: The annoying thing was that I had a whole lot of neatly turned phrases ready for him and he wouldn't let me use them.

CATHERINE: Such as?

JOHN: Oh—how proud and honoured I was by your acceptance of me, and how determined I was to make you a loyal and devoted husband—and to maintain you in the state to which you were accustomed—all that sort of thing. All very sincerely meant.

CATHERINE: Anything about loving me a little?

JOHN (*lightly*): That I thought we could take for granted. So did your father, incidentally.

CATHERINE: I see. (*She gazes at him.*) Goodness, you do look smart!

JOHN: Not bad, is it? Poole's.

CATHERINE: What about *your* father? How did he take it?

JOHN: All right.

CATHERINE: I bet he didn't.

JOHN: Oh, yes. He's been wanting me to get married for years. Getting worried about grandchildren, I suppose.

CATHERINE: He disapproves of me, doesn't he?

JOHN: Oh, no. Whatever makes you think that?

CATHERINE: He has a way of looking at me through his monocle that shrivels me up.

JOHN: He's just being a colonel, darling, that's all. All colonels look at you like that. Anyway, what about the way your father looks at me! Tell me, are all your family as scared of him as I am?

CATHERINE: Dickie is, of course; and Ronnie, though he doesn't need to be. Father worships him. I don't know about Mother being scared of him. Sometimes, perhaps. I'm not—ever.

JOHN: You're not scared of anything, are you?

CATHERINE: Oh, yes. Heaps of things.

JOHN: Such as?

CATHERINE (*with a smile*): Oh—they're nearly all concerned with you.

RONNIE *looks cautiously in at the window door. He now presents a very bedraggled and woebegone appearance, with his uniform wringing wet, and his damp hair over his eyes.*

JOHN: You might be a little more explicit——

RONNIE (*in a low voice*): Kate!

    CATHERINE *turns and sees him.*

CATHERINE (*amazed*): Ronnie! What on earth——

RONNIE: Where's Father?

CATHERINE: I'll go and tell him——

RONNIE (*urgently*): No, don't. Please, Kate, don't!

    CATHERINE, *half-way to the door, stops, puzzled.*

CATHERINE. What's the trouble, Ronnie?

RONNIE, *trembling on the edge of tears, does not answer her. She approaches him.*

You're wet through. You'd better go and change.

RONNIE: No.

CATHERINE (*gently*): What's the trouble, darling? You can tell me.

    RONNIE *looks at* JOHN.

You know John Watherstone, Ronnie. You met him last holidays, don't you remember?

    RONNIE *remains silent, obviously reluctant to talk in front of a comparative stranger.*

JOHN (*tactfully*): I'll disappear.

CATHERINE (*pointing to dining-room*): In there, do you mind?

    JOHN *goes out quietly.* CATHERINE *gently leads* RONNIE *further into the room.*

Now, darling, tell me. What is it? Have you run away?

    RONNIE *shakes his head, evidently not trusting himself to speak.*

What is it, then?

    RONNIE *pulls out the document from his pocket which we have seen him reading in an earlier scene, and slowly hands it to her.* CATHERINE *reads it quietly.*

Oh, God!

RONNIE: I didn't do it.

    CATHERINE *re-reads the letter in silence.*

RONNIE: Kate, I didn't. Really, I didn't.

CATHERINE (*abstractedly*): No, darling. (*She seems uncertain what to do.*) This letter is addressed to Father. Did you open it?

RONNIE: Yes.

CATHERINE: You shouldn't have done that——

RONNIE: I was going to tear it up. Then I heard you come in from church and ran into the garden—I didn't know what to do——

CATHERINE (*still distracted*): Did they send you up to London all by yourself?

RONNIE: They sent a petty officer up with me. He was supposed to wait and see Father, but I sent him away. (*Indicating letter.*) Kate—shall we tear it up, now?

CATHERINE: No, darling.

RONNIE: We could tell Father term had ended two days sooner——

CATHERINE: No, darling.

RONNIE: I didn't do it—really I didn't——

DICKIE *comes in from the hall. He does not seem surprised to see* RONNIE.

DICKIE (*cheerfully*): Hullor, Ronnie, old lad. How's everything?

RONNIE *turns away from him.*

CATHERINE: You knew he was here?

DICKIE: Oh, yes. His trunks and things are all over our room. Trouble?

CATHERINE: Yes.

DICKIE: I'm sorry.

CATHERINE: You stay here with him. I'll find Mother.

DICKIE: All right.

CATHERINE *goes out by the hall door. There is a pause.*

DICKIE: What's up, old chap?

RONNIE: Nothing.

DICKIE: Come on—tell me.

RONNIE: It's all right.

DICKIE: Have you been sacked.

RONNIE *nods.*

Bad luck. What for?

RONNIE: I didn't do it!

DICKIE (*reassuringly*): No, of course you didn't.

RONNIE: Honestly, I didn't.

DICKIE: That's all right, old chap. No need to go on about it. I believe you.

RONNIE: You don't.

DICKIE: Well, I don't know what it is they've sacked you for, yet——

RONNIE (*in a low voice*): Stealing.

DICKIE (*evidently relieved*): Oh, is that all? Good Lord! I didn't know they sacked chaps for *that*, these days.

RONNIE: I didn't do it.

DICKIE: Why, good Heavens, at school we used to pinch everything we could jolly well lay our hands on. All of us. I remember there was one chap—Carstairs his name was—captain of cricket believe it or not—absolutely nothing was safe with him—nothing at all. Pinched a squash racket of mine once, I remember——

He has quietly approached RONNIE, *and now puts his arm on his shoulder.*

Believe me, old chap, pinching's nothing. Nothing at all. I say —you're a bit damp, aren't you?

RONNIE: I've been out in the rain——

DICKIE: You're shivering a bit, too, aren't you? Oughtn't you to go and change? I mean, we don't want you catching pneumonia——

RONNIE: I'm all right.

GRACE *comes, in with* CATHERINE *following.* GRACE *comes quickly to* RONNIE, *who, as he sees her, turns away from* DICKIE *and runs into her arms.*

GRACE: There, darling! It's all right, now.

RONNIE *begins to cry quietly, his head buried in her dress.*

RONNIE (*his voice muffled*): I didn't do it, Mother.

GRACE: No, darling. Of course you didn't. We'll go upstairs now, shall we, and get out of these nasty wet clothes.

RONNIE: Don't tell Father.

GRACE: No, darling. Not yet. I promise. Come along, now.

She leads him towards the door held open by CATHERINE.

Your new uniform, too. What a shame.

She goes out with him.

DICKIE: I'd better go and keep "cave" for them. Ward off the old man if he looks like going upstairs.

CATHERINE *nods.*

(*At door.*) I say—who's going to break the news to him eventually? I mean, someone'll have to.

CATHERINE: Don't let's worry about that now.

DICKIE: Well, you can count me out. In fact, I don't want to be within a thousand miles of that explosion.

He goes out. CATHERINE *comes to the dining-room door, which she opens, and calls "John!"* JOHN *comes in.*

25

JOHN: Bad news?

CATHERINE *nods. She is plainly upset, and dabs her eyes with her handkerchief.*

That's rotten for you.   I'm awfully sorry.

CATHERINE (*violently*): How can people be so cruel!

JOHN (*uncomfortably*): Expelled, I suppose?

He gets his answer from her silence, while she recovers herself.

CATHERINE: God, how little imagination some people have! Why should they torture a child of that age, John, darling?   What's the point of it?

JOHN: What's he supposed to have done?

CATHERINE: Stolen some money.

JOHN: Oh.

CATHERINE: Ten days ago, it said in the letter.   Why, on earth didn't they let us know?   Just think what that poor little creature has been going through these last ten days down there, entirely alone, without anyone to look after him, knowing what he had to face at the end of it!   And then, finally, they send him up to London with a petty officer—Is it any wonder he's nearly out of his mind?

JOHN: It does seem pretty heartless, I admit.

CATHERINE: Heartless?   It's cold, calculated inhumanity.   God, how I'd love to have that Commanding Officer here for just two minutes!   I'd—I'd——

JOHN (*gently*): Darling, it's quite natural you should feel angry about it, but you must remember, he's not really at school.   He's in the Service.

CATHERINE: What difference does that make?

JOHN: Well, they have ways of doing things in the Service which may seem to an outsider horribly brutal—but at least they're always scrupulously fair.   You can take it from me, that there must have been a very full enquiry before they'd take a step of this sort.   What's more, if there's been a delay of ten days, it would only have been in order to give the boy a better chance to clear himself——

Pause. CATHERINE *is silent.*

I'm sorry, Catherine, darling.   I'd have done better to keep my mouth shut.

CATHERINE: No.   What you said was perfectly true——

JOHN: It was tactless of me to say it, though.   I'm sorry.

CATHERINE (*lightly*): That's all right.

JOHN: Forgive me?

 He lays his arm on her shoulder.

CATHERINE (*taking his hand*): Nothing to forgive.

JOHN: Believe me, I'm awfully sorry. (*After a pause.*) How will your father take it?

CATHERINE (*simply*): It might kill him——

 There is the sound of voices in the hall.

Oh, Heavens! We've got Desmond to lunch. I'd forgotten——

JOHN: Who?

CATHERINE: Desmond Curry—our family solicitor. Oh, Lord! (*In a hasty whisper.*) Darling—be polite to him, won't you?

JOHN: Why? Am I usually so rude to your guests?

CATHERINE: No, but he doesn't know about us yet——

JOHN: Who does?

CATHERINE (*still in a whisper*): Yes, but he's been in love with me for years—it's a family joke——

 VIOLET *comes in.*

VIOLET (*announcing*): Mr. Curry.

 DESMOND CURRY *comes in. He is a man of about forty-five, with the figure of an athlete gone to seed. He has a mildly furtive manner, rather as if he had just absconded with his firm's petty cash, but hopes no one is going to be too angry about it.* JOHN, *when he sees him, cannot repress a faint smile at the thought of his loving Catherine.* VIOLET *has made her exit.*

CATHERINE: Hullo, Desmond. I don't think you know John Watherstone——

DESMOND: No—but, of course, I've heard a lot about him——

JOHN: How do you do?

 He wipes the smile off his face, as he meets CATHERINE'S *glance. There is a pause.*

DESMOND: Well, well, well. I trust I'm not early.

CATHERINE: No. Dead on time, Desmond—as always.

DESMOND: Capital. Capital.

 There is another pause, broken by CATHERINE *and* JOHN *both suddenly speaking at once.*

CATHERINE { Tell me, Desmond—— } (*Simul-*
JOHN { Pretty ghastly this rain—— } *taneously.*)

JOHN: I'm so sorry——

CATHERINE: It's quite all right. I was only going to ask how you did in your cricket match yesterday, Desmond.

DESMOND: Not too well, I'm afraid. My shoulder's still giving me trouble——

There is another pause.

(*At length.*) Well, well. I hear I'm to congratulate you both——

CATHERINE: Desmond—you know?

DESMOND: Violet told me, just now—in the hall. Yes—I must congratulate you both.

CATHERINE: Thank you so much, Desmond.

JOHN: Thank you.

DESMOND: Of course, it's quite expected, I know. Quite expected. Still it was rather a surprise, hearing it like that—from Violet in the hall——

CATHERINE: We were going to tell you, Desmond dear. It was only official this morning, you know. In fact, you're the first person to hear it.

DESMOND: Am I? Am I, indeed? Well, I'm sure you'll both be very happy.

CATHERINE { (*Murmuring* } Thank you, Desmond.
JOHN   { *together.*) } Thank you.

DESMOND: Only this morning? Fancy.

GRACE *comes in.*

GRACE: Hullo, Desmond, dear.

DESMOND: Hullo, Mrs. Winslow.

GRACE (*to Catherine*): I've got him to bed——

CATHERINE: Good.

DESMOND: Nobody ill, I hope?

GRACE: No, no. Nothing wrong at all——

ARTHUR *comes in, with a bottle under his arm. He rings the bell.*

ARTHUR: Grace, when did we last have the cellars seen to?

GRACE: I can't remember, dear.

ARTHUR: Well, they're in a shocking condition. Hullo, Desmond. How are you? You're not looking well.

DESMOND: Am I not? I've strained my shoulder, you know——

ARTHUR: Well, why do you play these ridiculous games of yours? Resign yourself to the onrush of middle age, and abandon them, my dear Desmond.

DESMOND: Oh, I could never do that. Not give up cricket. Not altogether.

JOHN (*making conversation*): Are you any relation of D. W. H. Curry who used to play for Middlesex?

DESMOND (*whose moment has come*): I am D. W. H. Curry.

GRACE: Didn't you know we had a great man in the room?

JOHN: Gosh! Curry of Curry's match?

DESMOND: That's right.

JOHN: Hat trick against the Players in—what year was it?

DESMOND: 1895. At Lord's. Twenty-six overs, nine maidens, thirty-seven runs, eight wickets.

JOHN: Gosh! Do you know you used to be a schoolboy hero of mine?

DESMOND: Did I? Did I, indeed?

JOHN: Yes. I had a signed photograph of you.

DESMOND: Yes. I used to sign a lot once, for schoolboys, I remember.

ARTHUR: Only for schoolboys, Desmond?

DESMOND: I fear so—yes. Girls took no interest in cricket in those days.

JOHN: Gosh! D. W. H. Curry—in person. Well, I'd never have thought it.

DESMOND (*sadly*): I know. Very few people would nowadays——

CATHERINE (*quickly*): Oh, John didn't mean that, Desmond——

DESMOND: I fear he did. (*He moves his arm.*) This is the main trouble. Too much office work and too little exercise, I fear.

ARTHUR: Nonsense. Too much exercise and too little office work.

　　　VIOLET *comes in, in response to a bell rung by* ARTHUR *some moments before.*

VIOLET: You rang, sir?

ARTHUR: Yes, Violet. Bring some glasses, would you?

VIOLET: Very good, sir.

　　　She goes out.

ARTHUR: I thought we'd try a little of the Madeira before luncheon —we're celebrating, you know, Desmond——

　　　GRACE *jogs his arm furtively, indicating* DESMOND.
(*Adding hastily.*)—my wife's fifty-fourth birthday——

GRACE: Arthur! Really!

CATHERINE: It's all right, Father. Desmond knows——

DESMOND: Yes, indeed. It's wonderful news, isn't it? I'll most gladly drink a toast to the—er—to the——

ARTHUR (*politely*): Happy pair, I think, is the phrase that is eluding you——

DESMOND: Well, as a matter of fact, I was looking for something new to say——

ARTHUR (*murmuring*): A forlorn quest, my dear Desmond.

GRACE (*protestingly*): Arthur, really! You mustn't be so rude.

ARTHUR: I meant, naturally, that no one—with the possible exception of Voltaire—could find anything new to say about an engaged couple——

> DICKIE *comes in.*

Ah, my dear Dickie—just in time for a glass of Madeira in celebration of Kate's engagement to John——

> VIOLET *comes in with a tray of glasses.* ARTHUR *begins to pour out the wine.*

DICKIE: Oh, is that all finally spliced up now? Kate definitely being entered for the marriage stakes. Good egg!

ARTHUR: Quite so. I should have added just now—with the possible exception of Voltaire and Dickie Winslow. (*To Violet.*) Take these round, will you, Violet?

> VIOLET *goes first to* GRACE, *then to* CATHERINE, *then to* JOHN, DESMOND, DICKIE *and finally* ARTHUR.

CATHERINE: Are we allowed to drink our own healths?

ARTHUR: I think it's permissible.

GRACE: No. It's bad luck.

JOHN: We defy augury. Don't we, Kate?

GRACE: You mustn't say that, John dear. I know. You can drink each other's healths. That's all right.

ARTHUR: Are my wife's superstitious terrors finally allayed? Good.

> *The drinks have now been handed round.*

ARTHUR (*toasting*): Catherine and John!

> *All drink*—CATHERINE *and* JOHN *to each other.* VIOLET *lingers, smiling, in the doorway.*

(*Seeing* VIOLET) Ah, Violet. We mustn't leave you out. You must join this toast.

VIOLET: Well—thank you, sir.

> *He pours her out a glass.*

Not too much, sir, please. Just a sip.

ARTHUR: Quite so. Your reluctance would be more convincing if I hadn't noticed you'd brought an extra glass——

VIOLET (*taking glass from* ARTHUR): Oh, I didn't bring it for myself, sir. I brought it for Master Ronnie—— (*She extends her glass.*) Miss Kate and Mr. John.

She takes a sip, makes a wry face and hands the glass back to
ARTHUR.

ARTHUR: You brought an extra glass for Master Ronnie, Violet?

VIOLET (*mistaking his bewilderment*): Well—I thought you might
allow him just a sip, sir. Just to drink the toast. He's that grown
up these days.

She turns to go. The others, with the exception of DESMOND,
who is staring gloomily into his glass, are frozen with apprehension.

ARTHUR: Master Ronnie isn't due back from Osborne until
Tuesday, Violet.

VIOLET (*turning*): Oh, no, sir. He's back already. Came back
unexpectedly this morning, all by himself.

ARTHUR: No, Violet. That isn't true. Someone has been playing
a joke——

VIOLET: Well, I saw him with my own two eyes, sir, as large as
life, just before you come in from church—and then I heard Mrs.
Winslow talking to him in his room——

ARTHUR: Grace—what does this mean?

CATHERINE (*instinctively taking charge*): All right, Violet. You
can go——

VIOLET: Yes, miss.

She goes out.

ARTHUR (*to* CATHERINE): Did *you* know Ronnie was back?

CATHERINE: Yes——

ARTHUR: And you, Dickie?

DICKIE: Yes, Father.

ARTHUR: Grace.

GRACE (*helplessly*): We thought it best you shouldn't know—for
the time being. Only for the time being, Arthur.

ARTHUR (*slowly*): Is the boy very ill?

No one answers. ARTHUR *looks from one face to another in
bewilderment.*

Answer me, someone! Is the boy very ill? Why must I be kept
in the dark like this? Surely I have the right to know. If he's ill
I must be with him——

CATHERINE (*steadily*): No, Father. He's not ill.

ARTHUR suddenly realises the truth from her tone of voice.

ARTHUR: Will someone tell me what has happened, please?

GRACE looks at CATHERINE *with helpless enquiry.* CATHERINE
nods. GRACE *takes a letter from her dress.*

GRACE (*timidly*): He brought this letter for you—Arthur.

ARTHUR: Read it to me, please——

GRACE: Arthur—not in front of——

ARTHUR: Read it to me, please.

> GRACE *again looks at* CATHERINE *for advice, and again receives a nod.* GRACE *begins to read.*

GRACE (*reading*): "Confidential.   I am commanded by My Lords Commissioners of the Admiralty to inform you that they have received a communication from the Commanding Officer of the Royal Naval College at Osborne, reporting the theft of a five-shilling postal order at the College on the 7th instant, which was afterwards cashed at the Post Office.   Investigation of the circumstances of the case leaves no other conclusion possible than that the postal order was taken by your son, Cadet Ronald Arthur Winslow. My Lords deeply regret that they must therefore request you to withdraw your son from the College."   It's signed by someone—I can't quite read his name——

> *She turns away quickly to hide her tears.* CATHERINE *puts a comforting arm on her shoulder.* ARTHUR *has not changed his attitude. There is a pause, during which we can hear the sound of a gong in the hall outside.*

ARTHUR (*at length*): Desmond—be so good as to call Violet.

> DESMOND *does so.   There is another pause, until* VIOLET *comes in.*

VIOLET: Yes, sir.

ARTHUR: Violet, will you ask Master Ronnie to come down and see me, please?

GRACE: Arthur—he's in bed.

ARTHUR: You told me he wasn't ill.

GRACE: He's not at all well.

ARTHUR: Do as I say, please, Violet.

VIOLET: Very good, sir.

> *She goes out.*

ARTHUR: Perhaps the rest of you would go in to luncheon?   Grace would you take them in?

GRACE (*hovering*): Arthur—don't you think——

ARTHUR (*ignoring her*): Dickie, will you decant that bottle of claret I brought up from the cellar?   I put it on the sideboard in the dining-room.

DICKIE: Yes, Father.

He goes out.

ARTHUR: Will you go in, Desmond?   And John?

The two men go out into the dining-room, in silence. GRACE *still hovers.*

GRACE: Arthur?

ARTHUR: Yes, Grace?

GRACE: Please don't—please don't——   (*She stops, uncertainly.*)

ARTHUR: What mustn't I do?

GRACE: Please don't forget he's only a child——

ARTHUR *does not answer her.*   CATHERINE *takes her mother's arm.*

CATHERINE: Come on, Mother.

She leads her mother to the dining-room door. At the door GRACE *looks back at* ARTHUR. *He has still not altered his position and is ignoring her. She goes into the dining-room, followed by* CATHERINE.

ARTHUR *does not move after they are gone. After an appreciable pause there comes a timid knock on the door.*

ARTHUR: Come in.

RONNIE *appears in the doorway. He is in a dressing-gown. He stands on the threshold.*

Come in and shut the door.

RONNIE *closes the door behind him.*

Come over here.

RONNIE *walks slowly up to his father.* ARTHUR *gazes at him steadily for some time, without speaking.*

(*At length.*)   Why aren't you in your uniform?

RONNIE (*murmuring*): It got wet.

ARTHUR: How did it get wet?

RONNIE: I was out in the garden in the rain.

ARTHUR: Why?

RONNIE (*reluctantly*): I was hiding.

ARTHUR: From me.

RONNIE *nods.*

Do you remember once, you promised me that if ever you were in trouble of any sort you would come to me first?

RONNIE: Yes, Father.

ARTHUR: Why didn't you come to me now?   Why did you have to go and hide in the garden?

RONNIE: I don't know, Father.

ARTHUR: Are you so frightened of me?

RONNIE *does not reply.* ARTHUR *gazes at him for a moment,
then picks up the letter.*

In this letter it says you stole a postal order.

RONNIE *opens his mouth to speak.*

ARTHUR *stops him.*

Now, I don't want you to say a word until you've heard what *I've*
got to say. If you did it, you must tell me. I shan't be angry with
you, Ronnie—provided you tell me the truth. But if you tell me
a lie, I shall know it, because a lie between you and me can't be
hidden. I shall know it, Ronnie—so remember that before you
speak. (*Pause.*) Did you steal this postal order?

RONNIE (*without hesitation*): No, Father. I didn't.

ARTHUR (*staring into his eyes*): Did you steal this postal order?

RONNIE: No, Father. I didn't.

ARTHUR *continues to stare into his eyes for a second, then relaxes
and pushes him gently away.*

ARTHUR: Go on back to bed.

RONNIE *goes gratefully to the door.*

And in future I trust that a son of mine will at least show enough
sense to come in out of the rain.

RONNIE: Yes, Father.

He disappears. ARTHUR *gets up quite briskly and goes to the
telephone in the corner of the room.*

ARTHUR (*at telephone*): Hullo. Are you there? (*Speaking very
distinctly.*) I want to put a trunk call through, please. A trunk
call ... Yes ... The Royal Naval College, Osborne ... That's
right ... Replace receiver? Certainly.

*He replaces receiver and then, after a moment's meditation, turns
and walks briskly into the dining-room.*

CURTAIN

ACT II

SCENE: *The same, nine months later.   It is about six o'clock, of a spring evening.*

DICKIE is winding up his gramophone which, somehow or other, appears to have found its way back into the drawing-room.   A pile of books and an opened note-book on the table provide evidence of interrupted labours.

The gramophone, once started, emits a scratchy and muffled rendering of an early ragtime.   DICKIE listens for a few seconds with evident appreciation, then essays a little pas seul.

CATHERINE comes in.   She is in evening dress.   DICKIE switches off gramophone.

DICKIE: Hullo. Do you think the old man can hear this upstairs?

CATHERINE: I shouldn't think so.   I couldn't.

DICKIE: Soft needle and an old sweater down the horn. Is the doctor still with him?

CATHERINE *nods.*

What's the verdict, do you know?

CATHERINE: I heard him say Father needed a complete rest.

DICKIE: Don't we all.

CATHERINE (*indicating books*): It doesn't look as if *you* did.   He said he ought to go to the country and forget all his worries——

DICKIE: Fat chance there is of that, I'd say.

CATHERINE: I know.

DICKIE: I say, you look a treat.   New dress?

CATHERINE: Is it likely?   No, it's an old one I've had done up.

DICKIE; Where are you going to?

CATHERINE: Daly's.   Dinner first—at the Cri.

DICKIE: Nice.   You wouldn't care to take me along with you, I suppose?

CATHERINE: You suppose quite correctly.

DICKIE: John wouldn't mind.

CATHERINE: I dare say not.   I would.

DICKIE: I wish I had someone to take me out.   In your new

35

feminist world do you suppose women will be allowed to do some of the paying?

CATHERINE: Certainly.

DICKIE: Really? Then the next time you're looking for someone to chain themselves to Mr. Asquith you can jolly well call on me——

CATHERINE (*laughing*): Edwina might take you out if you gave her the hint. She's very rich——

DICKIE: If I gave Edwina a hint of that sort I wouldn't see her this side of doomsday.

CATHERINE: You sound a little bitter, Dickie dear.

DICKIE: Oh, no. Not bitter. Just realistic.

VIOLET *comes in with an evening paper on a salver.*

DICKIE: Good egg! The *Star*!

CATHERINE *makes a grab for it and gets it before* DICKIE.

VIOLET: You won't throw it away, will you, miss? If there's anything in it again, Cook and I would like to read it, after you.

CATHERINE *is hastily turning over the pages, with* DICKIE *craning his head over her shoulder.*

CATHERINE: No. That's all right, Violet.

VIOLET *goes out.*

Here it is. (*Reading.*) "The Osborne cadet." There are two more letters. (*Reading.*) "Sir. I am entirely in agreement with your correspondent, Democrat, concerning the scandalously high-handed treatment by the Admiralty of the case of the Osborne Cadet. The efforts of Mr. Arthur Winslow to secure a fair trial for his son have evidently been thwarted at every turn by a soulless oligarchy——"

DICKIE: Soulless oligarchy. That's rather good——

CATHERINE: "—it is high time private and peaceful citizens of this country awoke to the increasing encroachment of their ancient freedom by the new despotism of Whitehall. The Englishman's home was once said to be his castle. It seems it is rapidly becoming his prison. Your obedient servant, *Libertatis Amator.*"

DICKIE: Good for old Amator!

CATHERINE: The other's from Perplexed. (*Reading.*) "Dear Sir. I cannot understand what all the fuss is about in the case of the Osborne Cadet. Surely we have more important matters to get ourselves worked up about than a fourteen-year-old boy and a five-shilling postal order." Silly old fool!

DICKIE: How do you know he's old?

CATHERINE: Isn't it obvious? (*Reading.*) "With the present troubles in the Balkans and a certain major European Power rapidly outbuilding our navy, the Admiralty might be forgiven if it stated that it had rather more urgent affairs to deal with than Master Ronnie Winslow's little troubles. A further enquiry before the judge advocate of the Fleet has now fully confirmed the original findings that the boy was guilty. I sincerely trust that this will finally end this ridiculous and sordid little storm in a teacup. I am, sir, etc., Perplexed."

Pause.

DICKIE (*reading over her shoulder*): "This correspondence must now cease.—Editor." Damn!

CATHERINE: Oh, dear! How hopeless it seems, sometimes.

DICKIE: Yes, it does, doesn't it? (*Thoughtfully, after a pause.*) You know, Kate—don't give me away to the old man, will you—but the awful thing is, if it hadn't been my own brother, I think I might quite likely have seen Perplexed's point.

CATHERINE: Might you?

DICKIE: Well, I mean—looking at it from every angle and all that—it does seem rather a much ado about damn all. I mean to say—a mere matter of pinching. (*Bitterly.*) And it's all so beastly expensive. Let's cheer ourselves up with some music. (*He sets machine going.*)

CATHERINE (*listening to the record*): Is that what it's called?

DICKIE: Come and practise a few steps.

CATHERINE *joins him and they dance, in the manner of the period with arms fully outstretched and working up and down, pump-handle style.*

(*Surprised.*) I say! Jolly good!

CATHERINE: Thank you, Dickie.

DICKIE: Who taught you? John, I suppose.

CATHERINE: No, I taught John, as it happens——

DICKIE: Feminism—even in love?

CATHERINE *nods, smiling. Pause, while they continue to dance.* When's the happy date now?

CATHERINE: Postponed again.

DICKIE: Oh no. Why?

CATHERINE: His father's gone abroad for six months.

DICKIE: Why pay any attention to that old—(*he substitutes the word*)—gentleman?

CATHERINE: I wouldn't—but John does—so I have to.

Something in her tone makes DICKIE *stop dancing and gaze at her seriously.*

DICKIE: I say—nothing wrong, is there?

CATHERINE *shakes her head, smiling, but not too emphatically.*
I mean—you're not going to be left on the altar rails or anything are you?

CATHERINE: Oh, no. I'll get him past the altar rails, if I have to drag him there.

DICKIE (*as they resume their dance*): Do you think you might have to?

CATHERINE: Quite frankly, yes.

DICKIE: Competition?

CATHERINE: Not yet. Only—differences of opinion.

DICKIE: I see. Well, take some advice from an old hand, will you?

CATHERINE: Yes Dickie.

DICKIE: Suppress your opinions. Men don't like 'em in their lady friends, even if they agree with 'em. And if they don't—it's fatal. Pretend to be half-witted, like Edwina, then he'll adore you.

CATHERINE: I know. I do, sometimes, and then I forget. Still, you needn't worry. If there's ever a clash between what I believe and what I feel, there's not much doubt about which will win.

DICKIE: That's the girl. Of course, I don't know why you didn't fall in love with Ramsay MacDonald——

ARTHUR *comes in. He is walking with more difficulty than when we last saw him.* DICKIE *and* CATHERINE *hastily stop dancing, and* DICKIE *turns off the gramophone.*

CATHERINE (*quickly*): It was entirely my fault, Father. I enticed Dickie from his work to show me a few dance steps.

ARTHUR: Oh? I must admit I am surprised you succeeded.

DICKIE (*getting off the subject*): What did the doctor say, Father?

ARTHUR: He said, if I remember his exact words, that we weren't quite as well as when we last saw each other. That information seems expensive at a guinea. (*Seeing the evening paper.*) Oh, is that the *Star*? Let me see it, please.

CATHERINE *brings it over to him.*
John will be calling for you here, I take it?

CATHERINE: Yes, Father.

ARTHUR: It might be better, perhaps, if you didn't ask him in.

38

This room will shortly be a clutter of journalists, solicitors, barristers, and other impedimenta.

CATHERINE: Is Sir Robert Morton coming to see you here?

ARTHUR (*deep in the "Star"*): I could hardly go and see him, could I?

DICKIE, in deference to his father's presence, has returned to his books. ARTHUR reads the "Star". CATHERINE glances at herself in the mirror, and then wanders to the door.

CATHERINE: I must go and do something to my hair.

DICKIE: What's the matter with your hair?

CATHERINE: Nothing, except I don't like it very much.

She goes out. DICKIE opens two more books with a busy air and chews his pencil. ARTHUR finishes reading the "Star" and stares moodily into space.

ARTHUR (*at length*): I wonder if I could sue Perplexed.

DICKIE: It might be a way of getting the case into court.

ARTHUR: On the other hand, he has not been libellous. Merely base.

He throws the paper away and regards DICKIE thoughtfully. DICKIE, feeling his father's eye on him, is elaborately industrious.

ARTHUR (*at length, politely*): Do you mind if I disturb you for a moment?

DICKIE (*pushing books away*): No, Father.

ARTHUR: I want to ask you a question. But before I do I must impress on you the urgent necessity for an absolutely truthful answer.

DICKIE: Naturally.

ARTHUR: Naturally means by nature, and I'm afraid I have not yet noticed that it has invariably been your nature to answer my questions truthfully.

DICKIE: Oh. Well, I will, this one, Father, I promise.

ARTHUR: Very well. (*He stares at him for a moment.*) What do you suppose one of your bookmaker friends would lay in the way of odds against your getting a degree?

Pause.

DICKIE: Oh. Well, let's think. Say—about evens.

ARTHUR: Hm. I rather doubt if at that price your friend would find many takers.

DICKIE: Well—perhaps seven to four against.

ARTHUR: I see. And what about the odds against your eventually becoming a Civil Servant?

DICKIE: Well—a bit steeper, I suppose.

ARTHUR: Exactly.   Quite a bit steeper.

Pause.

DICKIE: You don't want to have a bet, do you?

ARTHUR: No, Dickie.   I'm not a gambler.   And that's exactly the trouble.   Unhappily I'm no longer in a position to gamble two hundred pounds a year on what you yourself admit is an outside chance.

DICKIE: Not an outside chance, Father.   A good chance.

ARTHUR: Not good enough, Dickie, I'm afraid—with things as they are at the moment.   Definitely not good enough.   I fear my mind is finally made up.

There is a long pause.

DICKIE: You want me to leave Oxford—is that it?

ARTHUR: I'm very much afraid so, Dickie.

DICKIE: Oh.   Straight away?

ARTHUR: No.   You can finish your second year.

DICKIE: And what then?

ARTHUR: I can get you a job in the bank.

DICKIE (*quietly*): Oh, Lord!

Pause.

ARTHUR (*rather apologetically*): It'll be quite a good job, you know. Luckily my influence in the bank still counts for something.

DICKIE gets up and wanders about, slightly in a daze.

DICKIE: Father—if I promised you—I mean, *really* promised you —that from now on I'll work like a black——

ARTHUR shakes his head slowly.

It's the case, I suppose?

ARTHUR: It's costing me a lot of money.

DICKIE: I know.   It must be.   Still, couldn't you—I mean, isn't there any way——

ARTHUR again shakes his head.

Oh, Lord!

ARTHUR: I'm afraid this is rather a shock for you.   I'm sorry.

DICKIE: What?   No.   No, it isn't, really.   I've been rather expecting it, as a matter of fact—especially since I've heard you are hoping to brief Sir Robert Morton.   Still, I can't say but what it isn't a bit of a slap in the face.

There is a ring at the front door.

ARTHUR: There is a journalist coming to see me.   Do you mind if we talk about this some other time?

DICKIE: No. Of course not, Father.

DICKIE begins forlornly to gather his books.

ARTHUR (*with a half-smile*): I should leave those there, if I were you.

DICKIE: Yes. I will. Good idea.

He goes to the door.

ARTHUR (*politely*): Tell me—how is your nice friend, Miss Edwina Gunn, these days?

DICKIE: Very well, thanks awfully.

ARTHUR: You don't suppose she'd mind if you took her to the theatre?—or gave her a little present perhaps?

DICKIE: Oh, I'm sure she wouldn't.

ARTHUR: I'm afraid I can only make it a couple of sovereigns.

ARTHUR has taken out his sovereign case and now extracts two sovereigns. DICKIE comes and takes them.

DICKIE: Thanks awfully, Father.

ARTHUR: With what's left over you can always buy something for yourself.

DICKIE: Oh. Well, as a matter of fact, I don't suppose there will be an awful lot left over. Still, it's jolly decent of you—I say, Father—I think I could do with a little spot of something. Would you mind?

ARTHUR: Of course not. You'll find the decanter in the dining-room.

DICKIE: Thanks awfully.

He goes to dining-room door.

ARTHUR: I must thank you, Dickie, for bearing what must have been a very unpleasant blow with some fortitude.

DICKIE (*uncomfortably*): Oh. Rot, Father.

He goes out. ARTHUR sighs deeply.

VIOLET comes in at the hall door.

VIOLET (*announcing proudly*): The *Daily News.*

MISS BARNES comes in. She is a rather untidily dressed woman of about forty with a gushing manner.

MISS BARNES: Mr. Winslow? So good of you to see me.

ARTHUR: How do you do?

MISS BARNES (*simpering*): You're surprised to see a lady reporter? I know. Everyone is. And yet why not? What could be more natural?

ARTHUR: What indeed? Pray sit down——

MISS BARNES: My paper usually sends me out on stories which have a special appeal to women—stories with a little heart, you know, like this one—a father's fight for his little boy's honour——

ARTHUR *visibly winces.*

ARTHUR: I venture to think this case has rather wider implications than that——

MISS BARNES: Oh, yes. The political angle. I know. Very interesting but not *quite* my line of country. Now, what I'd really like to do—is to get a nice picture of you and your little boy together. I've brought my assistant and camera. They're in the hall. Where is your little boy?

ARTHUR: My son is arriving from school in a few minutes. His mother has gone to the station to meet him.

MISS BARNES (*making a note*): From school? How interesting. So you got a school to take him? I mean, they didn't mind the unpleasantness?

ARTHUR: No.

MISS BARNES: And why is he coming back this time?

ARTHUR: He hasn't been expelled again, if that is what you're implying. He is coming to London to be examined by Sir Robert Morton, whom we are hoping to brief——

MISS BARNES: Sir Robert Morton! (*She whistles appreciatively.*) Well!

ARTHUR: Exactly.

MISS BARNES (*doubtingly*): But do you *really* think he'll take a little case like this?

ARTHUR (*explosively*): It is *not* a little case, madam——

MISS BARNES: No, no. Of course not. But still—Sir Robert Morton!

ARTHUR: I understand that he is the best advocate in the country. He is certainly the most expensive——

MISS BARNES: Oh, yes. I suppose if one is prepared to pay his fee one can get him for almost *any* case.

ARTHUR: Once more, madam—this is *not* almost any case——

MISS BARNES: No, no. Of course not. Well, now, perhaps you wouldn't mind giving me a few details. When did it all start?

ARTHUR: Nine months ago. The first I knew of the charge was when my son arrived home with a letter from the Admiralty informing me of his expulsion. I telephoned Osborne to protest and was referred by them to the Lords of the Admiralty. My solicitors then took the matter up, and demanded from the Admiralty the fullest possible enquiry. For weeks we were ignored, then met with a blank refusal, and only finally got reluctant permission to view the evidence.

MISS BARNES (*indifferently*): Really?

ARTHUR: My solicitors decided that the evidence was highly unsatisfactory, and fully justified the re-opening of proceedings. We applied to the Admiralty for a Court Martial. They ignored us. We applied for a civil trial. They ignored us again.

MISS BARNES: They ignored you?

ARTHUR: Yes. But after tremendous pressure had been brought to bear—letters to the papers, questions in the House and other means open to private citizens of this country—the Admiralty eventually agreed to what they called an independent enquiry.

MISS BARNES (*vaguely*): Oh, good!

ARTHUR: It was not good, madam. At that independent enquiry, conducted by the judge advocate of the Fleet—against whom I am saying nothing, mind you—my son—a child of fourteen, was not represented by counsel, solicitors or friends. What do you think of that?

MISS BARNES: Fancy!

ARTHUR: You may well say fancy.

MISS BARNES: And what happened at the enquiry?

ARTHUR: What do you think happened? Inevitably he was found guilty again, and thus branded for the second time before the world as a thief and a forger——

MISS BARNES (*her attention wandering*): What a shame!

ARTHUR: I need hardly tell you, madam, that I am not prepared to let the matter rest there. I shall continue to fight this monstrous injustice with every weapon and every means at my disposal. Now, it happens I have a plan——

MISS BARNES: Oh, what charming curtains! What are they made of? (*She rises and goes to the window.*)

ARTHUR *sits for a moment in paralysed silence.*

ARTHUR (*at length*): Madam—I fear I have no idea.

There is the sound of voices in the hall.

MISS BARNES: Ah. Do I hear the poor little chap himself?

The hall door opens and RONNIE *comes in boisterously, followed by* GRACE. *He is evidently in the highest of spirits.*

RONNIE: Hullo, Father! (*He runs to him.*)

ARTHUR: Hullo, Ronnie.

RONNIE: I say, Father! Mr. Moore says I'm to tell you I needn't come back until Monday if you like. So that gives me three whole days.

ARTHUR: Mind my leg!

RONNIE: Sorry, Father.

ARTHUR: How are you, my boy?

RONNIE: Oh, I'm absolutely tophole, Father. Mother says I've grown an inch——

MISS BARNES: Ah! Now that's exactly the way I'd like to take my picture. Would you hold it, Mr. Winslow? (*She goes to hall door and calls.*) Fred! Come in now, will you?

RONNIE (*in a sibilant whisper*): Who's she?

> FRED *appears. He is a listless photographer, complete with apparatus.*

FRED (*gloomily*): Afternoon, all.

MISS BARNES: That's the pose, I suggest.

FRED: Yes. It'll do.

> *He begins to set up his apparatus.* ARTHUR, *holding* RONNIE *close against him in the pose suggested, turns his head to* GRACE.

ARTHUR: Grace, dear, this lady is from the *Daily News*. She is extremely interested in your curtains.

GRACE (*delighted*): Oh, really! How nice!

MISS BARNES: Yes, indeed. I was wondering what they were made of.

GRACE: Well, it's an entirely new material, you know. I'm afraid I don't know what it's called, but I got them at Barkers last year. Apparently it's a sort of mixture of wild silk and——

MISS BARNES (*now genuinely busy with her pencil and pad*): Just a second, Mrs. Winslow. I'm afraid my shorthand isn't very good. I must get that down——

RONNIE (*to* ARTHUR): Father, are we going to be in the *Daily News?*

ARTHUR: It appears so——

RONNIE: Oh, good! They get the *Daily News* in the school library and everyone's bound to see it——

FRED: Quite still, please——

> *He takes his photograph.*

All right, Miss Barnes. (*He goes out.*)

MISS BARNES (*engrossed with* GRACE): Thank you, Fred. (*To*

ARTHUR.) Good-bye, Mr. Winslow, and the very best of good
fortune in your inspiring fight. (*Turning to* RONNIE.) Good-bye,
little chap. Remember, the darkest hour is just before the dawn.
Well, it was very good of you to tell me all that, Mrs.Winslow.
I'm sure our readers will be most interested.

    GRACE *shows her out.*

RONNIE: What's she talking about?

ARTHUR: The case, I imagine.

RONNIE: Oh, the case. Father, do you know the train had fourteen coaches?

ARTHUR: Did it indeed?

RONNIE: Yes. All corridor.

ARTHUR: Remarkable.

RONNIE: Of course, it was one of the very biggest expresses. I
walked all the way down it from one end to the other.

ARTHUR: I had your half-term report, Ronnie.

RONNIE (*suddenly silenced by perturbation*): Oh, yes?

ARTHUR: On the whole it was pretty fair.

RONNIE: Oh, good.

ARTHUR: I'm glad you seem to be settling down so well. Very
glad indeed.

    GRACE *comes in.*

GRACE: What a charming woman, Arthur!

ARTHUR: Charming. I trust you gave her full details about our
curtains?

GRACE: Oh, yes. I told her everything.

ARTHUR (*wearily*): I'm so glad.

GRACE: I do think women reporters are a good idea——

RONNIE (*excitedly*): I say, Father, will it be all right for me to
stay till Monday? I mean, I won't be missing any work—only
Divinity—— (*He jogs his father's leg again.*)

ARTHUR: Mind my leg.

RONNIE: Oh, sorry, Father. Is it bad?

ARTHUR: Yes, it is. (*To* GRACE.) Grace, take him upstairs and
get him washed. Sir Robert will be here in a few minutes.

GRACE (*to Ronnie*): Come on, darling.

RONNIE: All right. (*On his way to the door with his mother.*) I say,
do you know how long the train took? 123 miles in two hours
and fifty-two minutes. That's an average of 46.73 recurring miles
an hour—I worked it out. Violet! Violet! I'm back.

He disappears, still chattering shrilly.

GRACE *stops at the door.*

GRACE: Did the doctor say anything, dear?

ARTHUR: A great deal; but very little to the purpose.

GRACE: Violet says he left an ointment for your back. Four massages a day. Is that right?

ARTHUR: Something of the kind.

GRACE: I think you had better have one now, hadn't you, Arthur?

ARTHUR: No.

GRACE: But, dear, you've got plenty of time before Sir Robert comes, and if you don't have one now, you won't be able to have another before you go to bed.

ARTHUR: Precisely.

GRACE: But really, Arthur, it does seem awfully silly to spend all this money on doctors if you're not even going to do what they say.

ARTHUR (*impatiently*): All right, Grace. All right. All right.

GRACE: Thank you, dear.

CATHERINE *comes in.*

CATHERINE: Ronnie's back, judging by the noise——

GRACE (*examining her*): I must say that old frock has come out very well. John'll never know it isn't brand new——

CATHERINE: He's late, curse him.

ARTHUR: Grace, go on up and attend to Ronnie, and prepare the witch's brew for me. I'll come up when you are ready.

GRACE: Very well, dear. (*To* CATHERINE.) Yes, that does look good. I must say Mme Dupont's a treasure.

She goes out.

ARTHUR (*wearily*): Oh, Kate, Kate! Are we both mad, you and I?

CATHERINE: What's the matter, Father?

ARTHUR: I don't know. I suddenly feel suicidally inclined. (*Bitterly.*) A father's fight for his little boy's honour. Special appeal to all women. Photo inset of Mrs. Winslow's curtains! Is there any hope for the world?

CATHERINE (*smiling*): I think so, Father.

ARTHUR: Shall we drop the whole thing, Kate?

CATHERINE: I don't consider that a serious question, Father.

ARTHUR (*slowly*): You realise that, if we go on, your marriage settlement must go?

CATHERINE (*lightly*): Oh, yes. I gave that up for lost weeks ago.

ARTHUR: Things are all right between you and John, aren't they?

CATHERINE: Oh, yes, Father, of course.   Everything's perfect.

ARTHUR: I mean—it won't make any difference between you, will it?

CATHERINE: Good Heavens, no!

ARTHUR: Very well, then.   Let us pin our faith to Sir Robert Morton.

> CATHERINE *is silent.*   ARTHUR *looks at her as if he had expected an answer, then nods.*

I see I'm speaking only for myself in saying that.

CATHERINE (*lightly*): You know what I think of Sir Robert Morton, Father.   Don't let's go into it again, now.   It's too late, anyway.

ARTHUR: It's not too late.   He hasn't accepted the brief yet.

CATHERINE (*shortly*): Then I'm rather afraid I hope he never does. And that has nothing to do with my marriage settlement either.

> *Pause.*   ARTHUR *looks angry for a second, then subsides.*

ARTHUR (*mildly*): I made enquiries about that fellow you suggested —I am told he is not nearly as good an advocate as Morton——

CATHERINE: He's not nearly so fashionable.

ARTHUR (*doubtfully*): I want the best——

CATHERINE: The best in this case certainly isn't Morton.

ARTHUR: Then why does everyone say he is?

CATHERINE (*roused*): Because if one happens to be a large monopoly attacking a Trade Union or a Tory paper libelling a Labour Leader, he *is* the best.   But it utterly defeats me how you or anyone else could expect a man of his record to have even a tenth of his heart in a case where the boot is entirely on the other foot——

ARTHUR: Well, I imagine, if his heart isn't in it, he won't accept the brief.

CATHERINE: He might still.   It depends what there is in it for him. Luckily there isn't much——

ARTHUR (*bitterly*): There is a fairly substantial cheque——

CATHERINE: He doesn't want money.   He must be a very rich man.

ARTHUR: What does he want, then?

CATHERINE: Anything that advances his interests.

> ARTHUR *shrugs his shoulders.   Pause.*

ARTHUR: I believe you are prejudiced because he spoke against women's suffrage.

CATHERINE: I am.   I'm prejudiced because he is always speaking against what is right and just.   Did you read his speech in the House on the Trades Disputes Bill?

GRACE (*calling off*): Arthur!   Arthur!

ARTHUR (*smiling*): Oh, well—in the words of the Prime Minister —let us wait and see.

He turns to the door.   At the door.

You're my only ally, Kate.   Without you I believe I should have given up long ago.

CATHERINE: Rubbish.

ARTHUR: It's true.   Still, you must sometimes allow me to make my own decisions.   I have an instinct about Morton.

CATHERINE *does not reply.*

(*Doubtfully.*)   We'll see which is right—my instinct or your reason, eh?

He goes out.

CATHERINE (*half to herself*): I'm afraid we will.

DICKIE *comes out of the dining-room door.*

DICKIE (*bitterly*): Hullo, Kate.

CATHERINE: Hullo, Dickie.

DICKIE *crosses mournfully to the other door.*

What's the matter?   Edwina jilted you or something?

DICKIE: Haven't you heard?

CATHERINE *shakes her head.*

I'm being scratched from the Oxford Stakes at the end of the year——

CATHERINE: Oh, Dickie!   I'm awfully sorry——

DICKIE: Did you know it was in the wind?

CATHERINE: I knew there was a risk——

DICKIE: You might have warned a fellow.   I fell plumb into the old man's trap.   My gosh, I could just about murder that little brother of mine.   (*Bitterly.*)   What's he had to go about pinching postal orders for?   And why the hell does he have to get himself nabbed doing it?   Silly little blighter!

He goes out gloomily.   There is a ring at the front door. CATH-ERINE, *obviously believing it is John, picks up her cloak and goes to the hall door.*

CATHERINE (*calling*): All right, Violet.   It's only Mr. Watherstone. I'll answer it.

She goes out.   There is the sound of voices in the hall, and then CATHERINE *reappears, leading in* DESMOND *and* SIR ROBERT

MORTON, SIR ROBERT *is a man in the early forties, cadaverous and immensely elegant. He wears a long overcoat, and carries his hat and stick. He looks rather a fop, and his supercilious expression bears out this view.*

(*As she re-enters.*) I'm so sorry. I was expecting a friend. Won't you sit down, Sir Robert! My father won't be long.

SIR ROBERT *bows slightly, and sits down on a hard chair, still in his overcoat.*

Won't you sit here? It's far more comfortable.

SIR ROBERT: No, thank you.

DESMOND (*fussing*): Sir Robert has a most important dinner engagement, so we came a little early.

CATHERINE: I see.

DESMOND: I'm afraid he can only spare us a very few minutes of his most valuable time this evening. Of course, it's a long way for him to come—so far from his chambers—and very good of him to do it, too, if I may say so——

He bows to SIR ROBERT, *who bows slightly back.*

CATHERINE: I know. I can assure you we're very conscious of it.

SIR ROBERT *gives her a quick look, and a faint smile.*

DESMOND: Perhaps I had better advise your father of our presence——

CATHERINE: Yes, do, Desmond. You'll find him in his bedroom —having his back rubbed.

DESMOND: Oh. I see.

He goes out. There is a pause.

CATHERINE: Is there anything I can get you, Sir Robert? A whiskey and soda or a brandy?

SIR ROBERT: No thank you.

CATHERINE: Will you smoke?

SIR ROBERT: No, thank you.

CATHERINE (*holding her cigarette*): I hope you don't mind me smoking?

SIR ROBERT: Why should I?

CATHERINE: Some people find it shocking.

SIR ROBERT (*indifferently*): A lady in her own home is surely entitled to behave as she wishes.

Pause.

CATHERINE: Won't you take your coat off, Sir Robert?

SIR ROBERT: No, thank you.

CATHERINE: You find it cold in here? I'm sorry.

SIR ROBERT: It's perfectly all right.

    Conversation languishes again. SIR ROBERT looks at his watch.

CATHERINE: What time are you dining?

SIR ROBERT: Eight o'clock.

CATHERINE: Far from here?

SIR ROBERT: Devonshire House.

CATHERINE: Oh. Then of course you mustn't on any account be late.

SIR ROBERT. No.

    There is another pause.

CATHERINE: I suppose you know the history of this case, do you, Sir Robert?

SIR ROBERT (*examining his nails*): I believe I have seen most of the relevant documents.

CATHERINE: Do you think we can bring the case into Court by a collusive action?

SIR ROBERT: I really have no idea——

CATHERINE: Curry and Curry seem to think that might hold——

SIR ROBERT: Do they? They are a very reliable firm.

    Pause. CATHERINE *is on the verge of losing her temper.*

CATHERINE: I'm rather surprised that a case of this sort should interest you, Sir Robert.

SIR ROBERT: Are you?

CATHERINE: It seems such a very trivial affair, compared to most of your great forensic triumphs.

    SIR ROBERT, *staring languidly at the ceiling, does not reply.*

I was in Court during your cross-examination of Len Rogers, in the Trades Union embezzlement case.

SIR ROBERT: Really?

CATHERINE: It was masterly.

SIR ROBERT: Thank you.

CATHERINE: I suppose you heard that he committed suicide a few months ago?

SIR ROBERT: Yes. I had heard.

CATHERINE: Many people believed him innocent, you know.

SIR ROBERT: So I understand. (*After a faint pause.*) As it happens, however, he was guilty.

    GRACE *comes in hastily.*

GRACE: Sir Robert? My husband's so sorry to have kept you, but he's just coming.

SIR ROBERT: It's perfectly all right. How do you do?

CATHERINE: Sir Robert is dining at Devonshire House, Mother.

GRACE: Oh, really? Oh, then you have to be punctual, of course, I do see that. It's the politeness of princes, isn't it?

SIR ROBERT: So they say.

GRACE: In this case the other way round, of course. Ah, I think I hear my husband on the stairs. I hope Catherine entertained you all right?

SIR ROBERT (*with a faint bow to* CATHERINE.): Very well, thank you.

ARTHUR *comes in, followed by* DESMOND.

ARTHUR: Sir Robert? I am Arthur Winslow.

SIR ROBERT: How do you do?

ARTHUR: I understand you are rather pressed for time.

GRACE: Yes. He's dining at Devonshire House——

ARTHUR: Are you indeed? My son should be down in a minute. I expect you will wish to examine him.

SIR ROBERT (*indifferently*): Just a few questions. I fear that is all I will have time for this evening——

ARTHUR: I am rather sorry to hear that. He has made the journey especially from school for this interview and I was hoping that by the end of it I should know definitely yes or no if you would accept the brief.

DESMOND (*pacifically*): Well, perhaps Sir Robert would consent to finish his examination some other time?

SIR ROBERT: It might be arranged.

ARTHUR: To-morrow?

SIR ROBERT: To-morrow is impossible. I am in Court all the morning and in the House of Commons for the rest of the day. (*Carelessly.*) If a further examination should prove necessary it will have to be some time next week.

ARTHUR: I see. Will your forgive me if I sit down? (*He sits in his usual chair.*) Curry has been telling me you think it might be possible to proceed by Petition of Right.

CATHERINE: What's a Petition of Right?

DESMOND: Well—granting the assumption that the Admiralty, as the Crown, can do no wrong——

CATHERINE (*murmuring*): I thought that was exactly the assumption we refused to grant.

DESMOND: In law, I mean. Now, a subject can sue the Crown, nevertheless, by Petition of Right, redress being granted as a matter of grace—and the custom is for the Attorney-General—on behalf of the King—to endorse the Petition, and allow the case to come to Court.

SIR ROBERT: It is interesting to note that the exact words he uses on such occasions are: Let Right be done.

ARTHUR: Let Right be done? I like that phrase, sir.

SIR ROBERT: It has a certain ring about it—has it not? (*Languidly.*) Let Right be done.

RONNIE *comes in. He is in an Eton suit, looking very spick and span.*

ARTHUR: This is my son Ronald. Ronnie, this is Sir Robert Morton.

RONNIE: How do you do, sir?

ARTHUR: He is going to ask you a few questions. You must answer them all truthfully—as you always have. (*He begins to struggle out of his chair.*) I expect you would like us to leave——

SIR ROBERT: No. Provided, of course, that you don't interrupt. (*To* CATHERINE.) Miss Winslow, will you sit down, please?

CATHERINE *takes a seat abruptly.*

SIR ROBERT (*to* RONNIE): Will you stand at the table, facing me? (RONNIE *does so.*) That's right.

SIR ROBERT *and* RONNIE *now face each other across the table.* SIR ROBERT *begins his examination very quietly.*

Now, Ronald, how old are you?

RONNIE: Fourteen and seven months.

SIR ROBERT: You were, then, thirteen and ten months old when you left Osborne: is that right?

RONNIE: Yes, sir.

SIR ROBERT: Now I would like you to cast your mind back to July 7th of last year. Will you tell me in your own words exactly what happened to you on that day?

RONNIE: All right. Well, it was a half-holiday, so we didn't have any work after dinner——

SIR ROBERT: Dinner? At one o'clock?

RONNIE: Yes. At least, until prep at seven.

SIR ROBERT: Prep at seven?

RONNIE: Just before dinner I went to the Chief Petty Officer and asked him to let me have fifteen and six out of what I had in the school bank——

SIR ROBERT: Why did you do that?

RONNIE: I wanted to buy an air pistol.

SIR ROBERT: Which cost fifteen and six?

RONNIE: Yes, sir.

SIR ROBERT: And how much money did you have in the school bank at the time.?

RONNIE: Two pounds three shillings.

ARTHUR: So you see, sir, what incentive could there possibly be for him to steal five shillings?

SIR ROBERT (*coldly*): I must ask you to be good enough not to interrupt me, sir. (*To* RONNIE.) After you had withdrawn the fifteen and six what did you do?

RONNIE: I had dinner.

SIR ROBERT: Then what?

RONNIE: I went to the locker-room and put the fifteen and six in my locker.

SIR ROBERT: Yes. Then?

RONNIE: I went to get permission to go down to the Post Office. Then I went to the locker-room again, got out my money, and went down to the Post Office.

SIR ROBERT: I see. Go on.

RONNIE: I bought my postal order——

SIR ROBERT: For fifteen and six?

RONNIE: Yes. Then I went back to college. Then I met Elliot minor, and he said: "I say, isn't it rot? Someone's broken into my locker and pinched a postal order. I've reported it to the P.O."

SIR ROBERT: Those were Elliot minor's exact words?

RONNIE: He might have used another word for rot——

SIR ROBERT: I see. Continue——

RONNIE: Well, then just before prep I was told to go along and see Commander Flower. The woman from the Post Office was there, and the Commander said: "Is this the boy?" and she said: "It might be. I can't be sure. They all look so much alike."

ARTHUR: You see? She couldn't identify him.

SIR ROBERT *glares at him.*

SIR ROBERT (*to* RONNIE): Go on.

RONNIE: Then she said: "I only know that the boy who bought a postal order for fifteen and six was the same boy that cashed one for five shillings." So the Commander said: "Did you buy a postal order for fifteen and six?" And I said: "Yes," and then they made me write Elliot minor's name on an envelope, and compared it to the signature on the postal order—then they sent me to the sanatorium and ten days later I was sacked—I mean—expelled.

SIR ROBERT: I see. (*Quietly.*) Did you cash a postal order belonging to Elliot minor for five shillings?

RONNIE: No, sir.

SIR ROBERT: Did you break into his locker and steal it?

RONNIE: No, sir.

SIR ROBERT: And that is the truth, the whole truth and nothing but the truth?

RONNIE: Yes, sir.

DICKIE *has come in during this, and is standing furtively in the doorway, not knowing whether to come in or go out.* ARTHUR *waves him impatiently to a seat.*

SIR ROBERT: Right. When the Commander asked you to write Elliot's name on an envelope, how did you write it? With Christian name or initials?

RONNIE: I wrote Charles K. Elliot.

SIR ROBERT: Charles K. Elliot. Did you by any chance happen to see the forged postal order in the Commander's office?

RONNIE: Oh, yes. The Commander showed it to me.

SIR ROBERT: Before or after you had written Elliot's name on the envelope?

RONNIE: After.

SIR ROBERT: After. And did you happen to see how Elliot's name was written on the postal order?

RONNIE; Yes, sir. The same.

SIR ROBERT: The same? Charles K. Elliot?

RONNIE: Yes, sir.

SIR ROBERT: When you wrote on the envelope, what made you choose that particular form?

RONNIE: That was the way he usually signed his name——

SIR ROBERT: How did you know?

RONNIE: Well—he was a great friend of mine——

SIR ROBERT: That is no answer. How did you know?

RONNIE: I'd seen him sign things.

SIR ROBERT: What things?

RONNIE: Oh—ordinary things.

SIR ROBERT: I repeat: what things?

RONNIE (*reluctantly*): Bits of paper.

SIR ROBERT: Bits of paper? And why did he sign his name on bits of paper?

RONNIE: I don't know.

SIR ROBERT: You do know. Why did he sign his name on bits of paper?

RONNIE: He was practising his signature.

SIR ROBERT: And you saw him?

RONNIE: Yes.

SIR ROBERT: Did he know you saw him?

RONNIE: Well—yes——

SIR ROBERT: In other words he showed you exactly how he wrote his signature?

RONNIE: Yes. I suppose he did.

SIR ROBERT: Did you practise writing it yourself?

RONNIE: I might have done.

SIR ROBERT: What do you mean you might have done? Did you or did you not?

RONNIE: Yes——

ARTHUR (*sharply*): Ronnie! You never told me that.

RONNIE: It was only for a joke——

SIR ROBERT: Never mind whether it was for a joke or not. The fact is you practised forging Elliot's signature——

RONNIE: It wasn't forging——

SIR ROBERT: What do you call it then?

RONNIE: Writing.

SIR ROBERT: Very well. Writing. Whoever stole the postal order and cashed it also *wrote* Elliot's signature, didn't he?

RONNIE: Yes.

SIR ROBERT: And oddly enough, in the exact form in which you had earlier been practising *writing* his signature——

RONNIE (*indignantly*): I say. Which side are you on?

SIR ROBERT (*snarling*): Don't be impertinent! Are you aware that the Admiralty sent up the forged postal order to Mr. Ridgeley-Pearce—the greatest handwriting expert in England?

RONNIE: Yes.

SIR ROBERT: And you know that Mr. Ridgeley-Pearce affirmed that there was no doubt that the signature on the postal order and

the signature you wrote on the envelope were by one and the same
hand?

RONNIE: Yes.

SIR ROBERT: And you still say that you didn't forge that signature?

RONNIE: Yes, I do.

SIR ROBERT: In other words, Mr. Ridgeley-Pearce doesn't know
his job?

RONNIE: Well, he's wrong anyway.

SIR ROBERT: When you went into the locker-room after dinner,
were you alone?

RONNIE: I don't remember.

SIR ROBERT: I think you do.   Were you alone in the locker-
room?

RONNIE: Yes.

SIR ROBERT: And you knew which was Elliot's locker?

RONNIE: Yes.   Of course.

SIR ROBERT: Why did you go in there at all?

RONNIE: I've told you.   To put my fifteen and six away.

SIR ROBERT: Why?

RONNIE: I thought it would be safer.

SIR ROBERT: Why safer than your pocket?

RONNIE: I don't know.

SIR ROBERT: You had it in your pocket at dinner-time.   Why
this sudden fear for its safety?

RONNIE (*plainly rattled*): I tell you, I don't know——

SIR ROBERT: It was rather an odd thing to do, wasn't it?   The
money was perfectly safe in your pocket.   Why did you suddenly
feel yourself impelled to put it away in your locker?

RONNIE (*almost shouting*): I don't know.

SIR ROBERT: Was it because you knew you would be alone in
the locker-room at that time?

RONNIE: No.

SIR ROBERT: Where was Elliot's locker in relation to yours?

RONNIE: Next to it, but one.

SIR ROBERT: Next, but one.   What time did Elliot put his postal
order in his locker?

RONNIE: I don't know.   I didn't even know he had a postal order
in his locker.   I didn't know he had a postal order at all.

SIR ROBERT: Yet you say he was a great friend of yours——

RONNIE: He didn't tell me he had one.

SIR ROBERT: How very secretive of him.   What time did you go to the locker-room?

RONNIE: I don't remember.

SIR ROBERT: Was it directly after dinner?

RONNIE: Yes.   I think so.

SIR ROBERT: What did you do after leaving the locker-room?

RONNIE: I've told you.   I went for permission to go to the Post Office.

SIR ROBERT: What time was that?

RONNIE: About a quarter past two.

SIR ROBERT: Dinner is over at a quarter to two.   Which means that you were in the locker-room for half an hour?

RONNIE: I wasn't there all that time——

SIR ROBERT: How long were you there?

RONNIE: About five minutes.

SIR ROBERT: What were you doing for the other twenty-five?

RONNIE: I don't remember.

SIR ROBERT: It's odd that your memory is so good about some things and so bad about others——

RONNIE: Perhaps I waited outside the C.O.'s office.

SIR ROBERT (*with searing sarcasm*): Perhaps you waited outside the C.O.'s office!   And perhaps no one saw you there, either?

RONNIE: No.   I don't think they did.

SIR ROBERT: What were you thinking about outside the C.O.'s office for twenty-five minutes?

RONNIE (*wildly*): I don't even know if I was there.   I can't remember.   Perhaps I wasn't there at all.

SIR ROBERT: No.   Perhaps you were still in the locker-room rifling Elliot's locker——

ARTHUR (*indignantly*): Sir Robert, I must ask you——

SIR ROBERT: Quiet!

RONNIE: I remember now.   I remember.   Someone did see me outside the C.O.'s office.   A chap called Casey.   I remember I spoke to him.

SIR ROBERT: What did you say?

RONNIE: I said: "Come down to the Post Office with me.   I'm going to cash a postal order."

SIR ROBERT (*triumphantly*): *Cash* a postal order.

RONNIE: I mean get.

SIR ROBERT: You said cash.   Why did you say cash if you meant get?

RONNIE: I don't know.

SIR ROBERT: I suggest cash was the truth.

RONNIE: No, no.   It wasn't.   It wasn't really.   You're muddling me.

SIR ROBERT: You seem easily muddled.   How many other lies have you told?

RONNIE: None.   Really I haven't——

SIR ROBERT (*bending forward malevolently*): I suggest your whole testimony is a lie——

RONNIE: No!   It's the truth——

SIR ROBERT: I suggest there is barely one single word of truth in anything you have said either to me, or to the judge advocate or to the Commander.   I suggest that you broke into Elliot's locker, that you stole the postal order for five shillings belonging to Elliot, that you cashed it by means of forging his name——

RONNIE (*wailing*): I didn't.   I didn't.

SIR ROBERT: I suggest that you did it for a joke, meaning to give Elliot the five shillings back, but that when you met him and he said he had reported the matter you got frightened and decided to keep quiet——

RONNIE: No, no, no.   It isn't true——

SIR ROBERT: I suggest that by continuing to deny your guilt you are causing great hardship to your own family, and considerable annoyance to high and important persons in this country——

CATHERINE (*on her feet*): That's a disgraceful thing to say!

ARTHUR: I agree.

SIR ROBERT (*leaning forward and glaring at* RONNIE *with the utmost venom*): I suggest, that the time has at last come for you to undo some of the misery you have caused by confessing to us all now that you are a forger, a liar, and a thief!

RONNIE (*in tears*): I'm not!   I'm not!   I'm not!   I didn't do it——

GRACE *has flown to his side and now envelops him.*

ARTHUR: This is outrageous, sir——

JOHN *appears at the door, dressed in evening clothes.*

JOHN: Kate, dear, I'm late.   I'm most terribly sorry——

He stops short as he takes in the scene, with RONNIE *sobbing hysterically on his mother's breast, and* ARTHUR *and* CATHERINE *glaring indignantly at* SIR ROBERT, *who is engaged in putting his papers together.*

SIR ROBERT (*to* DESMOND): Can I drop you anywhere? My car is at the door.

DESMOND: Er—no—I thank you——

SIR ROBERT (*carelessly*): Well, send all this stuff round to my chambers to-morrow morning, will you?

DESMOND: But—but will you need it now?

SIR ROBERT: Oh, yes. The boy is plainly innocent. I accept the brief.

> *He bows to* ARTHUR *and* CATHERINE *and walks languidly to the door, past the bewildered* JOHN, *to whom he gives a polite nod as he goes out.* RONNIE *continues to sob hysterically.*

CURTAIN

ACT III

SCENE: *The same, nine months later. The time is about ten-thirty p.m. Arthur is sitting in his favourite armchair, reading aloud from an evening paper, whose wide headline:* "WINSLOW DEBATE : FIRST LORD REPLIES" *we can read on the front page. Listening to him are Ronnie and Grace, though neither of them seems to be doing so with much concentration. Ronnie is finding it hard to keep his eyes open, and Grace, darning socks in the other armchair has evidently other and, to her, more important matters on her mind.*

ARTHUR (*reading*): "—The Admiralty, during the whole of this long-drawn-out dispute, have at no time acted hastily or ill-advisedly, and it is a matter of mere histrionic hyperbole for the right honourable and learned gentleman opposite to characterise the conduct of my department as that of callousness so inhuman as to amount to deliberate malice towards the boy Winslow. Such unfounded accusations I can well choose to ignore. (*An honourable Member*: 'You can't.') Honourable Members opposite may interrupt as much as they please, but I repeat—there is nothing whatever that the Admiralty has done, or failed to do, in the case of this cadet for which I, as First Lord, need to apologise. (*Further Opposition interruptions.*)" (*He stops reading and looks up.*) I must say it looks as if the First Lord's having rather a rough passage—— (*He breaks off, noticing* RONNIE'S *head has fallen back on the cushions and he is asleep.*) I trust my reading isn't keeping you awake. (*There is no answer.*) I say I trust my reading isn't keeping you awake! (*Again there is no answer. Helplessly.*) Grace!

GRACE: My poor sleepy little lamb! It's long past his bedtime, Arthur.

ARTHUR: Grace, dear—at this very moment your poor sleepy little lamb is the subject of a very violent and heated debate in the House of Commons. I should have thought, in the circumstances, it might have been possible for him to contrive to stay awake for a few minutes past his bedtime——

GRACE: I expect he's over-excited.

ARTHUR *and* GRACE *both look at the tranquilly oblivious form on the sofa.*

ARTHUR: A picture of over-excitement. (*Sharply.*) Ronnie! (*No answer.*) Ronnie!

RONNIE (*opening his eyes*): Yes, Father?

ARTHUR: I am reading the account of the debate. Would you like to listen, or would you rather go to bed?

RONNIE: Oh, I'd like to listen, of course, Father. I was listening, too, only I had my eyes shut——

ARTHUR: Very well. (*Reading.*) "The First Lord continued amid further interruptions: The chief point of criticism against the Admiralty appears to centre in the purely legal question of the Petition of Right brought by Mr. Arthur Winslow and the Admiralty's demurrer thereto. Sir Robert Morton has made great play with his eloquent reference to the liberty of the individual menaced, as he puts it, by the new despotism of bureaucracy—and I was as moved as any honourable Member opposite by his resonant use of the words: Let Right be done—the time-honoured phrase with which in his opinion the Attorney-General should without question have endorsed Mr. Winslow's Petition of Right. Nevertheless, the matter is not nearly as simple as he appears to imagine. Cadet Ronald Winslow is a servant of the Crown, and has therefore no more right than any other member of His Majesty's forces to sue the Crown in open court. To allow him to do so would undoubtedly raise the most dangerous precedents. There is no doubt whatever in my mind that in certain cases private rights may have to be sacrificed for the public good—— (*He looks up.*) And what other excuse, pray, did Charles the First make for ship money and——

RONNIE, *after a manful attempt to keep his eyes open by self-pinchings and other devices, has once more succumbed to oblivion.*

(*Sharply.*) Ronnie! Ronnie!

RONNIE *stirs, turns over, and slides more comfortably into the cushions.*

Would you believe it!

GRACE: He's dead tired. I'd better take him up to his bed——

ARTHUR: No. If he must sleep, let him sleep there.

GRACE: Oh, but he'd be much more comfy in his little bed——

ARTHUR: I dare say: but the debate continues and until it's ended the cause of it all will certainly not make himself comfy in his little bed.

> VIOLET *comes in.*

VIOLET: There are three more reporters in the hall, sir.   Want to see you very urgently.   Shall I let them in?

ARTHUR: No.   Certainly not.   I issued a statement yesterday. Until the debate is over I have nothing more to say.

VIOLET: Yes, sir.   That's what I told them, but they wouldn't go.

ARTHUR: Well, make them.   Use force, if necessary.

VIOLET: Yes, sir.   And shall I cut some sandwiches for Miss Catherine, as she missed her dinner?

GRACE: Yes, Violet.   Good idea.

> VIOLET *goes out.*

VIOLET (*off*): It's no good.   No more statements.

> *Voices answer her, fading at length into silence.* GRACE *puts a rug over* RONNIE, *now sleeping very soundly.*

ARTHUR: Grace dear——

GRACE: Yes?

ARTHUR: I fancy this might be a good opportunity of talking to Violet.

GRACE (*quite firmly*): No, dear.

ARTHUR: Meaning that it isn't a good opportunity?   Or meaning that you have no intention at all of ever talking to Violet?

GRACE: I'll do it one day, Arthur.   To-morrow, perhaps.   Not now.

ARTHUR: I believe you'd do better to grasp the nettle.   Delay only adds to your worries——

GRACE (*bitterly*): My worries?   What do you know about my worries?

ARTHUR: A good deal, Grace.   But I feel they would be a lot lessened if you faced the situation squarely.

GRACE: It's easy for you to talk, Arthur.   You don't have to do it.

ARTHUR: I will, if you like.

GRACE: No, dear.

ARTHUR: If you explain the dilemma to her carefully—if you even show her the figures I jotted down for you yesterday—I venture to think you won't find her unreasonable.

GRACE: It won't be easy for her to find another place.

ARTHUR: We'll give her an excellent reference.

GRACE: That won't alter the fact that she's never been properly trained as a parlourmaid and—well—you know yourself how we're always having to explain her to people. No, Arthur, I don't mind how many figures she's shown, it's a brutal thing to do.

ARTHUR: Facts are brutal things.

GRACE (*a shade hysterically*): Facts? I don't think I know what facts are any more——

Arthur. The facts, at this moment, are that we have a half of the income we had a year ago and we're living at nearly the same rate. However you look at it that's bad economics——

GRACE: I'm not talking about economics, Arthur. I'm talking about ordinary, common or garden facts—things we took for granted a year ago and which now don't seem to matter any more.

ARTHUR: Such as?

GRACE (*with rising voice*): Such as a happy home and peace and quiet and an ordinary respectable life, and some sort of future for us and our children. In the last year you've thrown all that overboard, Arthur. There's your return for it, I suppose (*she indicates the headline in the paper*) and it's all very exciting and important, I'm sure, but it doesn't bring back any of the things that we've lost. I can only pray to God that you know what you're doing.

RONNIE *stirs in his sleep.* GRACE *lowers her voice at the end of her speech. There is a pause.*

ARTHUR: I know exactly what I'm doing, Grace. I'm going to publish my son's innocence before the world, and for that end I am not prepared to weigh the cost.

GRACE: But the cost may be out of all proportion——

ARTHUR: It may be. That doesn't concern me. I hate heroics, Grace, but you force me to say this. An injustice has been done. I am going to set it right, and there is no sacrifice in the world I am not prepared to make in order to do so.

GRACE (*with sudden violence*): Oh, I wish I could see the sense of it all! (*Pointing to* RONNIE.) He's perfectly happy, at a good school, doing very well. No one need ever have known about Osborne, if you hadn't gone and shouted it out to the whole world. As it is, whatever happens now, he'll go through the rest of his life as the boy in that Winslow case—the boy who stole that postal order——

ARTHUR (*grimly*): The boy who didn't steal that postal order.

GRACE (*wearily*): What's the difference? When millions are talking and gossiping about him, a did or a didn't hardly matters.

The Winslow boy is enough.   You talk about sacrificing everything
for him: but when he's grown up he won't thank you for it, Arthur
—even though you've given your life to—publish his innocence as
you call it.

> ARTHUR *makes an impatient gesture.*

Yes, Arthur—your life.   You talk gaily about arthritis and a touch
of gout and old age and the rest of it, but you know as well as any
of the doctors what really is the matter with you.   (*Nearly in tears.*)
You're destroying yourself, Arthur, and me and your family besides.
For what I'd like to know?   I've asked you and Kate to tell me a
hundred times—but you never will.   For what, Arthur?

> ARTHUR *has struggled painfully out of his seat and now approaches*
> *her.*

ARTHUR (*quietly*): For Justice, Grace.

GRACE: That sounds very noble.   Are you sure it's true?   Are
you sure it isn't just plain pride and self-importance and sheer brute
stubbornness?

ARTHUR (*putting a hand out*): No, Grace.   I don't think it is.   I
really don't think it is——

GRACE (*shaking off his hand*): No.   This time I'm not going to
cry and say I'm sorry, and make it all up again.   I can stand anything if there is a reason for it.   But for no reason at all, it's unfair
to ask so much of me.   It's unfair——

> *She breaks down.   As* ARTHUR *puts a comforting arm around her*
> *she pushes him off and goes out of the door.* RONNIE *has, mean-*
> *while, opened his eyes.*

RONNIE: What's the matter, Father?

ARTHUR (*turning from the door*): Your mother is a little upset——

RONNIE (*drowsily*): Why?   Aren't things going well?

ARTHUR: Oh, yes. (*Murmuring.*)   Very well. (*He sits with more*
than his usual difficulty, as if he were utterly exhausted.)   Very well
indeed.

> RONNIE *contentedly closes his eyes again.*

(*Gently.*)   You'd better go to bed now, Ronnie.   You'll be more
comfortable——

> *He sees* RONNIE *is asleep again.   He makes as if to wake him,*
> *then shrugs his shoulders and turns away.* VIOLET *comes in with*
> *sandwiches on a plate and a letter on a salver.*

Thank you, Violet.

> VIOLET *puts the sandwiches on the table and hands* ARTHUR *the*

letter. ARTHUR *puts it down on the table beside him without opening it.* VIOLET *turns to go out.*

ARTHUR: Oh, Violet——

VIOLET (*turning placidly*): Yes, sir?

ARTHUR: How long have you been with us?

VIOLET: Twenty-four years come April, sir.

ARTHUR: As long as that?

VIOLET: Yes, sir. Miss Kate was that high when I first came (*she indicates a small child*) and Mr. Dickie hadn't even been thought of——

ARTHUR: I remember you coming to us now. I remember it well. What do you think of this case, Violet?

VIOLET: A fine old rumpus that is, and no mistake.

ARTHUR: It is, isn't it? A fine old rumpus.

VIOLET: There was a bit in the *Evening News*. Did you read it, sir?

ARTHUR: No. What did it say?

VIOLET: Oh, about how it was a fuss about nothing and a shocking waste of the Government's time, but how it was a good thing all the same because it could only happen in England——

ARTHUR: There seems to be a certain lack of logic in that argument——

VIOLET: Well, perhaps they put it a bit different, sir. Still, that's what it said all right. And when you think it's all because of our Master Ronnie—I have to laugh about it sometimes, I really do. Wasting the Government's time at his age! I never did. Well, wonders will never cease.

ARTHUR: I know. Wonders will never cease.

VIOLET: Well—would that be all, sir?

ARTHUR: Yes, Violet. That'll be all.

> CATHERINE *comes in.*

CATHERINE: Good evening, Violet.

VIOLET: Good evening, miss.

> *She goes out.*

CATHERINE: Hullo, Father. (*She kisses him. Indicating* RONNIE.) An honourable Member described that this evening as a piteous little figure, crying aloud to humanity for justice and redress. I wish he could see him now.

ARTHUR (*testily*): It's long past his bedtime. What's happened? Is the debate over?

CATHERINE: As good as.   The First Lord gave an assurance that in future there would be no enquiry at Osborne or Dartmouth without informing the parents first.   That seemed to satisfy most Members——

ARTHUR: But what about *our* case?   Is he going to allow us a fair trial?

CATHERINE: Apparently not.

ARTHUR: But that's iniquitous.   I thought he would be forced to——

CATHERINE: I thought so, too.   The House evidently thought otherwise.

ARTHUR: Will there be a division?

CATHERINE: There may be.   If there is the Government will win.

ARTHUR: What is the motion?

CATHERINE: To reduce the First Lord's salary by a hundred pounds. (*With a faint smile.*)   Naturally no one really wants to do that. (*Indicating sandwiches.*)   Are these for me?

ARTHUR: Yes.

> CATHERINE *starts to eat the sandwiches.*

So we're back where we started, then?

CATHERINE: It looks like it.

ARTHUR: The debate has done us no good at all?

CATHERINE: It's aired the case a little, perhaps.   A few more thousand people will say to each other at breakfast to-morrow: "That boy ought to be allowed a fair trial."

ARTHUR: What's the good of that, if they can't make themselves heard?

CATHERINE: I think they can—given time.

ARTHUR: Given time?

> *Pause.*

But didn't Sir Robert make any protest when the First Lord refused a trial?

CATHERINE: Not a verbal protest.   Something far more spectacular and dramatic.   He'd had his feet on the Treasury table and his hat over his eyes during most of the First Lord's speech—and he suddenly got up very deliberately, glared at the First Lord, threw a whole bundle of notes on the floor, and stalked out of the House.   It made a magnificent effect.   If I hadn't known I could have sworn he was genuinely indignant——

ARTHUR: Of course he was genuinely indignant. So would any man of feeling be——

CATHERINE: Sir Robert, Father dear, is not a man of feeling. I don't think any emotion at all can stir that fishy heart——

ARTHUR: Except perhaps a single-minded love of justice.

CATHERINE: Nonsense. A single-minded love of Sir Robert Morton.

ARTHUR: You're very ungrateful to him considering all he's done for us these last months——

CATHERINE: I'm not ungrateful, Father. He's been wonderful— I admit it freely. No one could have fought a harder fight.

ARTHUR: Well, then——

CATHERINE: It's only his motives I question. At least I *don't* question them at all. I know them.

ARTHUR: What are they?

CATHERINE: First—publicity—you know—look at me, the staunch defender of the little man—and then second—a nice popular stick to beat the Government with. Both very useful to an ambitious man. Luckily for him we've provided them.

ARTHUR: Luckily for us too, Kate.

CATHERINE: Oh, I agree. But don't fool yourself about him, Father, for all that. The man is a fish, a hard, cold-blooded, supercilious, sneering fish.

 VIOLET *enters*.

VIOLET (*announcing*): Sir Robert Morton.

 CATHERINE *chokes over her sandwich*.

 SIR ROBERT *comes in*.

SIR ROBERT: Good evening.

CATHERINE (*still choking*): Good evening.

SIR ROBERT: Something gone down the wrong way?

CATHERINE: Yes.

SIR ROBERT: May I assist? (*He pats her on the back.*)

CATHERINE: Thank you.

SIR ROBERT (*to* ARTHUR): Good evening, sir. I thought I would call and give you an account of the day's proceedings, but I see your daughter has forestalled me.

CATHERINE: Did you know I was in the gallery?

SIR ROBERT (*gallantly*): With such a charming hat, how could I have missed you?

ARTHUR: It was very good of you to call, sir, nevertheless——

SIR ROBERT (*seeing* RONNIE): Ah.   The *casus belli*—dormant——
    ARTHUR *goes to waken him.*

SIR ROBERT: No, no.   I beg of you.   Please do not disturb his innocent slunmbers.

CATHERINE: *Innocent* slumbers?

SIR ROBERT: Exactly.   Besides, I fear since our first encounter he is, rather pardonably, a trifle nervous of me.

CATHERINE: Will you betray a technical secret, Sir Robert?   What happened in that first examination to make you so sure of his innocence?

SIR ROBERT: Three things.   First of all, he made far too many damaging admissions.   A guilty person would have been much more careful and on his guard.   Secondly, I laid him a trap; and thirdly, left him a loophole.   Anyone who was guilty would have fallen into the one and darted through the other.   He did neither.

CATHERINE: The trap was to ask him suddenly what time Elliot put the postal order in his locker, wasn't it?

SIR ROBERT: Yes.

ARTHUR: And the loophole?

SIR ROBERT: I then suggested to him that he had stolen the postal order for a joke—which, had he been guilty, he would surely have admitted to as being the lesser of two evils.

CATHERINE: I see.   It was very cleverly thought out.

SIR ROBERT (*with a little bow*): Thank you.

ARTHUR: May we offer you some refreshment, Sir Robert?   A whisky and soda?

SIR ROBERT: No, thank you.   Nothing at all.

ARTHUR: My daughter has told me of your demonstration during the First Lord's speech.   She described it as—magnificent.

SIR ROBERT (*with a glance at* CATHERINE): Did she?   That was good of her.   It's a very old trick, you know.   I've done it many times in the Courts.   It's nearly always surprisingly effective——
    CATHERINE *catches her father's eye and nods triumphantly.*
(*To* CATHERINE.)   Was the First Lord at all put out by it—did you notice?

CATHERINE: How could he have failed to be?   (*To* ARTHUR, *approaching his chair.*)   I wish you could have seen it, Father—it was——
(*She notices the letter on the table beside* ARTHUR *and snatches it up with a sudden gesture.   She examines the envelope.*)   When did this come?

ARTHUR: A few minutes ago.   Do you know the writing?

CATHERINE: Yes. (*She puts the letter back on the table.*)

ARTHUR: Whose is it?

CATHERINE: I shouldn't bother to read it, if I were you.

> ARTHUR *looks at her, puzzled, then takes up the letter.*

ARTHUR (*to* SIR ROBERT): Will you forgive me?

SIR ROBERT: Of course.

> ARTHUR *opens the letter and begins to read.* CATHERINE *watches him for a moment, and then turns with a certain forced liveliness to* SIR ROBERT.

CATHERINE: Well, what do you think the next step should be?

SIR ROBERT: I have already been considering that, Miss Winslow. I believe that perhaps the best plan would be to renew our efforts to get the Director of Public Prosecutions to act.

CATHERINE (*with one eye on her father*): But do you think there's any chance of that?

SIR ROBERT: Oh yes. In the main it will chiefly be a question of making ourselves a confounded nuisance——

CATHERINE: We've certainly done that quite successfully so far—thanks to you——

SIR ROBERT (*suavely*): Ah. That is perhaps the only quality I was born with—the ability to make myself a confounded nuisance.

> He, *too, has his eye on* ARTHUR, *sensing something amiss.* ARTHUR *finishes reading the letter.*

CATHERINE (*with false vivacity*): Father—Sir Robert thinks we might get the Director of Public Prosecutions to act——

ARTHUR: What?

SIR ROBERT: We were discussing how to proceed with the case——

ARTHUR: The case? (*He stares, a little blankly, from one to the other.*) Yes. We must think of that, mustn't we? (*Pause.*) How to proceed with the case? (*To* SIR ROBERT, *abruptly.*) I'm afraid I don't think, all things considered, that much purpose would be served by going on——

> SIR ROBERT *and* CATHERINE *stare at him blankly.* CATHERINE *goes quickly to him and snatches the letter from his lap. She begins to read.*

SIR ROBERT (*with a sudden change of tone*): Of course we must go on.

ARTHUR (*in a low voice*): It is not for you to choose, sir. The choice is mine.

SIR ROBERT (*harshly*): Then you must reconsider it. To give up now would be insane.

ARTHUR: Insane? My sanity has already been called in question to-night—for carrying the case as far as I have.

SIR ROBERT: Whatever the contents of that letter, or whatever has happened to make you lose heart, I insist that we continue the fight——

ARTHUR: Insist? We? It is my fight—my fight alone—and it is for me alone to judge when the time has come to give up.

SIR ROBERT (violently): But why give up? Why? In Heaven's name, man, why?

ARTHUR (slowly): I have made many sacrifices for this case. Some of them I had no right to make, but I made them none the less. But there is a limit and I have reached it. I am sorry, Sir Robert. More sorry, perhaps, than you are, but the Winslow case is now closed.

SIR ROBERT: Balderdash.

ARTHUR *looks surprised at this unparliamentary expression.* CATHERINE *has read and re-read the letter, and now breaks the silence in a calm, methodical voice.*

CATHERINE: My father doesn't mean what he says, Sir Robert.

SIR ROBERT: I am glad to hear it.

CATHERINE: Perhaps I should explain this letter——

ARTHUR: No, Kate.

CATHERINE: Sir Robert knows so much about our family affairs, Father, I don't see it will matter much if he learns a little more. (To SIR ROBERT.) This letter is from a certain Colonel Watherstone who is the father of the man I'm engaged to. We've always known he was opposed to the case, so it really comes as no surprise. In it he says that our efforts to discredit the Admiralty in the House of Commons to-day have resulted merely in our making the name of Winslow a nation-wide laughing-stock. I think that's his phrase. (She consults the letter.) Yes. That's right. A nation-wide laughing-stock.

SIR ROBERT: I don't care for his English.

CATHERINE: It's not very good, is it? He goes on to say that unless my father will give him a firm undertaking to drop this whining and reckless agitation—I suppose he means the case—he will exert every bit of influence he has over his son to prevent him marrying me.

SIR ROBERT: I see. An ultimatum.

CATHERINE: Yes—but a pointless one.

SIR ROBERT: He has no influence over his son?

CATHERINE: Oh yes. A little, naturally. But his son is of age, and his own master——

SIR ROBERT: Is he dependent on his father for money?

CATHERINE: He gets an allowance. But he can live perfectly well—we both can live perfectly well without it.

Pause. SIR ROBERT *stares hard at her, then turns abruptly to* ARTHUR.

SIR ROBERT: Well, sir?

ARTHUR: I'm afraid I can't go back on what I have already said. I will give you a decision in a few days——

SIR ROBERT: Your daughter seems prepared to take the risk——

ARTHUR: I am not. Not, at least, until I know how great a risk it is——

SIR ROBERT: How do you estimate the risk, Miss Winslow?

Pause. CATHERINE, *for all her bravado, is plainly scared. She is engaged in lighting a cigarette as* SIR ROBERT *asks his question.*

CATHERINE (*at length*): Negligible.

SIR ROBERT *stares at her again. Feeling his eyes on her, she returns his glance defiantly. Pause.*

SIR ROBERT (*returning abruptly to his languid manner*): I see. May I take a cigarette, too?

CATHERINE: Yes, of course. I thought you didn't smoke.

SIR ROBERT: Only occasionally. (*To* ARTHUR.) I really must apologise to you, sir, for speaking to you as I did just now. It was unforgivable.

ARTHUR: Not at all, sir. You were upset at giving up the case—and, to be frank, I liked you for it——

SIR ROBERT (*with a deprecating gesture*): It has been rather a tiring day. The House of Commons is a peculiarly exhausting place, you know. Too little ventilation, and far too much hot air—I really am most truly sorry.

ARTHUR: Please.

SIR ROBERT (*carelessly*): Of course, you must decide about the case as you wish. That really is a most charming hat, Miss Winslow——

CATHERINE: I'm glad you like it.

SIR ROBERT: It seems decidedly wrong to me that a lady of your political persuasion should be allowed to adorn herself with such a very feminine allurement. It really looks so awfully like trying to have the best of both worlds——

CATHERINE: I'm not a militant, you know, Sir Robert. I don't go about breaking shop windows with a hammer or pouring acid down pillar boxes.

SIR ROBERT (*languidly*): I am truly glad to hear it. Both those activities would be highly unsuitable in that hat——

> CATHERINE *glares at him but suppresses an angry retort.*

I have never yet fully grasped what active steps you take to propagate your cause, Miss Winslow.

CATHERINE (*shortly*): I'm an organising secretary at the West London Branch of the Woman's Suffrage Association.

SIR ROBERT: Indeed? Is the work hard?

CATHERINE: Very.

SIR ROBERT: But not, I should imagine, particularly lucrative.

CATHERINE: The work is voluntary and unpaid.

SIR ROBERT (*murmuring*): Dear me! What sacrifices you young ladies seem prepared to make for your convictions——

> VIOLET *enters.*

VIOLET (*to* CATHERINE): Mr. Watherstone is in the hall, miss. Says he would like to have a word with you in private—most particular——

> *Pause.*

CATHERINE: Oh. I'll come out to him——

ARTHUR: No. See him in here.

> *He begins to struggle out of his chair.* SIR ROBERT *assists him.*

You wouldn't mind coming to the dining-room, would you, Sir Robert, for a moment?

SIR ROBERT: Not in the least.

CATHERINE: All right, Violet.

VIOLET: Will you come in, sir?

> JOHN *comes in. He is looking depressed and anxious.* CATHERINE *greets him with a smile, which he returns only half-heartedly. This exchange is lost on* ARTHUR, *who has his back to them, but not on* SIR ROBERT.

CATHERINE: Hello, John.

JOHN: Hullo. (*To* ARTHUR.) Good evening, sir.

ARTHUR: Good evening, John. (*He goes on towards dining-room.*)

CATHERINE: I don't think you've met Sir Robert Morton.

JOHN: No, I haven't. How do you do, sir?

SIR ROBERT: I think you promised me a whisky and soda. (*Turning to* JOHN.) May I offer my very belated congratulations?

JOHN: Congratulations? Oh yes. Thank you.

ARTHUR *and* SIR ROBERT *go into dining-room.   There is a pause.*
CATHERINE *is watching* JOHN *with an anxious expression.*

JOHN (*indicating* RONNIE): Is he asleep?

CATHERINE: Yes.

JOHN: Sure he's not shamming?

CATHERINE: Yes.

JOHN (*after a pause*): My father's written your father a letter.

CATHERINE: I know.   I've read it.

JOHN: Oh.

CATHERINE: Did you?

JOHN: Yes.   He showed it to me.

Pause.   JOHN *is carefully not looking at her.*
(*At length.*)   Well, what's his answer?

CATHERINE: My father?   I don't suppose he'll send one.

JOHN: You think he'll ignore it?

CATHERINE: Isn't that the best answer to blackmail?

JOHN (*muttering*): It was damned high-handed of the old man, I admit.

CATHERINE: High-handed?

JOHN: I tried to get him not to send it——

CATHERINE: I'm glad.

JOHN: The trouble is—he's perfectly serious.

CATHERINE: I never thought he wasn't.

JOHN: If your father does decide to go on with the case, I'm very much afraid he'll do everything he threatens.

CATHERINE: Forbid the match?

JOHN: Yes.

CATHERINE (*almost pleadingly*): Isn't that rather an empty threat, John?

JOHN (*slowly*): Well, there's always the allowance——

CATHERINE (*dully*): Yes, I see.   There's always the allowance.

JOHN: I tell you, Kate darling, this is going to need damned careful handling; otherwise we'll find ourselves in the soup.

CATHERINE: Without your allowance would we be in the soup?

JOHN: And without your settlement.   My dear girl, of course we would.   Dash it all, I can't even live on my pay as it is, but with two of us——

CATHERINE: I've heard it said that two can live as cheaply as one.

JOHN: Don't you believe it.   Two can live as cheaply as two, and that's all there is to it.

CATHERINE: Yes, I see. I didn't know.

JOHN: Unlike you I have a practical mind, Kate. I'm sorry, but it's no good dashing blindly ahead without thinking of these things first. The problem has got to be faced.

CATHERINE: I'm ready to face it, John. What do you suggest?

JOHN (*cautiously*): Well—I think you should consider very carefully before you take the next step——

CATHERINE: I can assure you we will, John. The question is—what *is* the next step?

JOHN: Well—this is the way I see it. I'm going to be honest now. I hope you don't mind——

CATHERINE: No. I should welcome it.

JOHN: Your young brother over there pinches or doesn't pinch a five-bob postal order. For over a year you and your father fight a magnificent fight on his behalf, and I'm sure everyone admires you for it——

CATHERINE: Your father hardly seems to——

JOHN: Well, he's a diehard. Like these old Admirals you've been up against. I meant ordinary reasonable people, like myself. But now look—you've had two enquiries, the Petition of Right case which the Admiralty had thrown out of Court, and the Appeal. And now, good Heavens, you've had the whole damned House of Commons getting themselves worked up into a frenzy about it. Surely, darling, that's enough for you? My God! Surely the case can end there?

CATHERINE (*slowly*): Yes. I suppose the case can end there.

JOHN (Pointing to RONNIE): *He* won't mind.

CATHERINE: No. I know he won't.

JOHN: Look at him! Perfectly happy and content. Not a care in the world. How do you know what's going on in his mind? How can you be so sure he didn't do it?

CATHERINE (*also gazing down at* RONNIE): I'm not so sure he didn't do it.

JOHN (*appalled*): Good Lord! Then why in Heaven's name have you and your father spent all this time and money trying to prove his innocence?

CATHERINE (*quietly*): His innocence or guilt aren't important to me. They are to my father. Not to me. I believe he didn't do it; but I may be wrong. To prove that he didn't do it is of hardly more interest to me than the identity of the college servant, or whoever it was, who did it. All that I care about is that people should know that a Government department has ignored a fundamental human right and that it should be forced to acknowledge it. That's all that's important to me.

JOHN: But, darling, after all those long noble words, it does really resolve itself to a question of a fourteen-year-old kid and a five-bob postal order, doesn't it?

CATHERINE: Yes, it does.

JOHN (*reasonably*): Well now, look. There's a European war blowing up, there's a coal strike on, there's a fair chance of civil war in Ireland, and there's a hundred and one other things on the horizon at the moment that I think you genuinely could call *important*. And yet, with all that on its mind, the House of Commons takes a whole day to discuss him (*pointing to* RONNIE) and his bally postal order. Surely you must see that's a little out of proportion——

Pause. CATHERINE *raises her head slowly.*

CATHERINE (*with some spirit*): All I know is, John, that if ever the time comes that the House of Commons has so much on its mind that it can't find time to discuss a Ronnie Winslow and his bally postal order, this country will be a far poorer place than it is now. (*Wearily.*) But you needn't go on, John dear. You've said quite enough. I entirely see your point of view.

JOHN: I don't know whether you realise that all this publicity you're getting is making the name of Winslow a bit of a—well——

CATHERINE (*steadily*): A nation-wide laughing-stock, your father said.

JOHN: Well, that's putting it a bit steep. But people do find the case a bit ridiculous, you know. I mean, I get chaps coming up to me in the mess all the time and saying: "I say, is it true you're going to marry the Winslow girl? You'd better be careful. You'll find yourself up in front of the House of Lords for pinching the Adjutant's bath." Things like that. They're not awfully funny——

CATHERINE: That's nothing. They're singing a verse about us at the Alhambra:

> Winslow one day went to Heaven
> And found a poor fellow in quod.
> The fellow said I didn't do it,
> So naturally Winslow sued God.

JOHN: Well, darling—you see——

CATHERINE: Yes. I see. (*Quietly.*) Do you want to marry me, John?

JOHN: What?

CATHERINE: I said: do you want to marry me?

JOHN: Well, of course I do. You know I do. We've been engaged for over a year now. Have I ever wavered before?

CATHERINE: No. Never before.

JOHN (*correcting himself*): I'm not wavering now. Not a bit—I'm only telling you what I think is the best course for us to take.

CATHERINE: But isn't it already too late? Even if we gave up the case, would you still want to marry—the Winslow girl?

JOHN: All that would blow over in no time.

CATHERINE (*slowly*): And we'd have the allowance——

JOHN: Yes. We would.

CATHERINE: And that's so important——

JOHN (*quietly*): It is, darling. I'm sorry, but you can't shame me into saying it isn't.

CATHERINE: I didn't mean to shame you——

JOHN: Oh, yes, you did. I know that tone of voice.

CATHERINE (*humbly*): I'm sorry.

JOHN (*confidently*): Well, now—what's the answer?

CATHERINE (*slowly*): I love you, John, and I want to be your wife.

JOHN: Well, then, that's all I want to know. Darling! I was sure nothing so stupid and trivial could possibly come between us.

He kisses her. She responds wearily. The telephone rings. After a pause she releases herself and picks up the receiver.

CATHERINE: Hullo . . . Yes . . . Will you wait a minute? (*She goes to the dining-room door and calls.*) Sir Robert! Someone wants you on the telephone——

SIR ROBERT *comes out of the dining-room.*

SIR ROBERT: Thank you. I'm so sorry to interrupt.

CATHERINE: You didn't. We'd finished our talk.

SIR ROBERT *looks at her enquiringly. She gives him no sign. He walks to the telephone.*

SIR ROBERT (*noticing sandwiches*): How delicious! May I help myself?

CATHERINE: Do.

SIR ROBERT (*into receiver*): Hello . . . Yes, Michael . . . F.E.? I didn't know he was going to speak . . . I see . . . Go on. . . .

SIR ROBERT *listens, with closed eyelids, munching a sandwich, meanwhile.*

(*At length*)   Thank you, Michael.

He rings off. ARTHUR *has appeared in the dining-room doorway.*

SIR ROBERT (*to* ARTHUR): There has been a most interesting development in the House, sir.

ARTHUR: What?

SIR ROBERT: My secretary tells me that a barrister friend of mine who, quite unknown to me, was interested in the case, got on his feet shortly after nine-thirty and delivered one of the most scathing denunciations of a Government department ever heard in the House. (*To* CATHERINE.) What a shame we missed it—his style is quite superb——

ARTHUR: What happened?

SIR ROBERT: The debate revived, of course, and the First Lord, who must have felt himself fairly safe, suddenly found himself under attack from all parts of the House. It appears that rather than risk a division he has this moment given an undertaking that he will instruct the Attorney-General to endorse our Petition of Right. The case of Winslow versus Rex can now therefore come to court.

There is a pause. ARTHUR *and* CATHERINE *stare at him unbelievingly.*

(*At length.*)   Well, sir.   What are my instructions?

ARTHUR (*slowly*): The decision is no longer mine, sir.   You must ask my daughter.

SIR ROBERT: What are my instructions, Miss Winslow?

CATHERINE *looks down at the sleeping* RONNIE.   ARTHUR *is watching her intently.* SIR ROBERT, *munching sandwiches, is also looking at her.*

CATHERINE (*in a flat voice*): Do you need my instructions, Sir Robert?   Aren't they already on the Petition?   Doesn't it say: Let Right be done?

JOHN *makes a move of protest towards her.   She does not look at him.   He turns abruptly to the door.*

JOHN (*furiously*): Kate!   Good night.

He goes out. SIR ROBERT, *with languid speculation, watches him go.*

SIR ROBERT (*his mouth full*): Well, then—we must endeavour to see that it is.

CURTAIN

ACT IV

SCENE: *The same, about five months later. It is a stiflingly hot June day—nearly two years less one month since* RONNIE'S *dismissal from Osborne. The glass door to the garden stands open, and a bathchair, unoccupied, has been placed nearby.* ON THE RISE OF THE CURTAIN *the stage is empty and the telephone is ringing insistently.*

DICKIE *comes in from the hall carrying a suit-case, evidently very hot, his straw hat pushed on to the back of his head and panting from his exertions. He is wearing a neat, dark blue suit, a sober tie and a stiff collar. He puts the suit-case down and mops his face with his handkerchief. Then he goes to the hall door and calls:*

DICKIE: Mother! (*There is no reply.*) Violet! (*Again no reply.*) Anyone about?

He goes to the telephone—taking off the receiver.

Hullo . . . No, not senior—junior . . . I don't know where he is . . . *Daily Mail?* . . . No, I'm the brother . . . Elder brother—that's right . . . Well—I'm in the banking business . . . That's right. Following in father's footsteps . . . My views on the case? Well —I—er—I don't know I have any, except, I mean, I hope we win and all that . . . No, I haven't been in Court. I've only just arrived from Reading . . . Reading . . . Yes. That's where I work . . . Yes, I've come up for the last two days of the trial. Verdict's expected to-morrow, isn't it? . . . Twenty-two, last March . . . *Seven* years older. . . . No. He was thirteen when it happened, but now he's fifteen . . . Well, I suppose, if I'm anything I'm a sort of Liberal-Conservative . . . Single . . . No. No immediate prospects. I say, is this at all interesting to you? . . . Well, a perfectly ordinary kid, just like any other—makes a noise, does fretwork, doesn't wash and all that . . . Doesn't wash . . . (*Alarmed.*) I say, don't take that too literally. I mean he does, sometimes . . . Yes. All right. Good-bye. . . .

He rings off and exits through centre door. Telephone rings again. He comes back to answer it, when GRACE *dressed for going out, comes out of the dining-room.*

78

GRACE: Oh, hullo, darling. When did you get here?
She picks up the telephone receiver.
(*Into receiver.*) Everyone out.
She rings off and embraces DICKIE.
You're thinner. I like your new suit.

DICKIE: Straight from Reading's Savile Row. Off the peg at three and a half guineas. (*Pointing to telephone.*) I say—does that go on all the time?

GRACE: All blessed day. The last four days it simply hasn't stopped.

DICKIE: I had to fight my way in through an army of reporters and people——

GRACE: Yes, I know. You didn't say anything, I hope, Dickie dear. It's better not to say a word——

DICKIE: I don't think I said anything much. . . . (*Carelessly.*) Oh, yes. I did say that I personally thought he did it——

GRACE (*horrified*): Dickie! You didn't! (*He is smiling at her.*) Oh, I see. It's a joke. You mustn't say things like that, even in fun, Dickie dear——

DICKIE: How's it all going?

GRACE: I don't know. I've been there all four days now and I've hardly understood a word that's going on. Kate says the judge is against us, but he seems a charming old gentleman to me. (*Faintly shocked.*) Sir Robert's so rude to him——
Telephone rings. GRACE *answers it automatically.*
Nobody in.
She rings off and turns to garden door.
(*Calling.*) Arthur! Lunch! I'll come straight down. Dickie's here. (*To* DICKIE.) Kate takes the morning session, then she comes home and relieves me with Arthur, and I go to the Court in the afternoons, so you can come with me as soon as she's in.

DICKIE: Will there be room for me?

GRACE: Oh, yes. They reserve places for the family. You never saw such crowds in all your life. And such excitement! Cheers and applause and people being turned out. It's thrilling—you'll love it, Dickie.

DICKIE: Well—if I don't understand a word——

GRACE: Oh, that doesn't matter. They all get so terribly worked up you find yourself getting worked up, too. Sir Robert and the Attorney-General go at each other hammer and tongs—you wait and hear them—all about Petitions and demurrers and prerogatives and things.   Nothing to do with Ronnie at all—seems to me——

DICKIE: How did Ronnie get on in the witness-box?

GRACE: Two days he was cross-examined.   Two whole days. Imagine it, the poor little pet!   I must say he didn't seem to mind much.   He said two days with the Attorney-General wasn't nearly as bad as two minutes with Sir Robert.   Kate says he made a very good impression with the jury——

DICKIE: How is Kate, Mother?

GRACE: Oh, all right.   You heard about John, I suppose——

DICKIE: Yes.   That's what I meant.   How has she taken it?

GRACE: You can never tell with Kate.   She never lets you know what she's feeling.   We all think he's behaved very badly——

ARTHUR *appears at the garden door, walking very groggily.*
Arthur!   You shouldn't have come up the stairs by yourself.

ARTHUR: I had little alternative.

GRACE: I'm sorry, dear.   I was talking to Dickie.

GRACE *helps* ARTHUR *into the bath-chair.*

ARTHUR: How are you, Dickie?

DICKIE (*shaking hands*): Very well, thank you, Father.

ARTHUR: I've been forced to adopt this ludicrous form of propulsion.   I apologise.

He wheels himself into the room and examines DICKIE.
You look very well.   A trifle thinner, perhaps——

DICKIE: Hard work, Father.

ARTHUR: Or late hours?

DICKIE: You can't keep late hours in Reading.

ARTHUR: You could keep late hours anywhere.   I've had quite a good report about you from Mr. Lamb.

DICKIE: Good egg!   He's a decent old stick, the old baa-lamb. I took him racing last Saturday.   Had the time of his life and lost his shirt.

ARTHUR: Did he?   I have no doubt that, given the chance, you'll succeed in converting the entire Reading branch of the Westminster Bank into a bookmaking establishment.   Mr. Lamb says you've joined the territorials.

DICKIE: Yes, Father.

ARTHUR: Why have you done that?

DICKIE: Well, from all accounts there's a fair chance of a bit of a scrap quite soon. If there is I don't want it to be all over before I can get in on it——

ARTHUR: If there is what you call a scrap you'll do far better to stay in the bank——

DICKIE: Oh, no, Father. I mean, the bank's all right—but still —a chap can't help looking forward to a bit of a change—I can always go back to the bank afterwards——

> *The telephone rings.* ARTHUR *takes receiver off and puts it down on table.*

GRACE: Oh, no, dear. You can't do that.

ARTHUR: Why not?

GRACE: It annoys the exchange.

ARTHUR: I prefer to annoy the exchange rather than have the exchange annoy me. (*To* GRACE.) Catherine's late. She was in at half-past yesterday.

GRACE: Perhaps they're taking the lunch interval later to-day.

ARTHUR: Lunch interval? This isn't a cricket match. (*Looking at her.*) Nor, may I say, is it a matinée at the Gaiety. Why are you wearing that highly unsuitable get-up?

GRACE: Don't you like it, dear? I think it's Mme Dupont's best.

ARTHUR: Grace—your son is facing a charge of theft and forgery——

GRACE: Oh, dear! It's so difficult! I simply can't be seen in the same old dress, day after day. (*A thought strikes her.*) I tell you what, Arthur. I'll wear my black coat and skirt to-morrow— for the verdict.

> ARTHUR *glares at her, helplessly, then turns his chair to the dining-room.*

ARTHUR: Did you say my lunch was ready?

GRACE: Yes, dear. It's only cold. I did the salad myself. Violet and cook are at the trial.

DICKIE: Is Violet still with you? She was under sentence last time I saw you——

GRACE: She's been under sentence for the last six months, poor thing—only she doesn't know it. Neither your father nor I have the courage to tell her——

ARTHUR (*stopping at door*): I have the courage to tell her.

GRACE: It's funny that you don't, then, dear.

ARTHUR: I will.

GRACE (*hastily*): No, no, you mustn't. When it's to be done, I'll do it.

ARTHUR: You see, Dickie? These taunts of cowardice are daily flung at my head; but should I take them up I'm forbidden to move in the matter. Such is the logic of women.

> *He goes into the dining-room.* DICKIE, *who has been holding the door open, closes it after him.*

DICKIE (*seriously*): How *is* he?

> GRACE *shakes her head quietly.*

Will you take him away after the trial?

GRACE: He's promised to go into a nursing home.

DICKIE: Do you think he will?

GRACE: How do I know? He'll probably find some new excuse——

DICKIE: But surely, if he loses this time, he's lost for good, hasn't he?

GRACE (*slowly*): So they say, Dickie dear—I can only hope it's true.

DICKIE: How did you keep him away from the trial?

GRACE: Kate and Sir Robert together. He wouldn't listen to me or the doctor.

DICKIE: Poor old Mother! You must have been having a pretty rotten time of it, one way and another——

GRACE: I've said my say, Dickie. He knows what I think. Not that he cares. He never has—all his life. Anyway, I've given up worrying. He's always said he knew what he was doing. It's my job to try and pick up the pieces, I suppose.

> CATHERINE *comes in.*

CATHERINE: Lord! The heat! Mother, can't you get rid of those reporters—Hullo, Dickie.

DICKIE (*embracing her*): Hullo, Kate.

CATHERINE: Come to be in at the death?

DICKIE: Is that what it's going to be?

CATHERINE: Looks like it. I could cheerfully strangle that old brute of a judge, Mother. He's dead against us.

GRACE (*fixing her hat in the mirror*): Oh, dear?

CATHERINE: Sir Robert's very worried. He said the Attorney-General's speech made a great impression on the jury. I must say it was very clever. To listen to him yesterday you would have thought that a verdict for Ronnie would simultaneously cause a mutiny in the Royal Navy and triumphant jubilation in Berlin.

ARTHUR *appears in his chair, at the dining-room door.*

ARTHUR: You're late, Catherine.

CATHERINE: I know, Father. I'm sorry. There was such a huge crowd outside as well as inside the Court that I couldn't get a cab. And I stayed to talk to Sir Robert.

GRACE (*pleased*): Is there a bigger crowd even than yesterday, Kate?

CATHERINE: Yes, Mother. Far bigger.

ARTHUR: How did it go this morning?

CATHERINE: Sir Robert finished his cross-examination of the postmistress. I thought he'd demolished her completely. She admitted she couldn't identify Ronnie in the Commander's office. She admitted she couldn't be sure of the time he came in. She admitted that she was called away to the telephone while he was buying his fifteen-and-six postal order, and that all Osborne cadets looked alike to her in their uniforms, so that it might quite easily have been another cadet who cashed the five shillings. It was a brilliant cross-examination. So gentle and quiet. He didn't bully her, or frighten her—he just coaxed her into tying herself into knots. Then, when he'd finished the Attorney-General asked her again whether she was absolutely positive that the same boy that bought the fifteen-and six postal order also cashed the five-shilling one. She said yes. She was quite, quite sure because Ronnie was such a good-looking little boy that she had specially noticed him. She hadn't said that in her examination-in-chief. I could see those twelve good men and true nodding away to each other. I believe it undid the whole of that magnificent cross-examination.

ARTHUR: If she thought him so especially good-looking, why couldn't she identify him the same evening?

CATHERINE: Don't ask me, Father. Ask the Attorney-General. I'm sure he has a beautifully reasonable answer.

DICKIE: Ronnie good-looking! What utter rot! She must be lying, that woman.

GRACE: Nonsense, Dickie! I thought he looked very well in the box yesterday, didn't you, Kate?

CATHERINE: Yes, Mother.

ARTHUR: Who else gave evidence for the other side?

CATHERINE: The Commander, the Chief Petty Officer and one of the boys at the College.

ARTHUR: Anything very damaging?

CATHERINE: Nothing that we didn't expect. The boy showed obviously he hated Ronnie and was torn to shreds by Sir Robert. The Commander scored, though. He's an honest man and genuinely believes Ronnie did it.

GRACE: Did you see anybody interesting in Court, dear?

CATHERINE: Yes, Mother. John Watherstone.

GRACE: John? I hope you didn't speak to him, Kate.

CATHERINE: Of course I did.

GRACE: Kate, how could you! What did he say?

CATHERINE: He wished us luck.

GRACE: What impertinence! The idea of John Watherstone coming calmly up in Court to wish you luck—I think it's the most disgraceful, cold-blooded——

ARTHUR: Grace—you will be late for the resumption.

GRACE: Oh, will I? Are you ready, Dickie?

DICKIE: Yes, Mother.

GRACE: You don't think that nice, grey suit of yours you paid so much money for——

ARTHUR: What time are they resuming, Kate?

CATHERINE: Two o'clock.

ARTHUR: It's twenty past two now.

GRACE: Oh, dear! We'll be terribly late. Kate—that's your fault. Arthur, you must finish your lunch——

ARTHUR: Yes, Grace.

GRACE: Promise now.

ARTHUR: I promise.

GRACE (to herself): I wonder if Violet will remember to pick up those onions. Perhaps I'd better do it on the way back from the Court. (As she passes CATHERINE.) Kate, dear, I'm so sorry——

CATHERINE: What for, Mother?

GRACE: John proving such a bad hat. I never did like him very much, you know.

CATHERINE: No, I know.

GRACE: Now, Dickie, when you get to the front door put your head down, like me, and just charge through them all.

ARTHUR: Why don't you go out by the garden?

GRACE: I wouldn't like to risk this dress getting through that hedge. Come on, Dickie. I always shout: "I'm the maid and don't know nothing," so don't be surprised.

DICKIE: Right-oh, Mother.

GRACE *goes out.* DICKIE *follows her.*
There is a pause.

ARTHUR: Are we going to lose this case, Kate?

CATHERINE *quietly shrugs her shoulders.*

It's our last chance.

CATHERINE: I know.

ARTHUR (*with sudden violence*): We've got to win it.

CATHERINE *does not reply.*

What does Sir Robert think?

CATHERINE: He seems very worried.

ARTHUR (*thoughtfully*): I wonder if you were right, Kate. I wonder if we could have had a better man.

CATHERINE: No, Father. We couldn't have had a better man.

ARTHUR: You admit that now, do you?

CATHERINE: Only that he's the best advocate in England and for some reason—prestige, I suppose—he seems genuinely anxious to win this case. I don't go back on anything else I've ever said about him.

ARTHUR: The papers said that he began to-day by telling the judge he felt ill and might have to ask for an adjournment. I trust he won't collapse——

CATHERINE. He won't. It was just another of those brilliant tricks of his that he's always boasting about. It got him the sympathy of the Court and possibly—no, I won't say that——

ARTHUR: Say it.

CATHERINE (*slowly*): Possibly provided him with an excuse if he's beaten.

ARTHUR: You don't like him, do you?

CATHERINE (*indifferently*): There's nothing in him to like or dislike, Father. I admire him.

DESMOND *appears at the garden door. Standing inside the room, he knocks diffidently.* CATHERINE *and* ARTHUR *turn and see him.*

DESMOND: I trust you do not object to me employing this rather furtive entry. The crowds at the front door are most alarming——

ARTHUR: Come in, Desmond. Why have you left the Court?

DESMOND: My partner will be holding the fort. He is perfectly competent, I promise you.

ARTHUR: I'm glad to hear it.

DESMOND: I wonder if I might see Catherine alone. I have a matter of some urgency to communicate to her——

ARTHUR: Oh. Do you wish to hear this urgent matter, Kate?

CATHERINE: Yes, Father.

ARTHUR: Very well, I shall go and finish my lunch.

He wheels his chair to the dining-room. DESMOND *flies to help.*

DESMOND: Allow me.

ARTHUR: Thank you. I can manage this vehicle without assistance.

He goes out.

DESMOND: I fear I should have warned you of my visit. Perhaps I have interrupted——

CATHERINE: No, Desmond. Please sit down.

DESMOND: Thank you. I'm afraid I have only a very short time. I must get back to Court for the cross-examination of the judge-advocate.

CATHERINE: Yes, Desmond. Well?"

DESMOND: I have a taxicab waiting at the end of the street.

CATHERINE (*smiling*): How very extravagant of you, Desmond.

DESMOND (*also smiling*): Yes. But it shows you how rushed this visit must necessarily be. The fact of the matter is—it suddenly occurred to me during the lunch recess that I had far better see you to-day.

CATHERINE (*her thoughts far distant*): Why?

DESMOND: I have a question to put to you, Kate, which, if I had postponed putting until after the verdict, you might—who knows—have thought had been prompted by pity—if we had lost. Or—if we had won, your reply might—again who knows—have been influenced by gratitude. Do you follow me, Kate?

CATHERINE: Yes, Desmond. I think I do.

DESMOND: Ah. Then possibly you have some inkling of what the question is I have to put to you?

CATHERINE: Yes. I think I have.

DESMOND (*a trifle disconcerted*): Oh.

CATHERINE: I'm sorry, Desmond. I ought, I know, to have followed the usual practice in such cases, and told you I had no inkling whatever.

DESMOND: No, no. Your directness and honesty are two of the qualities I so much admire in you. I am glad you have guessed. It makes my task the easier——

CATHERINE (*in a matter-of-fact voice*): Will you give me a few days to think it over?

DESMOND: Of course. Of course.

CATHERINE: I need hardly tell you how grateful I am, Desmond.

DESMOND (*a trifle bewildered*): There is no need, Kate. No need at all——

CATHERINE *has risen brusquely.*

CATHERINE: You musn't keep your taxi waiting——

DESMOND: Oh, bother, my taxi! (*Recovering himself.*) Forgive me, Kate, but you see I know very well what your feelings for me really are.

CATHERINE (*gently*): You do, Desmond?

DESMOND: Yes, Kate. I know quite well they have never amounted to much more than a sort of—well—shall we say, friendliness? A warm friendliness, I hope. Yes, I think perhaps we can definitely say, warm. But no more than that. That's true, isn't it?

CATHERINE (*quietly*): Yes, Desmond.

DESMOND: I know, I know. Of course, the thing is that even if I proved the most devoted and adoring husband that ever lived— which, I may say—if you give me the chance, I intend to be—your feelings for me would never—could never—amount to more than that. When I was younger it might, perhaps, have been a different story. When I played cricket for England——

He notices the faintest expression of pity that has crossed CATHERINE'S *face.*

(*Apologetically.*) And, of course, perhaps even that would not have made so much difference. Perhaps you feel I cling too much to my past athletic prowess. I feel it myself, sometimes—but the truth is I have not much else to cling to save that and my love for you. The athletic prowess is fading, I'm afraid, with the years and the stiffening of the muscles—but my love for you will never fade.

CATHERINE (*smiling*): That's very charmingly said, Desmond.

DESMOND: Don't make fun of me, Kate, please. I meant it, every word. (*Clearing his throat.*) However, let's take a more mundane approach and examine the facts. Fact one: You don't love me, and never can. Fact two: I love you, always have, and always will. That is the situation—and it is a situation which, after most careful consideration, I am fully prepared to accept. I reached this decision some months ago, but thought at first it would be better to wait until this case, which is so much on all our minds, should be over. Then at lunch to-day I determined to anticipate the verdict to-morrow, and let you know what was in my mind at once. No matter what you feel or don't feel for me, no matter what you feel for anyone else, I want you to be my wife.

Pause.

CATHERINE (*at length*): I see. Thank you, Desmond. That makes everything much clearer.

DESMOND: There is much more that I had meant to say, but I shall put it in a letter.

CATHERINE: Yes, Desmond. Do.

DESMOND: Then I may expect your answer in a few days?

CATHERINE: Yes, Desmond.

DESMOND (*looking at his watch*): I must get back to Court. (*He collects his hat, stick and gloves.*) How did you think it went this morning.

CATHERINE: I thought the postmistress restored the Admiralty's case with that point about Ronnie's looks——

DESMOND: Oh, no, no. Not at all. There is still the overwhelming fact that she couldn't identify him. What a brilliant cross-examination, was it not?

CATHERINE: Brilliant.

DESMOND: He is a strange man, Sir Robert. At times, so cold and distant and—and——

CATHERINE: Fishlike.

DESMOND: Fishlike, exactly. And yet he has a real passion about this case. A real passion. I happen to know—of course this must on no account go any further—but I happen to know that he has made a very, very great personal sacrifice in order to bring it to court.

CATHERINE: Sacrifice? What? Of another brief?

DESMOND: No, no. That is no sacrifice to him. No—he was offered—you really promise to keep this to yourself?

CATHERINE: My dear Desmond, whatever the Government offered him can't be as startling as all that; he's in the Opposition.

DESMOND: As it happens it was quite startling, and a most graceful compliment, if I may say so, to his performance as Attorney-General under the last Government.

CATHERINE: What was he offered, Desmond?

DESMOND: The appointment of Lord Chief Justice. He turned it down simply in order to be able to carry on with the case of Winslow versus Rex. Strange are the ways of men are they not? Good-bye, my dear.

CATHERINE: Good-bye, Desmond.

Exit DESMOND.

> CATHERINE *turns from the window deep in thought. She has a puzzled, strained expression. It does not look as though it were Desmond she was thinking of.* ARTHUR *opens dining-room door and peers round.*

ARTHUR: May I come in now?

CATHERINE: Yes, Father. He's gone.

ARTHUR: I'm rather tired of being gazed at from the street while eating my mutton, as though I were an animal at the Zoo.

CATHERINE (*slowly*): I've been a fool, Father.

ARTHUR: Have you, my dear?

CATHERINE: An utter fool.

> ARTHUR *waits for* CATHERINE *to make herself plain. She does not do so.*

ARTHUR: In default of further information, I can only repeat, have you, my dear?

CATHERINE: There can be no further information. I'm under a pledge of secrecy.

ARTHUR: Oh. What did Desmond want?

CATHERINE: To marry me.

ARTHUR: I trust the folly you were referring to wasn't your acceptance of him?

CATHERINE (*smiling*): No, Father. (*She comes and sits on the arm of his chair.*) Would it be such folly, though?

ARTHUR: Lunacy.

CATHERINE: Oh, I don't know. He's nice, and he's doing very well as a solicitor.

ARTHUR: Neither very compelling reasons for marrying him.

CATHERINE: Seriously—I shall have to think it over.

ARTHUR: Think it over, by all means. But decide against it.

CATHERINE: I'm nearly thirty, you know.

ARTHUR: Thirty isn't the end of life.

Catherine: It might be—for an unmarried woman, with not much looks.

ARTHUR: Rubbish.

> CATHERINE *shakes her head.*

Better far to live and die an old maid than to marry Desmond.

CATHERINE: Even an old maid must eat. (*Pause.*)

ARTHUR: I am leaving you and your mother everything you know.

89

CATHERINE (*quietly*): Everything?

ARTHUR: There is still a little left. (*Pause.*) Did you take my suggestion as regards your Suffrage Association?

CATHERINE: Yes, Father.

ARTHUR: You demanded a salary?

CATHERINE: I asked for one.

ARTHUR: And they're going to give it to you, I trust?

CATHERINE: Yes, Father. Two pounds a week.

ARTHUR (*angrily*): That's insulting.

CATHERINE: No. It's generous. It's all they can afford. We're not a very rich organisation—you know.

ARTHUR: You'll have to think of something else.

CATHERINE: What else? Darning socks? That's about my only other accomplishment.

ARTHUR: There must be something useful you can do.

CATHERINE: You don't think the work I am doing at the W.S.A. is useful?

ARTHUR *is silent.*

You may be right. But it's the only work I'm fitted for, all the same. (*Pause.*) No, Father. The choice is quite simple. Either I marry Desmond and settle down into quite a comfortable and not really useless existence—or I go on for the rest of my life earning two pounds a week in the service of a hopeless cause.

ARTHUR: A hopeless cause? I've never heard you say that before.

CATHERINE: I've never felt it before.

ARTHUR *is silent.* CATHERINE *leans her head against his chair.*

CATHERINE: John's going to get married next month.

ARTHUR: Did he tell you?

CATHERINE: Yes. He was very apologetic.

ARTHUR: Apologetic!

CATHERINE: He didn't need to be. It's a girl I know slightly. She'll make him a good wife.

ARTHUR: Is he in love with her?

CATHERINE: No more than he was with me. Perhaps, even, a little less.

ARTHUR: Why is he marrying her so soon after—after——

CATHERINE: After jilting me? Because he thinks there's going to be a war. If there is, his regiment will be among the first to go overseas. Besides, his father approves strongly. She's a general's daughter. Very, very suitable.

ARTHUR: Poor Kate!

    Pause. He takes her hand slowly.

How I've messed up your life, haven't I?

CATHERINE: No, Father. Any messing-up that's been done has been done by me.

ARTHUR: I'm so sorry, Kate. I'm so sorry.

CATHERINE: Don't be, Father. We both knew what we were doing.

ARTHUR: Did we?

CATHERINE: I think we did.

ARTHUR: Yet our motives seem to have been different all along—yours and mine, Kate? Can we both have been right?

CATHERINE: I believe we can. I believe we have been.

ARTHUR: And yet they've always been so infernally logical, our opponents, haven't they?

CATHERINE: I'm afraid logic has never been on our side.

ARTHUR: Brute stubbornness—a selfish refusal to admit defeat. That's what your mother thinks have been our motives——

CATHERINE: Perhaps she's right. Perhaps that's all they've been.

ARTHUR: But perhaps brute stubbornness isn't such a bad quality in the face of injustice?

CATHERINE: Or in the face of tyranny. (*Pause.*) If you could go back, Father, and choose again—would your choice be different?

ARTHUR: Perhaps.

CATHERINE: I don't think so.

ARTHUR: I don't think so, either.

CATHERINE: I still say we both knew what we were doing. And we were right to do it.

    ARTHUR *kisses the top of her head.*

ARTHUR: Dear Kate. Thank you.

    There is a silence. A newsboy can be heard dimly, shouting from the street outside.

You aren't going to marry Desmond, are you?

CATHERINE (*with a smile*): In the words of the Prime Minister, Father—wait and see.

    He squeezes her hand. The newsboy can still be heard—now a little louder.

ARTHUR: What's that boy shouting, Kate?

CATHERINE: Only—Winslow case—Latest.

ARTHUR: It didn't sound to me like "Latest."

CATHERINE *gets up to listen at the window.* *Suddenly we hear it quite plainly:* "*Winslow Case Result! Winslow Case Result!*" Result?

CATHERINE: There must be some mistake.

There is another sudden outburst of noise from the hall as the front door is opened. It subsides again. VIOLET *comes in quickly with a broad smile.*

VIOLET: Oh sir! Oh, sir!

ARTHUR: What's happened?

VIOLET: Oh, Miss Kate, what a shame you missed it! Just after they come back from lunch, and Mrs. Winslow she wasn't there neither, nor Master Ronnie. The cheering and the shouting and the carrying-on—you never heard anything like it in all your life—and Sir Robert standing there at the table with his wig on crooked and the tears running down his face—running down his face they were, and not able to speak because of the noise. Cook and me we did a bit of crying too, we just couldn't help it—you couldn't, you know. Oh, it was lovely? We did enjoy ourselves. And then Cook had her hat knocked over her eyes by the man behind who was cheering and waving his arms about something chronic, and shouting about liberty—you would have laughed, Miss, to see her, she was that cross—but she didn't mind really, she was only pretending, and we kept on cheering and the judge kept on shouting, but it wasn't any good, because even the jury joined in, and some of them climbed out of the box to shake hands with Sir Robert. And then outside in the street it was just the same—you couldn't move for the crowd, and you'd think they'd all gone mad the way they were carrying on. Some of them were shouting "Good old Winslow!" and singing "For he's a jolly good fellow," and Cook had her hat knocked off again. Oh, it was lovely! (*To* ARTHUR.) Well, sir, you must be feeling nice and pleased, now it's all over?

ARTHUR: Yes, Violet. I am.

VIOLET. That's right. I always said it would come all right in the end, didn't I?

ARTHUR: Yes. You did.

VIOLET: Two years all but one month it's been, now, since Master Ronnie come back that day. Fancy.

ARTHUR: Yes.

VIOLET: I don't mind telling you, sir, I wondered sometimes

whether you and Miss Kate weren't just wasting your time carrying on the way you have all the time. Still—you couldn't have felt that if you'd been in Court to-day——

> *She turns to go and stops.*

Oh, sir, Mrs. Winslow asked me to remember most particular to pick up some onions from the green-grocer, but——

CATHERINE: That's all right, Violet. I think Mrs. Winslow is picking them up herself, on her way back——

VIOLET: I see, miss. Poor Madam! What a sell for her when she gets to the Court and finds it's all over. Well, sir—congratulations, I'm sure.

ARTHUR: Thank you, Violet.

> *Exit* VIOLET.

ARTHUR: It would appear, then, that we've won.

CATHERINE: Yes, Father, it would appear that we've won.

> *She breaks down and cries, her head on her father's lap.*

ARTHUR (*slowly*): I would have liked to have been there.

> *Pause.*
>
> *Enter* VIOLET.

VIOLET (*announcing*): Sir Robert Morton!

> SIR ROBERT *walks calmly and methodically into the room. He looks as spruce and neat as ever, and* VIOLET'S *description of him in Court does not seem to tally with his composed features.*
>
> CATHERINE *jumps up hastily and dabs her eyes.*
>
> *Exit* VIOLET.

SIR ROBERT: I thought you might like to hear the actual terms of the Attorney-General's statement—— (*He pulls out a scrap of paper.*) So I jotted it down for you. (*Reading.*) "I say now, on behalf of the Admiralty, that I accept the declaration of Ronald Arthur Winslow that he did not write the name on the postal order, that he did not take it and that he did not cash it, and that consequently he was innocent of the charge which was brought against him two years ago. I make that statement without any reservation of any description, intending it to be a complete acceptance of the boy's statements."

> *He folds the paper up and hands it to* ARTHUR.

ARTHUR: Thank you, sir. It is rather hard for me to find the words I should speak to you.

SIR ROBERT: Pray do not trouble yourself to search for them, sir. Let us take these rather tiresome and conventional expressions of gratitude for granted, shall we? Now, on the question of damages and costs. I fear we shall find the Admiralty rather niggardly. You are likely still to be left considerably out of pocket. However, doubtless we can apply a slight spur to the First Lord's posterior in the House of Commons——

ARTHUR: Please, sir—no more trouble—I beg. Let the matter rest here. (*He shows the piece of paper.*) This is all I have ever asked for.

SIR ROBERT (*turning to* CATHERINE): A pity you were not in Court, Miss Winslow. The verdict appeared to cause quite a stir.

CATHERINE: So I heard. Why did the Admiralty throw up the case?

SIR ROBERT: It was a foregone conclusion. Once the hand writing expert had been discredited—not for the first time in legal history— I knew we had a sporting chance, and no jury in the world would have convicted on the postmistress's evidence.

CATHERINE: But this morning you seemed so depressed.

SIR ROBERT: Did I? The heat in the court-room was very trying, you know. Perhaps I was a little fatigued——

Enter VIOLET.

VIOLET (*to* ARTHUR): Oh, sir, the gentlemen at the front door say please will you make a statement. They say they won't go away until you do.

ARTHUR: Very well, Violet. Thank you.

VIOLET: Yes, sir.

Exit VIOLET.

ARTHUR: What shall I say?

SIR ROBERT (*indifferently*): I hardly think it matters. Whatever you say will have little bearing on what they write.

ARTHUR: What shall I say, Kate?

CATHERINE: You'll think of something, Father.

She begins to wheel his chair towards the door.

ARTHUR (*sharply*): No! I refuse to meet the Press in this ridiculous chariot. (*To* CATHERINE.) Get me my stick!

CATHERINE (*protestingly*): Father—you know what the doctor——

ARTHUR: Get me my stick!

CATHERINE, *without more ado, gets his stick for him. She and* SIR ROBERT *help him out of his chair.*

How is this? I am happy to have lived long enough to have seen justice done to my son——

CATHERINE: It's a little gloomy, Father. You're going to live for ages yet——

ARTHUR: Am I? Wait and see. I could say: This victory is not mine. It is the people who have triumphed—as they always will triumph—over despotism. How does that strike you, sir? A trifle pretentious, perhaps.

SIR ROBERT: Perhaps, sir. I should say it, none the less. It will be very popular.

ARTHUR: Hm! Perhaps I had better say what I really feel, which is merely: Thank God we beat 'em.

He goes out. SIR ROBERT *turns abruptly to* CATHERINE.

SIR ROBERT: Miss Winslow—might I be rude enough to ask you for a little of your excellent whisky?

CATHERINE: Of course.

She goes into the dining-room. SIR ROBERT, *left alone, droops his shoulders wearily. He subsides into a chair. When* CATHERINE *comes back with the whisky he straightens his shoulders instinctively but does not rise.*

SIR ROBERT: That is very kind. Perhaps you would forgive me not getting up? The heat in that courtroom was really so infernal.

He takes the glass from her and drains it quickly. She notices his hand is trembling slightly.

CATHERINE: Are you feeling all right, Sir Robert?

SIR ROBERT: Just a slight nervous reaction—that's all. Besides, I have not been feeling myself all day. I told the judge so, this morning, if you remember, but I doubt if he believed me. He thought it was a trick. What suspicious minds people have, have they not?

CATHERINE: Yes.

SIR ROBERT (*handing her back the glass*). Thank you.

CATHERINE *puts the glass down, then turns slowly back to face him as if nerving herself for an ordeal.*

CATHERINE: Sir Robert—I'm afraid I have a confession and an apology to make to you.

SIR ROBERT (*sensing what is coming*): Dear lady—I am sure the one is rash and the other superfluous. I would far rather hear neither——

CATHERINE (*with a smile*): I am afraid you must. This is probably the last time I shall see you and it is a better penance for me to say this than to write it. I have entirely misjudged your attitude to this case, and if in doing so I have ever seemed to you either rude or ungrateful, I am sincerely and humbly sorry.

SIR ROBERT (*indifferently*): My dear Miss Winslow, you have never seemed to me either rude or ungrateful. And my attitude to this case has been the same as yours—a determination to win at all costs. Only—when you talk of gratitude—you must remember that those costs were not mine, but yours.

CATHERINE: Weren't they also yours, Sir Robert?

SIR ROBERT: I beg your pardon?

CATHERINE: Haven't you too made a certain sacrifice for the case?
    Pause.

SIR ROBERT: The robes of that office would not have suited me.

CATHERINE: Wouldn't they?

SIR ROBERT (*with venom*): And what is more, I fully intend to have Curry expelled from the Law Society.

CATHERINE: Please don't. He did me a great service by telling me——

SIR ROBERT: I must ask you never to divulge it to another living soul, and even to forget it yourself.

CATHERINE: I shall never divulge it. I'm afraid I can't promise to forget it myself.

SIR ROBERT: Very well. If you choose to endow an unimportant incident with a romantic significance, you are perfectly at liberty to do so. I must go. (*He gets up.*)

CATHERINE: Why are you always at such pains to prevent people knowing the truth about you, Sir Robert?

SIR ROBERT: Am I, indeed?

CATHERINE: You know you are. Why?

SIR ROBERT: Perhaps because *I* do not know the truth about myself.

CATHERINE: That is no answer.

SIR ROBERT: My dear Miss Winslow, are you cross-examining me?

CATHERINE: On this point, yes. Why are you so ashamed of your emotions?

SIR ROBERT: Because, as a lawyer, I must necessarily distrust them.

CATHERINE: Why?

SIR ROBERT: To fight a case on emotional grounds, Miss Winslow, is the surest way of losing it. Emotions muddy the issue. Cold, clear logic—and buckets of it—should be the lawyer's only equipment.

CATHERINE: Was it cold, clear logic that made you weep to-day at the verdict?
    Pause.

SIR ROBERT: Your maid, of course told you that? It doesn't matter. It will be in the papers to-morrow, anyway. (*Fiercely.*) Very well, then, if you must have it, here it is. I wept to-day because right had been done.

CATHERINE: Not justice?

SIR ROBERT: No. Not justice. Right. It is easy to do justice —very hard to do right. Unfortunately, while the appeal of justice is intellectual, the appeal of right appears for some odd reason to induce tears in court. That is my answer and my excuse. And now, may I leave the witness-box?

CATHERINE: No. One last question. How can you reconcile your support of Winslow against the Crown with your political beliefs?

SIR ROBERT: Very easily. No one party has a monopoly of concern for individual liberty. On that issue all parties are united.

CATHERINE: I don't think so.

SIR ROBERT: You don't?

CATHERINE: No. Not all parties. Only some people from all parties.

SIR ROBERT: That is a wise remark. We can only hope, then, that those same people will always prove enough people. You would make a good advocate.

CATHERINE: Would I?

SIR ROBERT: Yes. (*Playfully.*) Why do you not canalise your feministic impulses towards the law courts, Miss Winslow, and abandon the lost cause of women's suffrage?

CATHERINE: Because I don't believe it *is* a lost cause.

SIR ROBERT: No? Are you going to continue to pursue it?

CATHERINE: Certainly.

SIR ROBERT: You will be wasting your time.

CATHERINE: I don't think so.

SIR ROBERT: A pity. In the House of Commons in days to come I shall make a point of looking up at the Gallery in the hope of catching a glimpse of you in that provocative hat.

> RONNIE *comes in. He is fifteen now, and there are distinct signs of an incipient man-about-town. He is very smartly dressed in lounge suit and homburg hat.*

RONNIE: I say, Sir Robert, I'm most awfully sorry. I didn't know anything was going to happen.

SIR ROBERT: Where were you?

RONNIE: At the pictures.

SIR ROBERT: Pictures? What is that?

CATHERINE: Cinematograph show.

RONNIE: I'm most awfully sorry. I say—we won, didn't we?

SIR ROBERT: Yes. We won. Good-bye, Miss Winslow. Shall I see you in the House then, one day?

CATHERINE (*with a smile*): Yes, Sir Robert. One day. But not in the Gallery. Across the floor.

SIR ROBERT (*with a faint smile*): Perhaps. Good-bye. (*He turns to go.*)

CURTAIN

FRENCH WITHOUT TEARS

THE CHARACTERS
(in the order of their appearance)

KENNETH LAKE
BRIAN CURTIS
HON. ALAN HOWARD
MARIANNE
MONSIEUR MAINGOT
LT-CMDR. ROGERS
DIANA LAKE
KIT NEILAN
JACQUELINE MAINGOT
LORD HEYBROOK

ACT I
SCENE I: July 1.   Morning
SCENE II: July 14.   Afternoon.

ACT II
SCENE I: The same evening.
SCENE II: Later the same night.
SCENE III: The following morning.

The action passes in the living-room at "Miramar," a villa in a small seaside town on the west coast of France.

French without Tears was first produced at the Criterion Theatre, London, on November 6th, 1936, with the following cast:

KENNETH LAKE	Trevor Howard
BRIAN CURTIS	Guy Middleton
HON. ALAN HOWARD	Rex Harrison
MARIANNE	Yvonne Andre
MONSIEUR MAINGOT	Percy Walsh
LIEUT.-COMMANDER ROGERS	Roland Culver
DIANA LAKE	Kay Hammond
KIT NEILAN	Robert Flemyng
JACQUELINE MAINGOT	Jessica Tandy
LORD HEYBROOK	Gerald Campion

The play produced by Harold French

ACT I

Scene I

SCENE: *The living-room at "Miramar," a villa in a small seaside town on the west coast of France.*

TIME: *July 1st, about nine a.m.*

The room is rather bare of furniture. There is a large, plain table in the centre, surrounded by eight kitchen chairs. There are two dilapidated arm-chairs against the back wall. The wallpaper is grey and dirty-looking.

On the left two french windows open out on to a small garden. They are open at the moment, and the sun is streaming through. There is a door back right leading into the hall, and another down-stage right leading into the kitchen.

The table is laid for breakfast, with an enormous coffee-pot in the middle and a quantity of rolls.

As the curtain rises KENNETH *is discovered sitting at the table. He is about twenty, good-looking in a rather vacuous way. At the moment he is engaged in writing in a note-book with one hand, while with the other he is nibbling a roll. A dictionary lies open before him.*

There is the sound of someone heavily descending the stairs. The door at the back opens and BRIAN *comes in. He is older than* KENNETH, *about twenty-three or twenty-four, large, thick-set and red-faced. He wears an incredibly dirty pair of grey flannel trousers, a battered brown tweed coat, and a white sweater.*

BRIAN: Morning, Babe.

KENNETH doesn't look up. BRIAN goes to the table, picks up a letter and opens it.

KENNETH (*looking musingly ahead*): She has ideas above her station.

BRIAN: What's that?

KENNETH: How would you say that in French?

BRIAN: What?

KENNETH: She has ideas above her station.

BRIAN: She has ideas above her station.   She has ideas ...   (*He stuffs his letter in his pocket and goes to kitchen door calling*) Marianne!

VOICE (*from the kitchen*): Oui, Monsieur?

BRIAN (*with an appalling accent*): Deux oeufs, s'il vois plaît.

VOICE (*off*): Bien, Monsieur.

BRIAN: Avec un petit peu de jambon.

VOICE (*off*): Oui, Monsieur,   Des oeufs brouillés, n'est-ce pas?

BRIAN: Brouillés?   Ah, oui, brouillés.   (*He closes the door.*)   I'm getting pretty hot at this stuff, don't you think?   You know, nowadays it's quite an effort for me to go back to English.

KENNETH: If you're so hot, you'd better tell me how to say she has ideas above her station.

BRIAN: Oh, yes, I forgot.   It's fairly easy, old boy.   Elle a des idées au-dessus de sa gare.

KENNETH: You can't do it like that.   You can't say au-dessus de sa gare.   It isn't that sort of station.

BRIAN (*pouring himself out a cup of coffee*): Well, don't *ask* me.

KENNETH: I thought you were so hot at French.

BRIAN: Well, as a matter of fact, that wasn't strictly the truth. Now if a Frenchman asked me where the pen of his aunt was, the chances are I could give him a pretty snappy comeback and tell him it was in the pocket of the gardener.

KENNETH: Yes, but that doesn't help me much.

BRIAN: Sorry, old boy.

KENNETH: I suppose I'd better just do it literally.   Maingot'll throw a fit.

BRIAN: That doesn't bother you, does it?

KENNETH: You're not going into the diplomatic.   He doesn't really get worked up about you.

BRIAN: Well, I don't know about that.   The whole of his beard came off yesterday when I was having my lesson.

KENNETH: No, but he doesn't really mind.   It's absolute physical agony to him when I do something wrong.   He knows as well as I do that I haven't got one chance in a thousand of getting in.

BRIAN: (*cheerfully*): Don't say that, old boy.   You're breaking my heart.

KENNETH (*gloomily*): Yes, but it's true.   (*He starts to write again.*)

BRIAN: As a matter of fact. Alan told me you had a pretty good chance.

KENNETH (*looking up, pleased*): Did he really?

    BRIAN *nods*.

BRIAN: He ought to know, oughtn't he? Isn't he Maingot's red-hot tip for the diplomatic stakes?

KENNETH: If he was keener about getting in he'd walk it. He will anyway, I should think.

BRIAN: I think I'll make a book on the result this year. I'll lay evens on Alan—a class colt with a nice free action: will win if he can get the distance.

KENNETH: What about me?

BRIAN: I'll lay you threes about yourself.

KENNETH: Threes? More like twenties.

BRIAN: Oh, I don't know. Nice-looking colt—good stayer. Bit of a dog from the starting-gate, perhaps. Say seven to two, then.

    Enter ALAN *through the door at the back. He is about twenty-three, dark and saturnine. He wears carefully creased grey flannel trousers and a German "sport jacket"*)

Morning, Alan. We were just talking about you.

ALAN: Good morning, Brian. Good morning, Babe. (*He looks at his place at the head of the table.*) Not one blood-stained letter. What were you saying about me?

BRIAN: I'm making a book on the diplomatic stakes. I'm laying evens about you.

ALAN (*sitting down*): That's not very generous.

BRIAN: Hell, you're the favourite.

ALAN: What about the startling rumours that the favourite may be scratched?

KENNETH (*looking up quickly*): Why, have they accepted your novel?

ALAN: Do I look as if they'd accepted my novel?

BRIAN: I don't know how you do look when they accept your novels.

ALAN: I hope, my dear Brian, that one day you'll have a chance of finding out.

KENNETH: Well, what's this talk about your scratching?

ALAN: Perhaps just to give you a better chance, ducky.

BRIAN: You're not serious about it, though, old boy?

ALAN: Probably not.

KENNETH: But you must be mad, Alan. I mean even if you do

want to write you could still do it in the diplomatic. Honestly, it seems quite crazy——

BRIAN: What does His Excellency have to say about the idea, by the way?

ALAN: His Excellency says that he doesn't mind me choosing my own career a bit, provided always it's the one he's chosen for me.

BRIAN: Broad-minded, eh?

ALAN: That's right. Always sees two sides to every question— his own, which is the right one; and anyone else's, which is the wrong one.

He taps KENNETH *on the head with a brioche.* KENNETH *sulkily returns to his work.*

Enter MARIANNE, *the maid, with a plate of scrambled eggs and bacon, placing them in front of* BRIAN.

BRIAN: Ah, mes oeufs, as I live.

MARIANNE (*to* ALAN): Monsieur le Commandant, va-t-il aussi prendre des oeufs avec son déjeuner, Monsieur?

BRIAN: Oh, well—er—(*to* ALAN) she's talking to you, old boy.

ALAN: Je ne sais rien des habitudes de Monsieur le Commandant, Marianne.

MARIANNE: Bien, Monsieur. Alors voulez-vous lui demander s'il les veut, Monsieur, lorsqu'il descend?

ALAN: Bien.

Exit MARIANNE.

BRIAN: What did she want?

ALAN: She wanted to know if the Commander took eggs with his breakfast.

BRIAN: I meant to ask you. Did you see him when he arrived last night?

ALAN: Yes, I went to the station with Maingot to meet him.

BRIAN: What's he like?

ALAN: Very naval commander.

BRIAN: Yes, old boy, but what's that?

ALAN: You know. Carries with him the salty tang of the sea wherever he goes.

BRIAN: Pity he's carried it here. Paucot-sur-mer could do without any more salty tang than it's got already. Has he a rolling gait?

ALAN: He was sober when he arrived.

BRIAN: No, old boy, drunk or sober, all sailors have a rolling gait.

MONSIEUR MAINGOT *comes in hurriedly through the door at the back. He is about sixty, with a ferocious face and a white beard.*

MAINGOT: Bonjour—Bonjour—Bonjour!

All three rise. He shakes hands with each in turn, then sits down at the head of the table R. *at the opposite end to the three boys.*

Mon Dieu que je suis en retard ce matin. (*He opens a letter.*)

BRIAN (*speaking in a whisper to Alan*): What's he like, though, really?

ALAN (*also in a whisper*): Pretty hellish, I thought.

BRIAN: Po-faced, I suppose?

MAINGOT (*roaring into his letter*): Français! Voluez-vous parlez Français, Messieurs, s'il-vous plaît.

Pause.

(*Looking up from his letter.*) Qu'est-ce que c'est que ça, po-faced?

ALAN: Nous disions que Monsieur le Commandant avait une figure de vase de nuit, Monsieur.

MAINGOT: Ah! Mais c'est pas vrai.

ALAN: Nous exaggérons un peu.

MAINGOT: Je crois bien.

He returns his letters.

KENNETH *surreptitiously pushes his note-book towards* ALAN, *pointing at a certain sentence.* ALAN *reads it and shakes his head violently.* KENNETH *looks pleadingly at him.* ALAN *considers and is about to speak when* MAINGOT *looks up.*

Dites-moi, est-ce-que vous connaissez un Lord Heybrook? (*Looking at letter.*)

ALAN: Non, Monsieur.

MAINGOT: Il voudarit venir le quinze Juillet.

ALAN (*To* BRIAN): Do you know him?

BRIAN: Lord Heybrook? No, old boy. (*Confidentially.*) As a matter of fact, I knew a peer once, but he died. What about Lord Heybrook, anyway?

ALAN: He's coming here on the fifteenth.

MAINGOT (*roaring*): Français, Messiers—Français!

Pause.

MAINGOT *takes up the Matin and begins to read.*

(*Roaring.*) Ah! Ce Hitler. (*Throwing paper on floor.*) Quel phenomène!

(*To* BRIAN.) Aha, Monsieur Curtis, vous étiez saôul au Casino hier soir, n'est-ce pas?

BRIAN: (*puzzled*).   Saôul?

ALAN: Drunk.

BRIAN: Oh, non, Monsieur.   Pas ça.   Un peu huilé, peut-être.

    COMMANDER ROGERS *comes in.   He is about thirty-five, dark, small, very neat, rather solemn.   All get up.*

MAINGOT: Ah, Bonjour, Monsieur le Commandant, et comment allez-vous?   J'espère que vous avez bien dormi?

Ah, pardon!   (*Introducing the others.*)   Monsieur Curtis—Monsieur le Commandant Rogers.   Monsieur Lake—Monsieur le Commandant Rogers.   Monsieur Howard—vous connaissez déjà.

    BRIAN *and* KENNETH *shake hands.*

ALAN: Bonjour!   (*To* ROGERS.)

ROGERS: Yes, we met last night.   (*Indicating a chair.*)   Shall I sit here?

ALAN: That's Kit Neilan's place, as a matter of fact.   I think this is your place.   (*He shows a place next to* MAINGOT.)

MAINGOT (*rising*): Ah!   Pardon, Monsieur le Commandant. Voila votre place.   Asseyez-vous donc et soyez à votre aise.

ROGERS: Thanks.   (*He sits.*)

ALAN: I've been told to ask you if you like eggs with your breakfast.

MAINGOT: Oui, Monsieur.   Mais voulez-vous parlez Français, s'il-vous plaît.

ROGERS (*smiling apologetically*): I'm afraid I don't speak your lingo at all, you know.

MAINGOT: Lingo?   Ah, oui, langue.   C'est ça.   Mais il faut essayer.   You—must—try.

ROGERS (*turning to* MAINGOT, *then to* ALAN): Oui—Non.

ALAN: What?

MAINGOT: Pardon?

ROGERS: Oui, je ne—want any eggs.

ALAN: Right.   I'll tell Marianne.   (*He gets up and goes into the kitchen.*)

MAINGOT (*to* ROGERS): Il faut dire: Je ne veux pas des oeufs pour mon petit déjeuner.

    ROGERS *smiles vaguely.*   MAINGOT *laughs.*

Ça viendra, ça viendra.

    Re-enter ALAN.

BRIAN: I say, sir.   Did you have a good crossing?

ROGERS: Pretty bad, as a matter of fact.   Still, that didn't worry me.

BRIAN: You're a good sailor?

    ALAN *laughs.*

Oh, of course you would be. I mean you are, aren't you?

    MAINGOT *gets up.*

MAINGOT: Eh, bien. Par qui vais-je commencer?

KENNETH: Moi, Monsieur.

MAINGOT: *Par* Moi. (*Rising.*) Alors, allons dans le jardin. (*Bowing.*) *Messieurs!*

    He goes out into garden, followed by KENNETH.

ALAN: Poor Babe! He's going to be slaughtered.

ROGERS: Really. Why?

ALAN (*shaking his head sadly*): Elle a des idées au-dessus de sa gare.

ROGERS: What does that mean?

ALAN: It doesn't mean she has ideas above her station.

ROGERS: The Professor is pretty strict, I suppose.

ALAN: Where work is concerned, he's a sadist.

ROGERS: I'm glad to hear it. I want to learn as much French as I can, and I'm starting from scratch, you know.

BRIAN: Are you learning it for any special reason, sir?

ROGERS: Yes. Interpretership exam. in seven months' time.

ALAN: If you stay here for seven months you'll eather be dead or a Frenchman.

ROGERS: How long have you been here?

ALAN: On and off for a year.

    There is a pause, broken suddenly by a roar coming from the garden.

MAINGOT (*off*): Aha, ça c'est formidable. Qu'est ce que vous me fichez la donc? "Elle a des idées au-dessus de sa gare." Idiot! Idiot! Idiot!

    The noise subsides. ALAN *shakes his head.*

ALAN: Poor Babe. But he had it coming to him.

BRIAN: The Babe was having the horrors this morning before you came down. He said he hadn't one chance in a thousand of getting in.

ALAN: He hasn't.

ROGERS: Of getting in what?

ALAN: The diplomatic.

ROGERS: Oh, I suppose you're all budding diplomats?

BRIAN: All except me. I'm learning French for—er—commercial reasons.

ALAN: He's learnt a lot already. He can say "How much?" in

French, and you know how valuable that phrase is in the world of—er—commerce.

BRIAN (*laughing heartily*): Yes, old boy, and that's not all. I can say "Fifty francs? Do you think I'm made of money?"

ALAN (*laughing too*): "Cinquante francs? Crois-tu que je suis construit d'argent?"

They both suddenly become aware that ROGERS *isn't laughing. They stop and there is rather an awkward pause.* ALAN *and* BRIAN *exchange a brief glance.* BRIAN *silently frames the word* "*Po-faced*" *in his mouth.*

ROGERS (*with a wooden face*): Who else is staying here at the moment?

ALAN: There's only Kit Neilan, I think, that you haven't met.

ROGERS: Oh! Is he going into the diplomatic, too?

ALAN: Yes. (*To* BRIAN.) By the way, Brian, what odds did you lay against Kit in your book?

BRIAN: I didn't, but I should think five to two against would about meet the case.

ALAN: I don't know. The odds must have lengthened considerably these last few weeks.

BRIAN: Why? Oh, you mean Diana. I say, old boy, I hadn't thought of that. You don't think there's a chance of a well-fancied colt being withdrawn before the big contest?

ALAN: No. She won't marry him. That is, not until she's exhausted other possibilities.

ROGERS: Er—who is this girl?

BRIAN: Diana? She's Babe's—Kenneth Lake's sister. She's staying here.

ROGERS: Oh! is she learning French, too?

BRIAN: No. She just stops us from learning it. No, she's staying here because her people live in India and she's got nowhere else to go.

ROGERS: Pretty dull for her here, I should think.

ALAN: That girl wouldn't find it dull on a desert island.

BRIAN: Unless it *was* deserted.

ALAN: True. But one feels somehow it wouldn't be deserted long if she were on it.

ROGERS: What do you mean by that?

ALAN: I've no idea. She's a nice girl. You'll love her.

BRIAN *hides a smile.*

At least, it won't be her fault if you don't.

Rogers (*politely*): I don't quite follow you, I'm afraid.

Alan: I'm sorry, sir.   I was forgetting you're of an age to take care of yourself.

Rogers (*testily*): There's no need to call me "sir," you know.

Alan raises his eyebrows.

What you're implying is that this girl is—er—rather fast.

Alan: I'm not implying it.   I'm saying it.   That girl is the fastest worker you're ever likely to see.

Rogers: Oh!   (*He goes back to his food.*)

Brian (*conciliatorily*): What he means is that she's just naturally full of joie de vivre and all that.   She's all right really.   She just likes company.

Alan (*under his breath*): A battalion, you mean.

Rogers: You sound embittered.

Alan: Embittered?   Oh, no.   Oh, dear me, no.   (*He breaks a roll open rather violently*)   Both Brian and I, for reasons that I won't go into now, are immune.   Only I thought it just as well to let you know before you met her that Diana Lake, though a dear girl in many ways, is a little unreliable in her emotional life.

Rogers: You mean she isn't in love with this chap Kit What's-his-name, who wants to marry her.

Alan: The only reason I have for supposing she isn't is that she says that she is.   But that's good enough for me.

Pause.   Brian gets up.

Brian: Well, Maingot's simple French Phrases are calling me.

Rogers (*evidently glad to change the subject*): Maingot's Phrase-book.   He's given me that to do, too.

Brian: Good.   Then very soon now you will be able to walk into a chemist's and say in faultless French, "Please, sir, I wish a toothpaste with a slightly stronger scent."

Rogers: Oh, really.

Alan: Then think how nice it'll be if you're in a railway carriage, and you're able to inform a fellow traveller that the guard has just waved a red flag to signify that the locomotive has run off the line.

Rogers: Sounds a bit out of date, I must say.

Brian: Maingot's grandfather wrote it, I believe.

The telephone rings.   Brian turns round.

Do you know, I have a nasty feeling that's Chi-Chi.

Rogers: Who's Chi-Chi?

Brian: That's not her real name.

MAINGOT's *voice is heard from the garden.*

MAINGOT (*off*): Monsieur Howard.

ALAN (*getting up, calling*): Oui, Monsieur?

MAINGOT (*off*): Voulez-vous répondre au téléphone? Je vous empric?

ALAN: Bien, Monsieur. (*He goes to telephone and takes off the receiver.*) Hullo ... Bien. (*He holds out the receiver to* BRIAN.)

BRIAN: Me? Hell! (*He takes the receiver.*) Hullo ... Ah hullo, Chi-Chi, comment ça va? Comment-allez-vous? ... Quoi? ... Quoi? ... Wait a moment, Chi-Chi. (*Lowers receiver.*) Take it for me, old boy (*to* ALAN) I can't hear a word the girl's saying.

ALAN *comes and takes it.*

ALAN: Hullo. Oui, il ne comprend pas ... Bien. Je le liés demanderai.

(*To* BRIAN.) Can you see her to-night at the Casino? She wants you to meet her sister.

BRIAN: Ask her if it's the same one I met on Tuesday.

ALAN (*in phone*): Il voudrait savoir s'il a déjà rencontré votre soeur. ... Bon. (*To* BRIAN.) She says it's a different one.

BRIAN: Tell her it's O.K. I'll be there.

ALAN (*in phone*): Il dit qu'il sera enchanté. ... Oui ... Au revoir. (*He rings off.*)

BRIAN: I told that damn woman not to ring up here.

MAINGOT *enters from window.*

MAINGOT: Alors. Qui est ce qui vient de téléphoner?

BRIAN (*apologetically*): C'était quelqu'un pour moi, Monsieur.

MAINGOT: Pour vous?

BRIAN: Oui, une fille que je connais dans la ville.

MAINGOT: Une fille. *He bursts into a stentorian roar of laughter and goes back into the garden.*) Une fille qu'il connait! Ho! Ho!

BRIAN: Now what's bitten him?

ALAN: A fille doesn't mean a girl, Brian.

BRIAN: It says so in my dictionary. What does it mean, then?

ALAN: A tart.

BRIAN: Oh! (*He considers a second.*) Well, I hate to have to say it, old boy, but having a strict regard for the truth that's a fairly neat little description of Chi-Chi. See you two at lunch-time.

He goes out.

ALAN: There in a nutshell you have the reason for Brian's immunity to the charms of Diana Lake.

ROGERS (*icily*): Really?

ALAN (*easily*): Yes. (*Pause. He takes a cigarette.*) This place is going to be rather a change for you after your boat, isn't it?

ROGERS (*stung*): You mean my ship, don't you?

ALAN: Oh, is there a difference?

ROGERS: There is.

ALAN: Of course. It's a grave social error to say boat for ship, isn't it. Like mentioning a lady's name before the royal toast or talking about Harrow College.

ROGERS: Yes, that would be very wrong.

> DIANA LAKE *comes in from the garden. She is in a bathing wrap which she wears open, disclosing a bathing dress underneath. She is about twenty, very lovely.*

DIANA: Good morning. (*She stops at the sight of* ROGERS, *and decorously pulls her wrap more closely about her.*)

> ROGERS *and* ALAN *get up.*

ALAN: Good morning, Diana. I don't think you've met Commander Rogers.

> DIANA *comes forward and shakes hands.*

DIANA: How do you do?

ROGERS: How do you do?

DIANA (*to* ROGERS): I didn't know you'd—you must have arrived last night, I suppose.

ALAN: Don't you remember? You asked me what train he was coming by.

> DIANA *comes round the table; kisses him on the top of his head.*

DIANA: Do sit down, Commander Rogers. (*He sits.*) How are you this morning, Alan?

ALAN (*feeling her bathing dress*): I'll bet you didn't go in the water.

DIANA: Yes, I did.

ALAN: Right in?

DIANA: Yes, right in. Ask Kit.

ALAN (*really surprised*): Kit? You don't mean to say that you got Kit to go bathing with you.

DIANA: Yes, I did. He's fetching my towel. I left it behind.

ALAN: God! you women.

DIANA: What?

ALAN: Without the slightest qualm and just to gratify a passing whim, you force a high-souled young man to shatter one of his most sacred principles.

ROGERS: What principle is that, if I might ask?

DIANA (*emphatically*): Never, under any circumstances, to do anything hearty.

ROGERS (*challengingly*): Personally, I rather like an early morning dip.

ALAN (*as if the words burnt his mouth*): An—early—morning—dip?

ROGERS: Certainly. That's hearty, I suppose.

ALAN: Well——

DIANA: I quite agree with you, Commander Rogers. I don't think there's anything nicer than a swim before breakfast. Ashtray? (*Hands it to* ROGERS.)

ALAN: You'd like anything that gave you a chance to come down to breakfast in a bathing dress.

DIANA: Does it shock you, Alan?

ALAN: Unutterably.

DIANA: I'll go and dress then.

ALAN: No. There's no point in that. You've made one successful entrance. Don't spoil it by making another.

ROGERS: I don't think I quite understand you.

ALAN: Diana does, don't you, angel?

DIANA (*sweetly*): Has another publisher refused your novel, Alan?

(ALAN, *momentarily disconcerted, can find nothing to say. Pause. Enter* KIT *through the french window. He is about twenty-two, fair and good-looking. He wears a dressing-gown over his bathing dress, and carries two towels over his arm.*)

KIT (*sullenly*): Morning.

ALAN (*in gentle reproof*): Well, well, well.

KIT (*shamefacedly*): Well, why not?

ALAN *shakes his head sadly.*

ALAN: I don't think you've met Commander Rogers.

KIT (*shaking hands*): How do you do? I heard you were coming. (*He begins to dry his hair on a towel, throwing the other one to* DIANA.)

ALAN: Did Diana go in the water?

KIT: No.

DIANA: Kit, you dirty liar.

KIT: I've done enough for you already this morning. I'm not going to perjure myself as well. (*He sits down gloomily and pours himself out a cup of coffee.*) I had hoped you wouldn't be here, Alan, to witness my shame.

ALAN: You of all people an early morning dipper.

KIT (*shuddering*): Don't put it like that.   You make it sound worse than it is.   Say a nine o'clock bather.   Oh, hell, this coffee's cold. Marianne!

ALAN: Mere toying with words can't hide the truth.   Do you know I think that girl could make you go for a bicycle tour in the Pyrenees if she set her mind to it.

KIT: She could you know, Alan, that's the awful thing.
    Slight pause.

ROGERS: I once went for a bicycle tour in the Pyrenees.

ALAN: Really?
    KIT *splutters into his coffee simultaneously.*
    JACQUELINE *comes out of the kitchen.   She is about twenty-five or twenty-six, not unattractive, but nothing in looks to compare with* DIANA.   *She wears an apron and has a handkerchief tied over her hair.*

JACQUELINE: Marianne's upstairs.   (*She speaks with only the barest trace of accent.*)

KIT: Hello, Jack.

ALAN: Good morning, darling.

JACQUELINE (*going to Rogers*): How do you do, Commander Rogers.   I'm so glad you could come to us.

ROGERS (*shaking hands*): Er—how do you do?

JACQUELINE: I hope you've found everything you want.

ROGERS: Yes, thank you.

JACQUELINE: Did Marianne ask you if you wanted eggs for breakfast?

ROGERS: I don't want any, thanks.

JACQUELINE: I see.   Well, don't worry about asking for anything you need.   By the way, do you drink beer at meals or do you prefer wine?

ROGERS (*sitting*): Beer, please.   Nothing like a can of beer.

ALAN: No, I suppose there isn't.

JACQUELINE (*to Kit*): What were you shouting about, by the way?

KIT: Jack, darling, the coffee's cold.

JACQUELINE: Of course it's cold.   You're half an hour late for breakfast.

KIT: Yes, but . . .

JACQUELINE: You can't have any more because Marianne's doing the rooms.

KIT: I thought perhaps, Jack, darling, knowing how much you love me, you might be an angel and do something about it.

JACQUELINE: Certainly not. It's against all the rules of the house. Besides, you'd better go and get dressed. I'm giving you a lesson in five minutes.

KIT: In the near future, when I am Minister of Foreign Affairs, this incident will play a large part in my decision to declare war on France.

JACQUELINE pushes him back into his chair and grabs the coffee-pot.

JACQUELINE: Ooh! This is the last time I'm going to do this for you.

She goes back into the kitchen.

KIT (*to* DIANA): You see what a superb diplomat I should make.

ALAN: Rather the Palmerston tradition, wasn't it?

ROGERS: Was that Maingot's daughter?

KIT: Yes. Her name's Jacqueline.

ROGERS: Jacqueline? (*Brightly.*) I see. That's why you call her Jack.

KIT (*looking at him distastefully*): Yes, that's why we call her Jack.

ROGERS: She speaks English very well.

KIT: She's been in England half her life. I believe she's going to be an English school-marm. You'll like her. She's amusing. (*He continues to dry himself.*) Hell! I still feel wet.

He glares at DIANA who comes behind his chair and dries his hair with her own towel.

DIANA: You've got such lovely hair, darling. That's why it takes so long to dry.

KIT (*to* ALAN): You know, Alan, this is a nice girl.

ALAN (*tilting his chair back and gazing at DIANA*): Yes, she's nice. She's good, too.

ROGERS gets up.

ROGERS: Well, I must go upstairs. I want to get my room ship-shape.

ALAN: And above board.

ROGERS (*turning savagely on* ALAN): Yes, and above board. Any objection?

ALAN (*airily*): No, no objection at all. Make it as above board as you like.

ROGERS (*bowing stiffly*): Thank you. I'm most grateful.

Exit ROGERS.

ALAN (*pensively*): Do you know, I don't think he likes me.

KIT: Who does? I'm the only one who can stand you and then only in small doses.

DIANA: Kenneth adores you, anyway. He's quite silly the way he tries to imitate you.

ALAN: Your brother shows remarkable acumen sometimes.

DIANA: And then, of course, I adore you too. You know that.

KITS *wings his chair round and pulls her roughly down on his knee.*

KIT: Hey! I'm not going to have you adoring anybody except me. Do you understand? (*He kisses her.*)

DIANA: Darling, you're not jealous of Alan, are you?

KIT: I'm jealous of anyone you even look at.

DIANA: All right, then in future I won't look at anyone except you.

KIT: That's a promise?

DIANA: That's a promise.

ALAN, *still leaning back in his chair, whistles a tune softly.* (*Feeling* KIT's *hands.*) Darling, you *are* cold.

KIT: Yes, I know. I think I'll go and dress and not wait for the coffee. (*He gets up.*) You've probably given me pneumonia. But I don't mind. You could tear me up in little pieces and trample on them, and I'd still love you.

DIANA: Sweet little thing. Take these things upstairs, darling, will you? (*Gives him towels.*)

KIT *goes out.*

ALAN: That's no reason why you should, you know.

DIANA: Should what?

ALAN: Tear him up in little pieces and trample on them.

DIANA *crosses over to the window where she stands, looking out.* So you're not going to look at anyone except Kit.

DIANA *doesn't answer.* ALAN *gets up and walks over to the window. He puts his arm round her waist and his cheek against hers.* (*After a pause.*) This doesn't mean I'm falling for you.

DIANA (*gently*): Doesn't it, Alan?

ALAN: No, it doesn't.

He walks over to the arm-chair and sits.

DIANA: I *am* disappointed.

ALAN: What do you think of the Commander?

DIANA: I think he's quite nice.

ALAN: Yes. (*Gently.*) Yes. I want to tell you, it's no good starting anything with him.

DIANA: Don't be silly, Alan.

ALAN: It really isn't any good, darling, because you see I've warned him against you.

DIANA: You warned him? (*Coming to* ALAN.) What did you say?

ALAN: I told him what you are.

DIANA (*quietly*): What's that?

ALAN: Don't you know?

DIANA: Alan, much as I like you there *are* times when I could cheerfully strangle you.

ALAN: Is this one of them, darling?

DIANA: Yes, ducky, it is.

ALAN: Good, that's just what I hoped.

DIANA: This is rather a new rôle for you, isn't it, playing wet nurse to the Navy?

ALAN: You don't think it suits me?

DIANA: No, darling, I'm afraid I don't. What are you doing it for?

ALAN: Never you mind, only no hanky-panky with the Navy or . . .

DIANA: Or what?

ALAN: Or I shall have to be rather beastly to you, darling, and you know how you wouldn't like that.

DIANA: You don't understand me at all, Alan.

ALAN: I understand every little bit of you, Diana, through and through. That's why we get along so well together.

DIANA (*tearfully*): I ought to *hate* you.

ALAN: Well go on trying, darling, and you may succeed. (*He kisses her on the back of the neck.*) I've got to go and finish some stuff for Maingot. See you at lunch-time. (*He goes to the door.*)

DIANA: Alan?

ALAN (*turning at door*): Yes?

DIANA: What do you mean by hanky-panky?

ALAN: *I* should tell *you*.

He goes out.

DIANA *kicks petulantly at the window. She goes to the table, opens her handbag, takes out a small mirror and looks at herself. Enter* JACQUELINE *from the kitchen with the coffee-pot.*

DIANA: Oh, thank you so much.

JACQUELINE: Where's Kit?

DIANA: He's gone up to dress.   He felt cold.

JACQUELINE: Isn't that like him.   Well you can tell him that I'm not going to make him any more coffee however loud he screams.

DIANA: Yes, I'll tell him, and I think you're quite right.

    JACQUELINE *goes out into the kitchen.*

    Enter ROGERS *through the door at the back.*

ROGERS (*nervously*): Oh, hullo.

DIANA (*brightly*): Hullo, Commander Rogers.

    ROGERS *goes over to the bookcase at the back.*

Looking for something?

ROGERS: Yes, Maingot's Phrase Book, as a matter of fact.   (*He bends down and pulls a book out.*)   Here it is, I think.   (*He looks at the title.*)   No, it isn't.

DIANA: Let me help you.   I think I know where it is.

ROGERS: Oh, that's very good of you.

    DIANA *bends down at the bookcase and pulls a book out.*

DIANA: Here.   (*She hands it to him.*)

ROGERS: Oh, thanks most awfully.

DIANA (*going back to the table*): Well, what are your first impressions of Monsieur Maingot's establishment?

ROGERS: Oh, I—er—think it ought to be very cheery here.

DIANA: I'm sure you'll love it.

ROGERS: Yes, I'm sure I will.

DIANA: The boys are so nice, don't you think?

ROGERS: Er—yes, I think they are—some of them.   (*He makes a tentative move towards the door.*)

DIANA (*quickly*): I suppose you find Alan a bit startling, don't you?

ROGERS: Alan?

DIANA: The one with the navy pullover.

ROGERS: Oh, yes.   Yes, he is a bit startling.   Well, I ought to be getting along.

DIANA: Why?   You've got your room pretty well ship-shape by now, haven't you?

ROGERS: Oh, thanks, yes, I have.

DIANA: Well, don't go for a bit.   Stay and talk to me while I have my coffee.   Have you got a cigarette?

ROGERS (*coming to her*): Yes, I have.   (*Offers her one.*)

DIANA (*takes one*): Thanks.   I was saying about Alan——

ROGERS: Match?

DIANA: Thanks. (*He lights it.*) What was I saying?

ROGERS: About Alan.

DIANA: Oh, yes, about Alan—he's really very nice but that you mustn't take everything he says seriously.

ROGERS: Oh. Oh, I see. No, I won't.

DIANA: He's just the tiniest bit—you know (*he taps her forehead significantly*) unbalanced.

ROGERS: Oh, really.

DIANA: I thought it as well to warn you.

ROGERS: Yes. Thank you very much.

DIANA: Otherwise it might lead to trouble.

ROGERS: Yes, it might.

     Pause.

DIANA: Poor Alan. I'm afraid he's got it very badly.

ROGERS: Er—got what?

DIANA: Well—— (*She leans back and blows a puff of smoke into the air.*) Of course I oughtn't to say it. (*Pause. She throws him a quick glance to see if he has caught her meaning. Evidently he hasn't.*)

ROGERS: Oh.

DIANA: I'm awfully sorry for him of course.

ROGERS (*puzzled, but polite*): Of course.

DIANA: It's so funny, because from the way he behaves to me and the things he says about me, you'd think he hated me, wouldn't you?

ROGERS: Yes, you would. (*Pause.*) Doesn't he?

DIANA: (*laughing*) No. Oh, no. Far from it.

ROGERS (*The light of understanding in his face at last*): Oh, I see. You mean he's rather keen on you?

DIANA: I mustn't give him away. It wouldn't be fair. But if he ever talks to you about me, as he probably will, and tries to give you the impression that I'm a (*smiling*) scheming wrecker of men's lives, you needn't necessarily believe him.

ROGERS: No—no, I won't, of course. But I don't see why he should, you know.

DIANA (*embarrassedly*): Well, you see, Commander Rogers, I like Alan, but I don't like him as much as perhaps he wants me to, and I suppose that makes him feel rather embittered.

ROGERS: Ah, yes. I see.

DIANA (*gaily*): Well, don't let's talk any more about it, because it's not a very pleasant subject. Tell me about yourself. Tell me about the Navy. I'm always thrilled to death by anything to do with the sea.

ROGERS: Really, that's splendid.

    Pause.

DIANA: It must be a wonderful life.

ROGERS: Yes, it's a pretty good life on the whole.

DIANA: Marvellously interesting, I should think.

ROGERS: Yes, pretty interesting.

DIANA: I bet you've had any amount of wildly exciting experiences.

ROGERS: Oh, well, you know, things have a way of happening in the Navy.

DIANA: Yes, I'm sure they have. (*Pause.*) You naval people never talk about yourselves, do you?

ROGERS: Well, you know, silent service and all that.

DIANA: Yes, I know, but I do hope you're not going to be too silent with me, because honestly, I am so terribly interested.

ROGERS (*smiling*): I'll try not to be too silent then.

    Pause.

DIANA: What are you doing this morning?

ROGERS: Nothing special. Why?

DIANA: How would you like to have a look round the town?

    Enter JACQUELINE *from the kitchen.*

JACQUELINE: Hasn't Kit come down yet?

ROGERS (*to* DIANA): Oh, I'd love to.

DIANA: Good. I'll go and get dressed and we'll go for a little stroll.

ROGERS: But isn't it rather a bore for you?

DIANA: No, of course not. I'd love it. (*She goes to the door.*)

JACQUELINE: Diana?

DIANA: Yes?

JACQUELINE (*pouring out a cup of coffee*): If you're going past Kit's room you might give him this. (*She hands her the cup.*)

DIANA: Right, I will. (*To* ROGERS.) Are you sure I'm not dragging you away from your work or anything?

    JACQUELINE *goes back into the kitchen.*

ROGERS: Oh, no. That's quite all right. I haven't been given anything to do yet.

DIANA: Good. Well, I'll go and put some clothes on.

She turns to go. ALAN *comes in and almost collides with her in
the doorway.*

(*turning.*) I'll meet you down here then in about a quarter of an
hour?

ROGERS: Right.

DIANA *smiles at* ROGERS, *walks past* ALAN *without glancing at
him and goes out.*

ALAN (*going to the table and sitting*): Going for a little constitutional,
Commander? (*He has a note-book in his hands. He places them on
the table in front of him and opens the note-book.*)

ROGERS: Yes. (*He turns his back.*)

ALAN (*taking a fountain pen from his pocket and unscrewing the top*):
You've got a nice day for it. (*Pause. He writes in his note-book and
begins to sing the* "Lorelei". *Without looking up.*) It's a lovely song
the "Lorelei", don't you think?

ROGERS: It *could* be.

ALAN: True. (*He continues to write.*) It's a stupid fable anyway.
I ask you, what sailor would be lured to his doom after he had been
warned of his danger?

ROGERS (*turning quickly*): If you think that's funny, I don't.

Enter KENNETH *through the window.*

KENNETH: Oh, Commander Rogers, Maingot wants to see you a
moment.

Pause. ROGERS *is standing facing* ALAN *across the table, and
ALAN is still writing.*

ROGERS: Right. Thank you. (*He marches out into the garden.*)

ALAN (*after a pause*): Well, Babe, I suppose you were murdered
by the old man.

KENNETH (*wearily*): More so than usual this morning.

Pause. ALAN *goes on writing.*

ALAN (*without looking up*): Babe, I don't like your sister.

KENNETH (*walking round the table and looking over* ALAN's *shoulder
at what he is writing*): Don't you? I thought you did like her, rather
a lot.

ALAN *looks up. Pause.*

Enter JACQUELINE *from the kitchen. She has taken off her
apron and the handkerchief over her hair.*

JACQUELINE: Good morning, Kenneth.

KENNETH: Good morning, Mam'selle.

JACQUELINE: Had your lesson?

KENNETH: Yes. I've got to do the whole damn thing again. (*He goes to the door.*) Alan, I wish to God I had your brains.

He goes out.

ALAN *looks after him a moment, then goes back to his work.*

JACQUELINE (*looking at her watch*): Kit is a monster. He's never been on time for his lesson yet. (*She goes to the window and looks out.*)

ALAN (*looking up from his work*): What have you done to your hair, Jack?

JACQUELINE (*turning round*): Do you like it? (*Her hair is done in the same way as* DIANA's.)

ALAN (*he gets up and walks over to her, holding her out at arm's length and studying her hair. Doubtfully*): No, it's a mistake, Jack. You won't beat her by copying the way she does her hair.

JACQUELINE: He'll like it, Alan, I'm sure he will.

ALAN: He won't notice it.

JACQUELINE: He will, you see.

ALAN: I'll bet you fifty francs he doesn't.

JACQUELINE: All right. That's a bet.

ALAN: Go and change it while there's still time. Make it look hideous like it used to.

JACQUELINE (*laughing*): No, Alan.

Pause.

ALAN: Poor Jack. I must find you someone else to fall in love with.

JACQUELINE: So long as you don't tell him that I adore him, I don't mind what you do.

ALAN: Anyone less half-witted than Kit would have seen it years ago.

JACQUELINE: Am I very obvious, Alan? I don't want to bore him.

ALAN: Go and change that hair.

JACQUELINE: Do you think if Diana were out of the way I should stand a chance?

ALAN: You're not thinking of putting her out of the way, are you?

JACQUELINE (*smiling*): I'd do it painlessly, Alan.

ALAN: Why painlessly?

JACQUELINE: I'm not jealous of her really, though.

ALAN: Oh, no. Not a bit.

JACQUELINE: Honestly, Alan, I wouldn't mind if she made him happy. But she doesn't. She seems to enjoy making him miserable. And now that the Commander's here it's going to be much worse. You know what I mean, don't you?

ALAN: I have an idea.

JACQUELINE: Can't we do anything about it, Alan?

ALAN: Yes. Go and change that hair, Jack. It's the only chance.

JACQUELINE: No, I won't do anything of the sort.

Enter KIT dressed.

KIT (*walking right up to* JACQUELINE *and taking her hands earnestly*): Jack, I have something to tell you. (*To* ALAN.) Go away, Alan, this is confidential.

ALAN goes back to the table and his work.

JACQUELINE: What is it, Kit?

KIT: I haven't done that work you set me.

JACQUELINE: Oh, Kit. Why not?

KIT: Well, I took Diana to the Casino last night, and——

JACQUELINE: Kit, really——

KIT: But as a great treat I'll translate you some "La Bruyère" this morning. Come on. (*He pulls her towards one of the arm-chairs.*)

JACQUELINE: I set you that work specially because I thought it would interest you, and anyway you can't afford to slack off just now before your exam.

KIT (*hands her book*): Now sit down and read your nice "La Bruyrèe and be quiet. Are you comfortable? (*Opening his own book.*) Page one hundred and eight. Listen, Alan. You can learn a lot from hearing French beautifully translated. Chapter four. (*Translating.*) Of the heart . . .

JACQUELINE: Of love.

KIT: Of love, then. (*Translating.*) There is a fragrance in pure love . . .

JACQUELINE: In pure friendship.

KIT (*translating*): Friendship can exist between people of different sexes.

ALAN: You don't say.

KIT: I don't. "La Bruyère" does. (*Translating.*) Friendship can exist between people of different sexes, quite exempt from all grossness.

JACQUELINE: Quite free from all . . .

ALAN: Hanky-panky.

JACQUELINE: Quite free from all unworthy thoughts.

KIT: Quite exempt from all grossness. (*Looking up.*) I know what it is. It's been bothering me all the time. You've changed your hair, haven't you, Jack?

JACQUELINE (*giving* ALAN *a quick glance*): Yes, Kit, I've changed my hair.

KIT: Alan, do look at Jack.   She's changed her hair.

ALAN (*looking up*): So she has.   Well—well—well.

KIT: I knew you'd done something to yourself.   (*He studies her.*) It's queer, you know.   It makes you look quite . . .

JACQUELINE (*eagerly*): Quite what, Kit?

KIT: I was going to say alluring

 He laughs as if he'd made a joke; JACQUELINE *laughs, too.*

JACQUELINE: You do like it, anyway, Kit?

KIT: Yes, I do.   I think it's very nice.

JACQUELINE: You think I ought to keep it like this?

 Before Kit can answer, ROGERS *has appeared from garden.*

ROGERS: Sorry.   Maingot wants to take me now, so would one of you mind telling Diana—er—I mean Miss Lake, that we'll have to postpone our walk.

 Pause.

ALAN: Yes, I'll tell her.

ROGERS: Thank you.

 He goes back into garden.

JACQUELINE (*breaking a silence*): You think I ought to keep it like this?

KIT (*turning slowly*): Keep what?

JACQUELINE: My hair.

KIT: Oh, don't be such a bore about your hair, Jack.   Yes, keep it like that.   It'll get a laugh anyway.

 He goes out quickly.   Pause. JACQUELINE *closes her book with a slam and rises.*

JACQUELINE: Fifty francs please, Alan.

CURTAIN

ACT I

SCENE II

SCENE: *Same as Act I.*

TIME: *A fortnight later, about two p.m.*

Lunch is just finished. All the characters seen in Act I are still sitting at the table. MAINGOT sits at one end, ALAN facing him at the other end. On MAINGOT's right are ROGERS, DIANA and KIT, in that order, facing the audience. On his left are BRIAN, KENNETH and JACQUELINE, also in that order, with their backs to the audience.

On the rise of the CURTAIN conversation is general. ALAN is talking to JACQUELINE, BRIAN to MAINGOT, and ROGERS to DIANA. After a few seconds conversation lapses and ROGERS' voice can be heard.

ROGERS: Oh, yes, Tuppy Jones. Yes, he's in Belligerent. I know him quite well. Cheery cove. (*He chuckles.*) There's an amusing story about him as a matter of fact. He got a bit tight in Portsmouth, and broke seven Belisha Beacons with an air pistol.

MAINGOT (*turning politely to* ROGERS): Eh, bien, Monsieur le Commandant, voulez-vous raconter votre petite histoire en Française. Please to tell your little story in French.

ROGERS (*confused*): Oh, no, sir. That's a bit unfair. I don't know enough.

MAINGOT: You should have learnt enough, my Commander.

ROGERS: But, dash it, sir, I've only been here a few days.

MAINGOT: Two weeks, my Commander. After two weeks my pupils are usually enough advanced to tell me little stories in French.

ROGERS: Well, I'm afraid I can't tell this one, sir. It wasn't a story anyway.

ALAN (*leaning forward malevolently*): Au contraire, Monsieur, l'histoire de Monsieur le Commandant était excessivement rigolo.

MAINGOT: Bien. Alors, racontex-la vous même.

ALAN: Il parait qu'il connait un type qui s'appelle Tuppy Jones. Alors ce bonhomme, se promenant un soir par les rues de Portsmouth. et ayant un peu trop bu, a brisé, à coupe de pistolet à vent, sept Belisha Beacons.

MAINGOT (*who has been listening attentively, his ear cupped in his hand*): Et puis?

ALAN: C'est tout, Monsieur.

MAINGOT: C'est tout?

KIT: Vous savez que ce Tuppy Jones était d'un esprit le plus fin du monde.

MAINGOT: Je crois bien.   Au même temps, je n'ai pas tout a fait compris.   Qu'est-ce que ça veut dire—Belisha Beacons?

ALAN: Ah, ça c'est un peu compliqué.

BRIAN (*showing off his French*): Belisha Beacons sont des objets—comme de grandes pommes de toffee.

ALAN: Qui se trouvent actuellement dans les rues de Londres——

KIT: Et qui sont dédiés au salut des passants.

MAINGOT: Aha.   Des emblèmes religieux?

ALAN: C'est ça.   Des emblèmes religieux.

MAINGOT (*to* ROGERS): So one finds it funny in England to break these religious emblems with a pistol of wind?

ROGERS (*not having understood*): Well—— (MAINGOT *shrugs his shoulders sadly.*)

(*Angrily to* ALAN.)   Damn you, Howard.

BRIAN: That's not fair.

ALAN: It was a very good story, I thought.

MAINGOT (*rising, having finished his wine*): Bien, Messieurs, Mesdames, la session est terminée. (*He gets up.* ALL *get up after him.*)

(*Holding up his hand.*)   One moment, please.   I speak in English for those who cannot understand.   How many of you are going to-night to the Costume Ball and great battle of flowers at the Casino? Please hold up your hands?

KIT (*to* ALAN): Good lord!   Is it July the fourteenth?   I'd no idea.

All hold up their hands.

MAINGOT: All of you!   Good.   The festivities commence at eight o'clock; there will be no dinner 'ere.   All right.

MAINGOT *moves to window and stops.*

One moment please.   I give my history lecture at two-thirty, that is to say in twenty minutes' time.   All right.

He goes out into garden.

ROGERS *and* DIANA *are moving towards the french windows.* KIT *catches them up.*

KIT (*to* DIANA): What about a game of Japanese billiards, Diana?

DIANA (*indicating* ROGERS): Bill's just asked me to play, Kit. I'll play you afterwards. Come on, Bill.

ROGERS: Sorry, Neilan.

> ROGERS *and* DIANA *go out together.* KIT *goes to an arm-chair and sits sulkily.* MAINGOT *wanders out through the window.* BRIAN *has pulled out a wallet and is fumbling inside it.* ALAN *is going out through the window when* KENNETH *catches him up.*

KENNETH: Alan, will you help me with that essay now? You said you would.

ALAN: Oh, hell! Can't you do it yourself?

KENNETH: Well, I could, but it might mean missing this dance to-night, and I'd hate that. Do help me. It's on Robespierre, and I know nothing about him.

ALAN: There's a chapter on him in Lavisse. Why don't you copy that out? The old man won't notice. He'll probably say it isn't French, but still——

> *He goes out.*

KENNETH (*shouting after him*): Alan, be a sportsman.

ALAN (*off*): Nothing I should hate more.

KENNETH: Oh, hell!

> KENNETH *turns sadly and goes past* KIT *to the door at the back.*

KIT (*moodily*): What Alan wants is a good kick in the pants.

KENNETH (*at door*): Oh, I don't know.

> *He goes out.* BRIAN *puts his wallet back in his pocket.*

BRIAN: I say, old boy, I suppose you couldn't lend me five hundred francs, could you?

KIT: No, I couldn't. At any rate, not until you've paid me back that thousand you owe me.

BRIAN: Ah, I see your point. (*Cheerfully.*) Well, old boy, no ill feelings. I'll have to put off Chi-Chi for to-night, that's all.

KIT: You weren't thinking of taking her to this thing at the Casino, were you?

BRIAN: Yes.

KIT: What do you think Maingot would have said if he'd seen her.

BRIAN: That would have been all right. I told him I was taking the daughter of the British Consul.

KIT: But she doesn't exactly look like the daughter of the British Consul, does she?

BRIAN: Well, after all, it's fancy dress. It's just possible the daughter of the British Consul might go dressed as Nana of the Boulevards. Still, I admit that if he'd actually met her he might have found it odd that the only English she knew was "I love you, Big Boy."

KIT: How do you manage to talk to her, then?

BRIAN: Oh, we get along, old boy, we get along. (*Going to window.*) You couldn't make it thirty francs, I suppose.

KIT: No, and I don't suppose Chi-Chi could either.

BRIAN: Oh, well, you may be right. I'd better pop round in the car and tell her I won't be there to-night.

KIT: Oh, listen, Brian, if you want someone to take, why don't you take Jack?

BRIAN: Isn't anyone taking her?

KIT: Yes, I'm supposed to be, but——

BRIAN (*surprised*): You, old boy. What about Diana?

KIT: Oh, she's being taken by the Commander.

BRIAN: Oh.

    Pause.

As a matter of fact, I don't think I'll go at all. I don't fancy myself at a battle of flowers.

KIT: Nor do I, if it comes to that.

BRIAN: Oh, I don't know. I think you'd hurl a prettier bloom than I would. Well, so long.

    He goes out. KIT *sits biting his nails. The ferocious din of a sports car tuning up comes through the window.* KIT *jumps up.*

KIT (*shouting through the window*): Must you make all that noise?

BRIAN (*off, his voice coming faintly above the din*): Can't hear, old boy.

    The noise lessens as the car moves off down the street. JACQUELINE *and* MARIANNE *come in, the latter bearing a tray.*

KIT (*turning*): God knows why Brian finds it necessary to have a car that sounds like—like a sessions of foreign ministers.

JACQUELINE (*helping* MARIANNE *clear*): It goes with his character, Kit. He'd think it was effeminate to have a car that was possible to sit in without getting cramp and that didn't deafen one.

KIT (*sitting again*): I wonder what it's like to be as hearty as Brian?

JACQUELINE: Awful, I should think.

KIT: No, I should think very pleasant. Have you ever seen Brian bad-tempered?

E   129

JACQUELINE: No, but then I think he's too stupid to be bad-tempered.

KIT: It doesn't follow. Cats and dogs are bad-tempered, sometimes. No, Brian may be stupid but he's right-minded. He's solved the problem of living better than any of us.

MARIANNE *goes out with a loaded tray.*

It seems a simple solution, too. All it needs, apparently, is the occasional outlay of five hundred francs. I wish I could do the same.

JACQUELINE: I expect you could if you tried.

KIT: I have tried. Often.

JACQUELINE *is folding up the table-cloth.*

Does that shock you?

JACQUELINE: Why should it?

KIT: I just wondered.

JACQUELINE: I'm a woman of the world.

KIT (*smiling*): That's the last thing you are. But I'll tell you this, Jack. I like you so much that it's sometimes quite an effort to remember that you're a woman at all.

JACQUELINE: Oh.

She pnts the table-cloth in a drawer of the table and shuts it with something of a slam.

I thought you liked women.

KIT: I don't think one likes women, does one? One loves them sometimes, but that's a different thing altogether. Still, I like you. That's what's so odd.

JACQUELINE (*brightly*): Thank you, Kit. I like you, too.

KIT: Good. That's nice for both of us, isn't it?

He returns his gaze to the window. JACQUELINE, *in a sudden fit of temper, kicks the leg of the table.*

Clumsy!

JACQUELINE (*limping over to the other arm-chair and sitting*): Have you found anything to wear to-night?

KIT: Supposing I didn't go, would you mind?

JACQUELINE: Well, I have been rather looking forward to to-night.

KIT: Alan could take you. He's a better dancer than I am.

JACQUELINE (*after a pause*): Why don't you wear that Greek dress of my brother's?

KIT: Jack, you know, I don't think I could cope with a battle of flowers. (*He turns and meets her eyes.*)   Could I get into this dress of your brothers?

JACQUELINE: Yes, easily.   It may be a bit tight.

ALAN *comes in through the window.*

KIT: That reminds me.   I hope there'll be plenty to drink at this affair.

ALAN (*morosely*): There's nothing else for it.   I shall have to murder that man.

JACQUELINE: Who?

ALAN: The Commander.

KIT: Surely that's my privilege, isn't it?

ALAN: I've just been watching him play Japanese billiards with Diana.   Now you would think, wouldn't you, that Japanese billiards was a fairly simple game.   You either roll wooden balls into holes or you don't.   That should be the end of it.   But as played by the Commander it becomes a sort of naval battle.   Every shot he makes is either a plunging salvo or a blasting broadside, or a direct hit amidships.

KIT: At least he has the excuse that it amuses Diana.   (*He gets up.*)   Will you explain to me, Alan, as an impartial observer, how she can bear to be more than two minutes in that man's company?

ALAN: Certainly.   He's in the process of falling in love with her.

KIT: Yes, that's obvious, but——

ALAN: When one hooks a salmon one has to spend a certain amount of time playing it.   If one doesn't, it escapes.

KIT: Is that meant to be funny?

ALAN: Of course.   When the salmon is landed, all that's necessary is an occasional kick to prevent it slipping back into the water.

KIT (*angrily*): Don't be a damned fool.

ALAN: To-morrow a certain Lord Heybrook is arriving.   Diana is naturally rather anxious to bring the Commander to the gaff as quickly as possible, so that she can have two nice fat fish gasping and squirming about on the bank, before she starts to fish for what'll be the best catch of all of you, if she can bring it off.

Pause.   KIT suddenly bursts out laughing.

KIT: No wonder you can't get anyone to take your novel.

ALAN (*hurt*): I can't quite see what my novel has got to do with the machinations of a scalp-hunter.

JACQUELINE *rises in alarm.*

KIT (*walking over to* ALAN): Listen, Alan. One more crack like that——

JACQUELINE (*hurriedly to* ALAN): Kit's quite right. You shouldn't say things like that.

KIT (*turning to her savagely*): What do you know about it, anyway?

JACQUELINE: Nothing, only——

KIT: Well, please go away. This is between Alan and me.

JACQUELINE: Oh, I'm sorry.

JACQUELINE *goes into garden.*

KIT (*rising*): Now. Will you please understand this. I am in love with Diana, and Diana is in love with me. Now that's not too hard for you to grasp, is it? Because I'll repeat it again slowly if you like.

ALAN (*genially*): No, no. I've read about that sort of thing in books. The Commander, of course, is just an old friend who's known her since she was so high.

KIT: The Commander's in love with her, but you can't blame Diana for that.

ALAN: Of course I don't. It was a very smart piece of work on her part.

KIT (*swallowing his anger*): She's too kind-hearted to tell him to go to hell——

ALAN: I suppose it's because she's so kind-hearted that she calls him "darling," and plays these peculiar games with him all over the place.

Pause.

KIT: I called you an impartial observer a moment ago. Well, you're not. I believe you're in love with Diana yourself.

ALAN: My dear Kit! As a matter of fact, I admit it's quite possible I shall end by marrying her.

KIT: You'll what?

ALAN: But that'll only be—to take another sporting metaphor—like the stag who turns at bay through sheer exhaustion at being hunted.

Pause.

DIANA *appears at window,* ROGERS *following.*

ROGERS (*coming in through window*): Well, of course, there was only one thing to do. So I gave the order—all hands on deck—— (*Stops at sight of* KIT *and* ALAN.)

ALAN: And did they come?

ROGERS (*ignoring* ALAN, *to* DIANA): Let's go out in the garden, Diana?

DIANA (*languidly throwing herself into an arm-chair*): It's so hot, Bill. Let's stay here.

KIT: Aren't you going to play me a game of Japanese billiards, Diana?

DIANA: You don't mind, do you, Kit? I'm quite exhausted as a matter of fact.

KIT (*furious*): Oh, no. I don't mind a bit.

> *He goes out into the garden. Pause.* ALAN *begins to hum the "Lorelei".* ROGERS *walks towards window.*

ALAN: Don't leave us, Commander. If one of us has to go, let it be myself.

> ROGERS *stops.* ALAN *walks to door at back.*

I shall go aloft.

> *He goes out.*

ROGERS: Silly young fool. I'd like to have him in my ship. Do him all the good in the world.

DIANA: Yes. It might knock some of the conceit out of him.

ROGERS: Y-e-s. Has he been—bothering you at all lately?

DIANA (*with a gesture or resignation*): Oh, well. I'm awfully sorry for him, you know.

ROGERS: I find it hard to understand you sometimes, Diana.

> *He sits in chair beside her. She pats his hand.*

At least I think I do understand you, but it you don't mind me saying it, I think you're too kind-hearted—far too kind-hearted.

DIANA (*with a sigh*): Yes, I think I am.

ROGERS: For instance—I can't understand why you don't tell Kit.

DIANA: Oh, Bill, please——

ROGERS: I'm sorry to keep on at you about it, Diana, but you don't know how much I resent him behaving as if you were still in love with him.

DIANA: But I can't tell him—not yet, anyway. (*Gently.*) Surely you must see how cruel that would be?

ROGERS: This is a case where you must be cruel only to be kind.

DIANA: Yes, Bill, that's true. Terribly true. But you know, cruelty is something that's physically impossible to me. I'm the sort of person who's miserable if I tread on a snail.

ROGERS: You must tell him, Diana. Otherwise it's so unfair on him. Tell him now.

DIANA: (*Quickly*): No, not now.

ROGERS: Well, this evening.

DIANA: Well, I'll try. It's a terribly hard thing to do. It's like —it's like kicking someone when he's down.

    ROGERS *puts his arms round her.*

ROGERS: I know, old girl, it's a rotten thing to have to do. Poor little thing, you mustn't think I don't sympathise with you, you know.

DIANA (*laying her head on his chest*): Oh, Bill, I do feel such a beast.

ROGERS: Yes, yes, of course. But these things happen, you know.

DIANA: I can't understand it even yet. I loved Kit—at least I thought I did, and then you happened—and—and—— Oh, Bill, do you do this to all the women you meet?

ROGERS: Er—do what?

DIANA: Sweep them off their feet so that they forget everything in the world except yourself.

ROGERS: Diana, will you give me a truthful answer to a question I'm going to ask you?

DIANA: Yes, of course, Bill.

ROGERS: Is your feeling for me mere—infatuation, or do you really, really love me?

DIANA: Oh, you know I do, Bill.

ROGERS (*he kisses her*): Oh, darling. And you really don't love Kit any more?

DIANA: I'm still fond of him.

ROGERS: But you don't love him?

DIANA: No, Bill, I don't love him.

    JACQUELINE *comes in through the window.* ROGERS, *his back to her, doesn't see her.* DIANA *breaks away.*

ROGERS: And you *will* tell him so?

DIANA: Hullo, Jacqueline.

JACQUELINE: Hullo, Diana. Rather warm, isn't it?

    She walks across the room and into the kitchen.

DIANA (*alarmed*): You don't think she saw anything, do you?

ROGERS: I don't know.

DIANA: She may have been standing outside the window the whole time. I wouldn't put it past her.

ROGERS: What does it matter anyway? Everyone will know soon enough.

DIANA (*thoughtfully*): She's the sort of girl who'll talk.

ROGERS: Let her.

DIANA (*turning to him*): Bill, you don't understand. Our feelings for each other are too sacred to be soiled by vulgar gossip.

ROGERS: Er—yes, yes. But, dash it, we can't go on keeping it a secret for ever.

DIANA: Not for ever. But don't you find it thrilling to have such a lovely secret just between us and no one else? After all, it's our love. Why should others know about it and bandy it about?

ROGERS: Yes, I know, but——

> KIT *comes in through window. He glances moodily at* DIANA *and* ROGERS *and throws himself into an arm-chair, picking up a paper and beginning to read.* ROGERS *points significantly at him and frames the words "Tell him now" in his mouth.* DIANA *shakes her head violently.* ROGERS *nods his head urgently.* KIT *looks up.*

DIANA (*hurriedly*): You people have got a lecture now, haven't you?

KIT: In about five minutes.

DIANA: Oh. Then I think I'll go for a little walk by myself. (*Going to window.*) We'll have our bathe about four, don't you think, Bill?

ROGERS: Right.

> DIANA *goes out. Pause.*

(*Breezily.*) Well, Neilan, how's the world treating you these days.

KIT: Bloodily.

ROGERS: I'm sorry to hear that. What's the trouble?

KIT: Everything.   (*He takes up paper.*)

ROGERS (*after a pause*): This show to-night at the Casino ought to be rather cheery, don't you think?

> KIT *lowers his paper, looks at him, and raises it again.*

Who are you taking?

KIT (*into the paper*): Jacqueline.

ROGERS: Jacqueline?

KIT (*Loudly*): Yes, Jacqueline.

ROGERS: Oh. (*Cheerfully.*) That's a charming girl, I think. Clever. Amusing. Pretty. She'll make somebody a fine wife.

> KIT *emits a kind of snort.*

Did you say anything?

> KIT *doesn't answer.*

She's what the French call a sympathetic person.

KIT: Do they? I didn't know.

ROGERS: Oh, yes they do. Much nicer than most modern girls. Take some of these English girls, for instance——

KIT: You take them. I want to work.

He goes to bookcase and takes out a note-book.

Might I trouble you for your indiarubber?

ROGERS: Of course, my dear fellow. Delighted.

He gives it to him.

KIT (*examining it*): Hullo. Are you quite sure this *is* your indiarubber, Commander?

ROGERS: Yes, positive.

KIT: I only ask because my indiarubber happens to be missing.

ROGERS: Oh. I'm sorry to hear that, old chap. But that does happen to be my indiarubber, because, you see, I always make a pencil mark on mine——

KIT: Indeed? Well, I always chew mine, and I would say that this indiarubber has quite definitely been chewed.

ROGERS (*examining it*): Nonsense. That's a pencil mark.

KIT: I'm sorry, but to me that just isn't a pencil mark.

ROGERS: Then all I can say is—there must be something wrong with your eyesight——

KIT: There is nothing wrong with my eyesight, Commander, and I can assure you that I am perfectly capable of distinguishing between a pencil mark and a tooth mark on an indiarubber.

ROGERS: Just because you chew your indiarubber—which is a disgusting habit anyway—is no earthly reason why you should lay claim to all the indiarubbers in the world.

KIT: I am not laying claim to all the indiarubbers in the world. I am simply laying claim to this one particular indiarubber.

ROGERS: Are you accusing me of stealing your indiarubber?

KIT: I'm not accusing anybody of anything. I'm only saying that the whole thing looks extremely peculiar to me——

ROGERS: Neilan—I'll trouble you to return my indiarubber.

KIT: I see no reason why I should give you *my* indiarubber.

ROGERS: It's not your indiarubber. It's my indiarubber.

He snatches it.

KIT: Then what's happened to mine?

ROGERS: How should I know? Judging by your habits the likeliest contingency is that you've eaten it——

KIT: My God—Commander——

He makes a threatening move towards him, but is interrupted by
BRIAN *who enters singing "Somebody Stole My Girl."*

Blast you, Brian.

BRIAN (*appearing at window*): What's the matter, old boy? Don't
you like my voice?

KIT: No, and I don't like that song.

BRIAN: "Somebody Stole my Girl"? Why, it's a—— (*He
looks from* KIT *to* ROGERS.) Perhaps you're right. It's not one
of my better efforts. (*He puts a parcel on the table.*) This has just
come for Alan. It feels suspiciously like his novel. (*He goes to
bookcase and takes out his note-book.*) You won't believe it, but I used
to sing in my school choir. Only because I was in the rugger
fifteen, I admit. (*Sits next* KIT.) What's the old boy lecturing
on to-day?

KIT: The Near East, I suppose. He didn't finish it yesterday.

BRIAN: Good lord! Was it the Near East yesterday? I thought
it was the Franco-Prussian war.

KIT: You must get a lot of value out of these lectures.

BRIAN: Well, I only understood one word in a hundred.

ROGERS: It's rather the same in my case.

BRIAN: Give me your notes in case the old boy has the impertinence
to ask me a question.

He takes KIT'S *notes and starts to read them.* ALAN *comes in
through door at the back, followed by* KENNETH.

ALAN (*Going to table and picking up parcel*): Ah, I see the novel has
come home to father again.

BRIAN: Open it, old boy. There may be a marvellous letter
inside.

ALAN: There'll be a letter all right. But I don't need to read it.
(*He sits down at table and pushes the parcel away.*)

BRIAN: Bad luck, old boy.

KENNETH *grabs the parcel and unties the string.*

You mustn't give up hope yet, though. First novels are always
refused hundreds of times. I know a bloke who's been writing
novels and plays and things all his life. He's fifty now, and he's
still hoping to get something accepted.

ALAN: Thank you, Brian. That's very comforting.

KENNETH *has extracted a letter from the parcel and is reading it.*

ROGERS (*amicably*): Will you let me read it sometime?

ALAN (*pleased*): Would you like to? I'm afraid you'd hate it.

ROGERS: Why? What's it about?

KENNETH *hands down the letter to* ALAN.

ALAN (*Glancing over letter. He crumples the letter up and throws it away*): It's about two young men who take a vow to desert their country instantly in the case of war and to go and live on a farm in Central Africa.

ROGERS (*uncomfortably*): Oh.

ALAN: War breaks out and they go. One of them takes his wife. They go, not because they are any more afraid to fight than the next man, but because they believe violence in any circumstances to be a crime and that, if the world goes mad, it's their duty to remain sane.

ROGERS: I see. Conchies.

ALAN: Yes. Conchies. When they get to their farm one of them makes love to the other's wife and they fight over her.

ROGERS: Ah. That's a good point.

ALAN: But in fighting for her they are perfectly aware that the motive that made them do it is as vile as the impulse they feel to go back and fight for their country. In both cases they are letting their passions get the better of their reason—becoming animals instead of men.

ROGERS: But that's nonsense. If a man fights for his country or his wife he's—well, he's a man and not a damned conchie.

ALAN: The characters in my book have the honesty not to rationalise the animal instinct to fight, into something noble like patriotism or manliness. They admit that it's an ignoble instinct—something to be ashamed of.

ROGERS (*heated*): Ashamed of! Crikey!

ALAN: But they also admit that their reason isn't strong enough to stand out against this ignoble instinct, so they go back and fight.

ROGERS: Ah. That's more like it. So they were proved wrong in the end.

ALAN: Their ideal wasn't proved wrong because they were unable to live up to it. That's the point of the book.

KIT (*from his corner, morosely*): What's the use of an ideal if you can't live up to it?

ALAN: In a hundred years' time men may be able to live up to our ideals even if they can't live up to their own.

KENNETH (*excitedly*): That's it. Progress.

KIT: Progress my fanny.

ROGERS: Still, I mean to say—— Look here, supposing some rotter came along and stole your best girl, wouldn't you fight him?

KIT (*looking up*): You'd better ask me that question, hadn't you?

ROGERS (*swinging round*): What the devil do you mean?

KIT (*getting up*): And the answer would be yes.

ROGERS (*with heavy sarcasm*): That's very interesting, I'm sure.

ALAN (*enjoying himself*): By the way, I forgot to tell you, in my novel, when the two men go back to fight for their country they leave the woman in Central Africa. You see after fighting over her they come to the conclusion that she's a bitch. It would have been so much better, don't you think, if they had discovered that sooner?

KIT: All right, you asked for it.

He raises his arm to hit ALAN, *who grapples with him and holds him.*

ALAN: Don't be a damned fool.

ROGERS *strides over and knocks* ALAN *down.*

KIT (*turning furiously on* ROGERS): What the hell do you think you're doing?

KIT *aims a blow at* ROGERS, *who dodges it, overturning a chair.*
KENNETH *runs in to attack* ROGERS. BRIAN, *also running in, tries to restrain both* KENNETH *and* KIT.

BRIAN: Shut up, you damned lot of fools. (*Shouting.*) Kit, Babe, show some sense, for God's sake! Look out—Maingot!

ALAN *gets up and is about to go for* ROGERS *when* MAINGOT *comes in from the garden, carrying a large note-book under his arm.* KIT, KENNETH *and* BRIAN *sit down.* ROGERS *and* ALAN *stand glaring at each other.* MAINGOT *picks up the chair that has been knocked over, pulls it to the table, sits down and spreads his note-book out on the table.*

MAINGOT: Alors, asseyez-vous, Messieurs. Le sujet cet apres-midi sera la crise de mille huit cent quarante en Turquie.

ALAN *and* ROGERS *sit down, still glaring at each other.*

Or la dernière fois je vous ai expliqué comment le gouverneur ottomane d'Egypte, Mehemet Ali, s'était battu contre son souverain, le Sultain de Turquie. Constatons donc que la chute du Sultanat. . . .

CURTAIN

ACT II

Scene I

SCENE: *The same.*

TIME: *About six hours later.*

> DIANA *is discovered sitting in one arm-chair, her feet up on the other. She is smoking a cigarette and gazing listlessly out of the window.* JACQUELINE *comes in through door at back, dressed in a Bavarian costume.*

JACQUELINE: Hullo! Aren't you getting dressed?

DIANA (*turning her head. She gets up and examines* JACQUELINE): Darling, you look too lovely.

JACQUELINE: Do you like it.

DIANA: I adore it. I think it's sweet. (*She continues her examination*): If I were you, dear, I'd wear that hat just a little more on the back of the head. Look, I'll show you. (*She arranges* JACQUELINE'S *hat.*) No, that's not quite right. I wonder if it'd look better without a hat at all. (*She removes hat.*) No, you must wear a hat.

JACQUELINE: I suppose my hair's wrong.

DIANA: Well, it isn't quite Bavarian, is it, darling? Very nice, of course. (*Pulling* JACQUELINE'S *dress about.*) There's something wrong here. (*She kneels down and begins to rearrange the dress.*)

> *Pause.*

JACQUELINE: I've got something to say to you, Diana. Do you mind if I say it now?

DIANA: Of course not. (*Tugging dress.*) Oh, lord, there's a bit of braid coming off here.

JACQUELINE: Oh!

DIANA: I'll fix it for you.

JACQUELINE: If you look in that basket over there you'll find a needle and thread. (*She points to a work-basket which is lying on the seat of one of the chairs.*)

DIANA: Right. (*She goes to basket.*)

JACQUELINE: But you needn't trouble——

DIANA (*extracting needle and thread*): That's all right. It's no trouble. I enjoy doing this sort of thing. (*Threading needle.*) Well, what was it you wanted to say to me?

JACQUELINE: I overheard your conversation with the Commander this afternoon.

DIANA (*making a bad shot with the thread. She turns to the light*): All of it, or just a part of it?

JACQUELINE: I heard you say that you were in love with the Commander and that you didn't love Kit.

DIANA: Oh! (*Kneeling at* JACQUELINE'S *feet*). Now, scream if I stick a needle into you, won't you? (*She begins to sew.*) Is that what you wanted to tell me?

JACQUELINE: I wanted to know if you were going to tell Kit that you didn't love him.

DIANA (*sewing industriously*): Why?

JACQUELINE: Because if you don't tell him, I will.

DIANA (*after a slight pause*): My poor Jacqueline, I never knew you felt like that about Kit.

JACQUELINE: Yes, you did. You've known for some time, and you've had a lot of fun out of it.

DIANA: Well, I wish you the best of luck.

JACQUELINE: Thank you. Are you going to tell him?

DIANA: I don't think so.

JACQUELINE: I shall, then.

DIANA: My dear, I think that would be very silly. He won't believe you, it'll make him very unhappy, and, worst of all, he'll be furious with you.

JACQUELINE (*thoughtfully*): Yes, that's true, I suppose.

DIANA (*biting off the thread and standing up*): There. How's that?

JACQUELINE: Thank you so much. That's splendid. So you won't leave Kit alone?

DIANA: Now, let's be honest, for a moment. Don't let's talk about love and things like that, but just plain facts. You and I both want the same man.

JACQUELINE: But you don't——

DIANA: Oh yes, I do.

JACQUELINE: But what about the Commander?

DIANA: I want him too.

JACQUELINE: Oh!

DIANA: Don't look shocked, darling. You see, I'm not like you. You're clever—you can talk intelligently, and you're nice.

JACQUELINE: That's a horrid word.

DIANA: Now I'm not nice. I'm not clever and I can't talk intelligently. There's only one thing I've got, and I don't think you'll deny it. I have got a sort of gift for making men fall in love with me.

JACQUELINE: Oh, no. I don't deny that at all.

DIANA: Thank you, darling. I didn't think you would. Well, now, you have been sent into the world with lots of gifts, and you make use of them. Well, what about me, with just my one gift? I must use that too, mustn't I?

JACQUELINE: Well, what you call my gifts are at any rate social. Yours are definitely anti-social.

DIANA: Oh, I can't be bothered with all that. The fact remains that having men in love with me is my whole life. Its hard for you to understand, I know. You see, you're the sort of person that people *like*. But nobody *likes* me.

JACQUELINE: Oh, I wish you wouldn't keep harping on that. I wouldn't mind if everybody hated me, provided Kit loved me.

DIANA: You can't have it both ways, darling. Kit looks on you as a very nice person.

JACQUELINE (*with sudden anger*): Oh, God! What I'd give to be anything but nice!

DIANA: In a way, you know, I envy you. It must be very pleasant to be able to make friends with people.

JACQUELINE: You could be friends with Kit if you were honest with him.

DIANA: Darling! And I called you intelligent! Kit despises me. If he didn't love me he'd loathe me. That's why I can't let him go.

JACQUELINE (*pleadingly*): Oh, Diana, I do see your point of view. I do see that you must have men in love with you, but couldn't you, please, couldn't you make the Commander do?

DIANA: No—I always act on the principle that there's safety in numbers.

JACQUELINE: Well, there's this Lord Heybrook arriving to-morrow. Supposing I let you have the Commander and him.

DIANA: No, darling. I'm sorry. I'd do anything else for you, but if you want Kit, you must win him in fair fight.

JACQUELINE (*a shade tearfully*): But I don't stand a chance against you.

DIANA: To be perfectly honest, I agree with you, darling.

JACQUELINE: I only hope you make some awful blunder, so that he finds out the game you're playing.

DIANA (*with dignity*): I don't make blunders.   He's taking you to the Casino to-night, isn't he?

JACQUELINE: Yes, but he's so furious because you're going with the Commander that he'll give me the most dreadful evening.

DIANA: That's all right.   I'm not going.   I don't feel like it, as a matter of fact.

JACQUELINE: But have you told the Commander?

DIANA: Yes: he's furious, poor poppet, but it's very good for him.

JACQUELINE (*after a pause*): I wonder if you realise the trouble you cause?   You know there was a fight about you this afternoon?

DIANA: Yes.   I hear Alan was in it.   That's *very* interesting.

JACQUELINE *is surprised.* DIANA *smiles.* KIT's *voice is heard off, calling "Jack, where are you?"* JACQUELINE *turns to Diana in sudden fright.*

JACQUELINE: Does Kit know you're not going to-night?

KIT *comes in through door at back. His lower half is enclosed in the frilly skirt of a Greek Evzone, beneath which can be seen an ordinary pair of socks with suspenders. In addition he wears a cricket shirt and tie. He carries the tunic over his arm.*

KIT: Jack, I can't get into this damned coat.

DIANA *bursts into a shriek of laughter.*

DIANA: Kit, you look angelic!   I wish you could see yourself.

KIT: You shut up.

JACQUELINE: I told you it might be rather à tight fit.

KIT: But it's miles too small.   Your brother must be a pigmy.

JACQUELINE: Take that shirt off and then try.

KIT: Jack, would you mind terribly if I didn't come?   I can't go dressed as an inebriated danseuse.

DIANA *shrieks with laughter again.*

JACQUELINE: Don't be silly, Kit.   It's going to look lovely.

KIT: Honestly, though, I don't think I'll come.   You wouldn't mind?

JACQUELINE: I'd mind—awfully.

KIT: Alan's not going.   I don't think I can face it really.   I've asked Babe if he'll take you, and he says he'd love to. (*Turning to* DIANA—*offhandedly.*)   I hear you're not going, Diana.

DIANA: No.   I feel rather like you about it.

KIT (*to* DIANA): You know, they have dancing in the streets to-night. We might get rid of the others later and go out and join them—what do you say?

DIANA: Yes, that's a lovely idea, Kit.

KIT (*turning to* JACQUELINE): I'm awfully sorry, Jack, but honestly——

JACQUELINE: It's all right. I'll have a lovely time with Kenneth. (*She goes out quickly through door at back.*)

KIT: She seems rather odd. You don't think she minds, do you?

DIANA: Well, how on earth should I know.

KIT: Darling, if we go out to-night, you will get rid of the Commander, won't you? If he comes I won't be answerable for the consequences.

DIANA: He's not so easy to get rid of. He clings like a limpet. Still, I'll do my best.

KIT: I can't understand why you don't just tell him to go to hell.

DIANA (*gently*): That'd be a little cruel, wouldn't it, Kit?

KIT: As someone said once, why not be cruel only to be kind?

DIANA: Yes, that's true, but, you know, Kit, cruelty is something that's physically impossible to me. I'm the sort of person who's miserable if I tread on a snail.

KIT: But you can't, you see, darling. It's unfair on him to let him go on thinking he's got a hope.

DIANA: Poor old Bill. Oh, well, darling, come and give me a kiss and say you love me.

　　　ROGERS *comes in through garden door.*

KIT: With pleasure. (*He kisses her, although she tries to push him away.*) I love you.

ROGERS (*to* KIT): What the devil do you think you're doing?

KIT: I'll give you three guesses.

ROGERS: I've had enough of this. I'm going to give this young puppy a good hiding.

DIANA (*trying to separate them*): Don't be silly, Bill.

ROGERS: Out of the way, Diana.

KIT: Do what the Commander says, Diana.

DIANA (*still separating them*): You're both quite mad.

　　　MAINGOT *comes in through door at back dressed in Scottish Highland costume.* BRIAN *and* ALAN *follow, gazing at him with rapture.*

KIT *and* ROGERS *and* DIANA *break apart.*

ALAN (*clasping his hands in admiration*): Mais c'est exquis, Monsieur! Parfait!

MAINGOT: N'est-ce pas que c'est beau? Je l'ai choisi moi-même. Ça me va bien, hein?

ALAN: C'est tout ce qu'il y a de plus chic.

BRIAN: Vous ne pouvez pas dire le difféernce entre vous et un réel Highlander.

MAINGOT: Mais oui. Ça—c'est un véritable costume écossais.

DIANA: Oh, yes, that is formidable.

MAINGOT (*crossing to Diana*): Vous croyez? Et aussi je connais quelques pas du can-can écossais.

ALAN: Amusez-vous bien, Monsieur.

MAINGOT: Merci.

BRIAN: J'espère que vous baiserez beaucoup de dames, Monsieur.

MAINGOT (*turning, appalled*): Ha? Qu'est qu'il dit, ce garçon là?

BRIAN: Ai-je dit quelque chose?

MAINGOT: Une bétise, Monsieur. On ne dit jamais baiser—embrasser. Une faut pas me donner des idées.

> *He goes out chuckling.* ALAN, BRIAN *and* DIANA *go to the window to watch him go down the street.* KIT *and* ROGERS *stand looking at each other rather sheepishly.*

ALAN: My God! What *does* he look like?

DIANA: He looks perfectly sweet.

> JACQUELINE *comes in, followed by* KENNETH, *in sailor costume.*

BRIAN: Your father's just gone off, Jack. If you hurry you can catch him.

JACQUELINE: Right. (*Gaily.*) Good-bye, everyone. You're all fools not to be coming. We're going to have a lovely time.

KENNETH (*to* ALAN): Alan, do change your mind and come.

ALAN: No, thank you, Babe—have a good time.

KENNETH: Alan——

ALAN: Well, I'm going to have a drink. Anyone coming with me?

BRIAN: I'm ahead of you, old boy.

DIANA: Yes, I'm coming.

ALAN: I suppose that means I'll have to pay for both of you.

DIANA: Yes, it does.

ALAN: Are you two coming?

> ROGERS *and* KIT *look at each other and then shake their heads.*

ROGERS and KIT: No.

    DIANA *and* BRIAN *go out talking.*

ALAN: Oh, no. I see you're going to have a musical evening! (*He follows the other two out.*)

KIT: Now we can have our little talk.

ROGERS: I don't mean to do much talking.

KIT: But I do. Diana has just this minute given me a message to give you. She wants you to understand that she knows what you feel about her, and she's sorry for you. But she must ask you not to take advantage of her pity for you to make her life a burden.

ROGERS: Right. Now that you've had your joke, let me tell you the truth. This afternoon Diana asked me to let you know, in as kindly a way as possible, that her feelings for you have changed entirely, and that she is now in love with me.

KIT (*astounded*): God! What nerve! Do you know what she's just said about you? (*Shouting.*) She called you a silly old bore, who stuck like a limpet and weren't worth bothering about.

ROGERS: Oh, she did, did she?

KIT: Yes, she did, and a lot more besides that wouldn't bear repeating.

ROGERS: All right, you lying young fool. I've felt sorry for you up to this, but now I see I've got to teach you a lesson. Put your hands up.

KIT (*putting up his fists*): It's a pleasure.

    They stand facing each other, ready for battle. Pause. ROGERS *suddenly begins to laugh.*

ROGERS (*collapsing, doubled up with laughter, into a chair*): You look so damned funny in that get-up.

KIT (*looking down at his legs, and beginning to giggle*): A little eccentric, I admit.

ROGERS: Like a bedraggled old fairy queen.

KIT: I'll go and change.

ROGERS (*becoming serious*): No, don't. If you do I'll have to fight you. I can't when you're looking like that, and if you go on looking like that it'll save us from making idiots of ourselves.

KIT: You know, that's rather sensible. I am surprised.

ROGERS: You know, I'm not quite such a damned fool as you youngsters seem to think. As a matter of fact, I'm a perfectly rational being, and I'm prepared to discuss this particular situation rationally. Now, I'm ready to admit that you have a grievance against me.

KIT: But I haven't—speaking rationally.

ROGERS: Oh, yes. Rationally speaking, you might say that I've alienated the affections of your sweetheart.

KIT (*smiling*): But you haven't done anything of the sort.

ROGERS (*raising his hand*): Please don't interrupt. Now, I'm perfectly ready to apologise for something that isn't altogether my fault. I hope you will accept it in the spirit in which it is offered.

KIT (*incredulous*): But do you really think Diana's in love with you?

ROGERS: Certainly.

KIT: Why do you think that?

ROGERS: She told me so, of course.

KIT: (*laughing*): My poor dear Commander——

ROGERS: I thought we were going to discuss this matter rationally.

KIT: Yes, but when you begin with a flagrant misrepresentation of the facts——

ROGERS: You mean, I'm a liar?

KIT: Yes, that's exactly what I do mean.

ROGERS (*jumping to his feet*): Come on. Get up. I see I've got to fight you, skirt or no skirt.

KIT: No, no. Let reason have one last fling. If that fails we can give way to our animal passions. Let me tell you my side of the case.

ROGERS (*sitting*): All right.

KIT: I've just had a talk with Diana. She said you were in love with her. I suggested to her that it was only fair to you to let you know exactly where you stood—in other words, that she was in love with me and that you had no chance. She answered that, though what I'd said was the truth——

ROGERS: She never said that.

KIT (*raising his hand*): Please don't interrupt. (*Continuing.*) Though what I'd said was the truth, she couldn't tell you because it would be too cruel.

    ROGERS *starts slightly.*

I then said, rather aptly, that this was a case where she should be cruel only to be kind.

ROGERS: You said what?

KIT: Cruel only to be kind.

ROGERS: What did she say?

KIT: She said she found it physically impossible to be cruel. She said she was the sort of person who was miserable if she trod on a snail.

ROGERS: What? You're sure of that?

KIT: Certainly.

ROGERS: She said she was miserable if she trod on a snail?

KIT: Yes.

ROGERS (*with a word of feeling*): Good God!

KIT: What's the matter?

ROGERS: It's awful! (*Rising and walking about.*) I can't believe it. I don't believe it. This is all a monstrous plot. (*Swinging round.*) I believe you listened in to my conversation with Diana this afternoon.

KIT: Why?

ROGERS: Because I also told her she ought to be cruel only to be kind, and she made precisely the same answer as she made to you.

KIT (*after a pause*): You mean about the snail?

ROGERS: Yes, about the snail.

KIT: In other words she's been double-crossing us. No, you've made all that up.

ROGERS: I only wish I had.

KIT: How do I know you're telling the truth?

ROGERS: You'll have to take my word for it.

KIT: Why should I?

ROGERS: Do you want to make me fight you?

KIT: Yes, I do.

   Pause.

ROGERS: Well, I'm not going to.

KIT (*sitting down suddenly*): I wonder why it's such a comfort to get away from reason.

ROGERS: Because in this case reason tells us something our vanity won't let us accept.

KIT: It tells us that Diana's a bitch. Reason! Reason!

ROGERS: You're right. We'd better face it. Diana's in love with neither of us, and she's made a fool out of both of us.

KIT: We don't know that—I mean that she's in love with neither of us. She may be telling lies to one and the truth to the other.

ROGERS: Is that what your reason tells you?

KIT: No.

    Pause.   They are both sunk in gloom.
I feel rather sick.

ROGERS: I must have a stronger stomach than you.

    Pause.
I suppose you loved her more than I did?

KIT: Loved her? I still do love her, damn it.

ROGERS: But you can't, now that you know what you do.

KIT: What difference does that make? I love her face, I love the way she walks, I love her voice, I love her figure. None of that has changed.

ROGERS (*sympathetically*): Poor boy. It's simpler for me, though it's far more of a shock. You see, what I loved about her was her character.

    Pause.

KIT: You used to kiss her, I suppose?

ROGERS (*sadly*): Oh, yes.

KIT: You didn't—you didn't——?

ROGERS (*severely*): I loved her for her character. (*After a pause.*) Did you?

KIT: Well, no, not really.

ROGERS: I see.

    Pause.

KIT: What are we going to do?

ROGERS: We'd better face her together. We'll ask her point-blank which of us she really does love.

KIT: If she says me, I'm done for.

ROGERS: But you won't believe her?

KIT: I'll know she's lying, but I'll believe her all the same.

ROGERS: Well, supposing she says me?

KIT: That's my only hope.

ROGERS: Then, for your sake, I hope she says me.

KIT: That's terribly kind of you, Bill. I say, I may call you Bill, mayn't I?

ROGERS: Oh, my dear Kit.

    Pause.
You know, what I feel like doing is to go out and get very drunk.

KIT: Suppose we go and throw ourselves into the sea instead of going to the Casino.

ROGERS: I think my idea is better.

KIT: Yes, perhaps you're right.　Then let's start now.

ROGERS: You can't go out like that, my dear Kit.

KIT: Then let's go to the Casino.

ROGERS: I haven't got anything to wear.

KIT (*holding out tunic*): Wear this over your flannels.

ROGERS: All right.　Help me put it on.

　　ALAN and BRIAN come in.　KIT is buttoning up ROGERS' tunic.
　　They both stop in amazement.

ALAN: What on earth——?

KIT (*excitedly*): Bill and I are going to the Casino, Alan.　You've got to come, too.

ALAN: Bill and you?　What is this?　Some new sort of game?

KIT: Go and put something on.　You come, too, Brian.

BRIAN: No, old boy.　Not me.

KIT: Go on, Alan.　We want to get out of the house before Diana arrives.　Where is she, by the way?

ROGERS: Who cares!

　　KIT laughs.

ALAN (*scratching his head*): Let me get this straight.　You want me to come to the Ball with you and the Commander——

KIT: Don't call him the Commander, Alan.　His name is Bill.

ALAN: Bill?

KIT: Yes, Bill.　He's one of the best fellows in the world.

ROGERS: We're going to get drunk together, aren't we, Kit?

ALAN: Kit?

KIT: Screaming drunk, Bill.

ALAN (*dashing to door*): I won't be a minute.

　　Exit ALAN.

BRIAN: This sounds like a party.

KIT: Brian, tell me how I can get hold of your Chi-Chi?　Is she going to the Casino to-night?

BRIAN: Yes, old boy.

KIT: How can I recognise her?

BRIAN: I don't think you can miss her.　She's not likely to miss you, anyway, if you go into the bar alone.

KIT: Has she got a good figure?

BRIAN: I like it, but I'm easy to please.　From sideways on it's a bit S-shaped, if you know what I mean.

　　ALAN comes down, wearing his German coat.

ALAN: I shall probably be lynched in this thing.

KIT: Come on, Let's go.

They go to the window. KIT *with his arm across* ROGERS' *shoulder.*

BRIAN: Hi! Wait a minute. What am I to tell Diana?

They stop.

ROGERS: Tell her we're being cruel only to be kind.

KIT: Tell her to be careful she doesn't go treading on any snails.

ALAN: Just tell her to go to hell. That leaves no room for doubt.

They go out. BRIAN *gazes after them as the*

CURTAIN FALLS

ACT II

Scene II

SCENE: *The same.*

TIME: *A few hours later.*

The curtain rises to disclose ALAN *on the sofa,* KIT *in the arm-chair,* ROGERS *on the floor by the end of the sofa, each smoking a cigar. They are still in the clothes in which they had gone to the Casino.* ROGERS *is half asleep.*

KIT (*drowsily*): I don't agree with you. I don't agree with you at all. You can't judge women by our standards of Right and Wrong.

ALAN: They have none of their own, so how can you judge them.

KIT: Why judge them at all. There they are—all of them, I grant you, behaving absolutely nohow—still, that's what they're for, I mean they're built that way, and you've just got to take them or leave them. I'll take them.

ROGERS (*murmuring dreamily*): I'll take vanilla.

KIT: Now, you tell me that Diana's a cow. All right. I shan't deny it. I shall only say that I, personally, like cows.

ALAN: But you can like them without loving them. I mean, love is only sublimated sex, isn't it?

ROGERS (*rousing himself a little*): Devilish funny thing—my old friend Freud, the last time I met him, said *exactly* the same thing. Bill, old man, he said, take my word for it, love is only sublimated sex. (*Composing himself for sleep again.*) That's what Old Freudie said.

ALAN: I fear that Bill is what he'd describe himself as half seas over.

KIT: He's lucky. The more I drank up at that foul Casino the more sober I became. What were you saying about sublimated sex?

ALAN: Only that if that's what you feel for Diana, why sublimate?

KIT: Ah! Because she's clever enough to give me no choice.

ALAN: How simple everything would be if that sort of so-called virtue were made illegal—if it were just a question of will you or won't you.

> ROGERS' *head falls back on to the chair.*

No one ought to be allowed to get away with that—I'd like to but I mustn't. It's that that leads to all the trouble. The Commander has now definitely passed out. You know (*excitedly*) I like him, Kit. It's quite amazing how pleasant he is when you get to know him.

> *A slight smile appears on* ROGERS' *face.*

KIT: Yes, I know.

ALAN: Do you realise that if it hadn't been for Diana, we'd probably have gone on disliking him for ever?

KIT: Yes. We've got to be grateful to her for that.

ALAN: I wonder *why* we disliked him so much before to-night.

ROGERS (*from a horizontal position*): I'll tell you.

ALAN: Good lord! I thought you'd passed out.

ROGERS: Officers in the Royal Navy never pass out.

ALAN: They just fall on the floor in an alcoholic stupor, I suppose?

ROGERS: Exactly.

KIT: Well, tell us why we disliked you so much.

ROGERS: Right.

> ALAN *helps him to a sitting position.*

Because you all made up your mind to dislike me before I ever came into this house. All except Diana, that's to say. From the moment I arrived, you all treated me as if I were some interesting old relic of a bygone age. I've never known such an unfriendly lot of blighters as you all were.

ALAN: We thought you were a bumptious old bore.

ROGERS: Oh, I may have seemed a bortious old bump, but that was only because I was in a blue funk of you all. Here was I who'd never been away from my ship for more than a few days at a time, suddenly plumped down in a house full of strange people, all talking either French, which I couldn't understand, or your own brand of English, which was almost as hard, and all convinced I was a half-wit. Of course I was in a blue funk.

ALAN: Well, I'm damned.

ROGERS: As a matter of fact, I liked you all.

ALAN: Oh, that's very gratifying.

ROGERS: I didn't agree with most of your opinions, but I enjoyed listening to them. I wanted to discuss them with you, but I was never given the chance. You all seemed to think that because I was in the Navy I was incapable of consecutive thought—I say, brandy doesn't half loosen the old tongue.

ALAN: But you always seemed so aggressive.

ROGERS: I was only defending myself. You attacked first, you know.

ALAN (*contritely*): I'm terribly sorry.

ROGERS: That's all right. As a matter of fact it's done me a lot of good being here. One gets into a bit of a rut, you know, in the Service. One's apt to forget that there are some people in the world who have different ideas and opinions to one's own. You'll find the same in the diplomatic.

ALAN: I know. That's one of the reasons I want to chuck it.

ROGERS: Will you let me give you a bit of advice about that? I've been wanting to for a long time, but I've always been afraid you'd bite my head off if I did.

ALAN: Of course.

ROGERS: Well, chuck it. Go and do your writing.

ALAN *looks surprised. He takes a deep puff at his cigar.*

ALAN: I'd go back to England to-morrow, only—— (*He stops.*)

ROGERS: Only what?

ALAN: I don't know if I can write, for one thing.

ROGERS: It's ten to one you can't, but I shouldn't let that stop you. If it's what you want to do, I should do it.

ALAN: That isn't the real reason.

ROGERS: You haven't got the guts, is that it?

ALAN: That isn't quite my way of putting it, but I suppose it's true. I can't bring myself to make a definite decision. Oh, what the hell? I shall become a diplomat.

ROGERS: You'll be a damned bad one.

ALAN: I can adapt myself.

ROGERS (*rising, yawning*): Well, I've given you my advice for what it's worth. I shall now go to bed to sleep the sleep of the very drunk.

ALAN: You mustn't go yet. You've got to wait for Diana.

ROGERS (*with a magnificent gesture*): Diana—pooh!

ALAN: It's all very well for you to say "Diana—pooh," but this weak-kneed, jelly-livered protoplasm here is still in her clutches.

KIT (*who has been musing*): Are you referring to me?

ALAN: Diana's only got to raise her little finger and he'll go rushing back to her, screaming to be forgiven.

ROGERS: Then we must stop her raising her little finger.

ALAN: Exactly. That's why we must face her together.

ROGERS (*sitting heavily*): The United Front. We must scupper her with a plunging salvo.

ALAN: Oh, no, don't let's do that.

KIT (*dismally*): She's only got to say she still loves me.

ALAN: My dear Kit, if she has to choose between you and Bill, she'll choose you. You're younger, you're better-looking, and you've got more money. Don't you agree, Bill?

ROGERS: He's certainly younger and he's certainly got more money.

ALAN (*to* KIT): You must be firm, you must be strong. If you show any weakness, you'll be a traitor to our sex.

ROGERS: By jove, yes. We must put up a good show in this engagement.

KIT: It's all very well for you to talk. You don't know what it's like——

ALAN: Haven't I resisted her attacks for a whole month?

KIT: They were only little skirmishes. You don't know what it is to receive the whole brunt of her attack. It's quite hopeless. You can help me as much as you like, but if she attacks me directly, I shall go under, I know that.

ALAN: Do you hear that, Commander? I submit that he be tried for Extreme Cowardice in the face of the Enemy.

ROGERS: The Court finds the prisoner guilty. (*Rising with dignity.*) Mr. Neilan, I must call upon you to surrender your trousers. Ah? I see you have come into court without them. Very well, I have no option but to ask you for your skirt.

KIT: Come and get it.

ROGERS: I've been longing to get my hands on that damn thing all the evening. Come on, Alan.

    KIT *leaps out of his chair, and runs across the room pursued by* ROGERS *and* ALAN. *He is cornered and there is a scuffle.*

    DIANA, *stately and sad, comes through the french windows. She stands in the doorway for some five seconds before* ROGERS *sees her.*

ROGERS: Crikey! (*He taps the two others on the shoulders and they straighten themselves.*)

    There is a rather nervous silence.

DIANA (*coming into the room*): Well—I hope you all enjoyed yourselves at the Casino.

ROGERS (*after glancing at the others*): Oh, yes.   Thanks very much.

ALAN and KIT: Jolly nice.   Wonderful time, etc.

DIANA: Brian gave me a message from you which I found rather hard to understand.   Perhaps you'd explain it now.

Pause.   ALAN looks enquiringly from KIT to ROGERS.

ROGERS *looks appealingly at ALAN.*

ALAN: Well, who is to fire the first shot of the salvo?

No answer.

Come, come, gentlemen.

No answer.

Very well, I must engage the enemy on your behalf.   Diana, these two gentlemen have good reason to believe that you have been trifling with their affections.   You have told Kit that you are in love with him and are bored by Bill, and you have told Bill that you are in love with him and are bored by Kit.   So now they naturally want to know who exactly you are in love with and who exactly you are bored by.

ROGERS (*nodding vigorously*): Yes, that's right.

DIANA (*with scorn*): Oh, do they?

ALAN: Are you going to answer their question?

DIANA: Certainly not.   Whom I love and whom I don't love is entirely my own affair.   I've never heard such insolence.

ALAN (*turning to* ROGERS *and* KIT, *chuckling*): Insolence!   She's good, this girl, she's very good.

DIANA (*patiently*): May I please be allowed to go to my room?

ALAN (*barring her way*): Not until you've answered our question.

DIANA: I think you'd better let me go.

ALAN: Just as soon as you've given a straight answer to a straight question.

Pause.   DIANA at length takes a step back.

DIANA: All right.   You want to know who I'm in love with. Well, I'll tell you.   (*To* ALAN.)   I'm in love with you.

ALAN recoils.   There is a dead silence.

DIANA brushes past ALAN.   *He seizes her wrist.*

DIANA: Good night!

ALAN drops his hands and steps back.   He falls limply into a chair.

ROGERS (*scratching his head*): Now will someone tell me, was our engagement a success?

ALAN (*bitterly*): A success? (*Groaning.*)

KIT (*gloomily*): It was a success as far as I'm concerned.

    Pause.

ALAN: I'm frightened. I'm really frightened.

ROGERS: What? (*Sternly.*) Alan, I never thought to hear such words from you.

ALAN: I can't help it. I shall fall. Oh, God! I know it, I shall fall.

ROGERS: You must be firm. You must be strong. The United Front must not be broken.

ALAN: I want you to promise me something, you two. You must never, never leave me alone with that girl.

ROGERS: That sounds like rank cowardice.

ALAN: Cowardice be damned! You don't realise the appalling danger I'm in. If I'm left alone with her for a minute, I shudder to think what might happen. She might even (*in a whisper*) marry me.

ROGERS: Oh, not that.

ALAN: It's true. God help me. I think she may easily try to marry me. (*Turning imploringly to the others.*) So you see, you can't desert me now. Don't let me out of your sight for a second. Even if I beg you on my knees to leave me alone with her, don't do it. Will you promise?

ROGERS: I promise.

ALAN: And you, Kit?

KIT (*nods*): All right.

ALAN: Thank you. I've only got three weeks before the exam, but that's a long time with Diana in the house.

ROGERS: I think your hope lies in this Lord Heybrook fellow who's coming to-morrow. She may easily find that a peer in hand is worth more than one in the vague future. (*Getting up.*) I shall go to bed. Good night, Kit. Good night, Alan. You have my best wishes. (*At door.*) Don't go down to breakfast to-morrow until I come and fetch you. (*He goes out.*)

ALAN: There's a real friend. I hope you're going to show the same self-sacrifice.

KIT: I don't know what you're making all the fuss about. You ought to be very happy.

ALAN: Happy? (*Sarcastically.*) I've noticed how happy you've been these last few weeks.

KIT: I have in a way.

ALAN: That's not my way.   Damn it, Kit, I'm a man with principles and ideals.   I'm a romantic.   Let me give you a little word-
picture of the girl I should like to fall in love with.   Then you
can tell me how far it resembles Diana.   First of all, she must not be
a cow.

KIT (*shrugging indifferently*): Oh, well, of course——

ALAN: Secondly, she will be able to converse freely and intelligently with me on all subjects.   Thirdly, she will have all the
masculine virtues and none of the feminine vices.   Fourthly, she
will be physically unattractive enough to keep her faithful to me, and
attractive enough to make me desire her.   Fifthly, she will be in
love with me.   That's all, I think.

KIT: You don't want much do you?   I admit it isn't a close
description of Diana, but where on earth do you expect to find this
love-dream?

ALAN: They do exist, you know.   There's someone here, in this
house, who answers to all the qualifications, except the last.

KIT (*sitting forward*): Good lord!   You don't mean, Jack, do you?

ALAN: Why not?

KIT: But—but you couldn't be in love with Jack.

ALAN: I'm not, but she's exactly the sort of girl I should like to
be in love with.

KIT (*smiling*): Love and Jack.   They just don't seem to connect.
I'm frightfully fond of her, but somehow—I don't know—I mean
you couldn't kiss her or make love to her.

ALAN: Why not try it and see?

KIT: Who?   Me?   Good lord, no.

ALAN: Don't you think she's attractive?

KIT: Yes, I suppose she is, in a way, very attractive.   But don't
you see, Alan, I know her far too well to start any hanky-panky.
She'd just scream with laughter.

ALAN: Really?   She'd just scream with laughter?   (*Turning on
him.*)   You poor idiot, don't you realise the girl's been madly in
love with you for two months now?

KIT (*after a pause, derisively*): Ha, ha!

ALAN: All right.   Say ha, ha!   Don't believe it and forget I ever
said it.   I promised her I'd never tell you.

        Pause.

KIT: What did you have to drink up at the Casino?

ALAN: Less than you.

...pose. (*Pathetically.*) I've told so many lies before that
...ct you to believe me when I'm telling the truth.
...oor little Matilda.
...comes back to Alan): But this is the truth now. This is
...ompletely sincere feeling I've ever had for anyone in all
...(*Simply.*) I do love you, Alan. I always have and
...always will.
...n agony): Oh, go away. Please go away.
...All right. I know you have every right to think I'm
...I'm not, Alan, really, I'm not. That's what's so funny.
...imploringly): Oh, God help me!
...(at door): Good night, Alan. (*Simply.*) I do love you.
...e smiles tearfully at him. He throws away his cigarette, and
...s over to her.
...Say that again, blast you!
...: I love you.
...e embraces her fervently.
...(emerging from embrace, ecstatically): I suppose this is true.
...You know damn well it is.
...: Say it, darling.
...(hedging): Say what?
...: Say you love me.
...: Must I? Oh, this is hell! (*Shouting.*) I love you.
...A (turning back rapturously): Alan, darling——
...BRIAN comes in through window.
...N: Hello, Alan, hello, Diana, old thing.
...DIANA looks through BRIAN and turns hurriedly to the door.
...NA (softly): Good night, Alan. I'll see you in the morni...
...She goes out. ALAN sinks into a chair.
...N: Did you see that, old boy? She cut me...
...s with me. I must tell you about it, becau...
...story. After you boys had gone I took...
...ner with me. Well, we had a bott...
...nd all the time she was giving...
...AN: The green light?
...IAN: Yes. The go-ahe...
...ed out an invitation to...
...AN: Yes. I follow you...
...IAN: I mean, everybody...
...o be missed. Well, do yo...

KIT: Are you stone-cold sober?

ALAN: As sober as ten Lady Astors.

KIT: And you stand there and tell me——

Voices heard outside.

KIT (*getting up in alarm*): Oh, lord!

MAINGOT *comes in, followed by* JACQUELINE *and* KENNETH.

MAINGOT: Aha! Le Grec et l'Allemand. Vous vous êtes bien amusés au Casino?

JACQUELINE: Hello, Kit.

ALAN: Très bien, Monsieur. Et vous?

KIT *is gaping open-mouthed at* JACQUELINE.

MAINGOT: Ah, oui! C'était assez gai, mais on y a mangé excessivement mal, et le champagne était tres mauvais et m'a couté les yeux de la tête. Quand même le quartorze ne vieut qu'une fois par an. Alors je vais me coucher. Bonsoir, bonne nuit et dormez bicn.

ALL: Bonsoir.

MAINGOT *goes out through door at back, carrying his Highland shoes which he has changed for slippers.*

JACQUELINE: Why did you all leave so early?

KIT (*gaping*): Oh, I don't know.

JACQUELINE: Your costume caused a sensation, Kit. Everyone was asking me what it was meant to be.

KIT (*nervously*): Really.

ALAN: Did you have a good time, Kenneth?

KENNETH: Oh, all right. I'll say good night. I've got an essay to finish before to-morrow.

JACQUELINE: Good night, Kenneth, and thank you.

KENNETH: Good night.

KENNETH *goes out, looking sulky, through door at back.*

ALAN: You must have had a wonderful time with the Babe in that mood.

JACQUELINE: What's the matter with him, Alan?

ALAN: He's angry with me for not doing his essay for him. I think I'd better go and make my peace with him. (*At door.*) Don't go to bed for a few minutes. I want to talk to you, Jack.

He goes out. There is a pause. KIT *is plainly uncomfortable.*

KIT: Did you have a good time to-night?

JACQUELINE (*puzzled*): Yes, thank you, Kit.

KIT: Good. I—er—I'm sorry I couldn't take you.

JACQUELINE: That's all right. (*Smiling.*) That was Brian's girl you and Alan were dancing with, wasn't it? What's she like?

KIT: Pretty hellish.

Pause.

Jack?

JACQUELINE: Yes?

KIT: Oh, nothing. (*He sits.*) Was it raining when you came back?

JACQUELINE: No, it wasn't raining.

KIT: It was when we came back.

JACQUELINE: Really?

Pause.

KIT: Yes, quite heavily.

JACQUELINE: It must have cleared up, then.

Pause. KIT is fiddling with a box of matches.

KIT (*turns with sudden decision*): Jack, there's something I must—— (*In turning he upsets matches.*) · Damn, I'm sorry.

JACQUELINE: I've never seen a clumsier idiot than you, Kit. (*She goes on her knees.*) I seem to spend my life cleaning up after you. There!

She gets up. KIT kisses her suddenly and clumsily on the mouth. She pushes him away. They are both embarrassed and puzzled. (*After a long pause.*) You smell of whisky, Kit.

Enter ALAN.

ALAN: Oh!

KIT: I'm going to bed. Good night. (*He goes out.*)

JACQUELINE: What's the matter with him? Is he drunk?

ALAN: No, Jack, but I've a confession to make to you.

JACQUELINE (*in alarm*): You haven't told him?

ALAN: I couldn't help it.

JACQUELINE: Oh, Alan, no.

ALAN: Will you forgive me?

JACQUELINE: I'll never forgive you. It's ruined everything. · (*A shade tearfully.*) He's just been talking to me about the weather.

ALAN: Well, he's a bit embarrassed. That's natural.

JACQUELINE: But he'll spend all his time running away from me now, and when he is with me he'll always be wondering if I want him to kiss me, and he'll go on talking about the weather, and— (*turning away*)—oh, it's awful!

ALAN: I'm sorry, Jack. I meant well.

ALAN: No.

BRIAN: She gave me a sharp buffet on the kisser.

ALAN: What did you do?

BRIAN: I said, well, if that isn't what you want, what the hell do you want? Then she got up and left me. I never laughed so much in my life.

ALAN (*dazedly*): You laughed?

BRIAN: Wouldn't you, old boy?

> ALAN *gazes at him with amazed admiration.*

Well, I'm for bed. I say, I met the most charming little girl just now on the front—fantastic piece she was. She gave me her card—yes, here it is, Colette, chez Mme Pontet, Rue Lafayette, 23. Bains. 500 francs. I think I shall pop round to-morrow and have a bain.

ALAN (*rising and gazing at* BRIAN *with awe*): Oh, Brian! How right-minded you are!

BRIAN: Me?

ALAN: Thank God you came in when you did. You don't know what you've done for me with your splendid, shining example. I now see my way clear before me. A great light has dawned.

BRIAN: I say, old boy, are you feeling all right?

ALAN: Listen, Brian. You weren't the only person to get the old green light from Diana to-night. I got it, too.

BRIAN: Doesn't surprise me. I should think she's pretty stingy with her yellows and reds.

ALAN: Yes, but I didn't respond to it in the same glorious way as you. However, what's done can be undone. (*Going to door.*) I am now going upstairs to put the same question to Diana as you did earlier in the evening.

BRIAN: I shouldn't, old boy. She'll say no, and believe me, she's got rather a painful way of saying it.

ALAN: If she says no, then, lacking your own sterling qualities, I shan't pay a visit to Rue Lafayette 23. No. I shall run away. I shall go back to London to-morrow.

BRIAN: But what about your exam and so forth?

ALAN: I shall chuck that. Well (*opening door*) I am now about to throw my future life into the balance of fate. Diplomat or writer. Which shall it be? Diana shall choose.

> ALAN *goes out.*

BRIAN (*to himself*): Crackers!

He shakes his head wonderingly. After a bit he rises, crosses to table and stops to think.

BRIAN (*musing*): Bains. 500 francs! (*Fumbles for money and starts to count.*) 100, 200, 300, 400, 450—— Damn.

Slamming of door is heard. ALAN *comes in.*

ALAN: I'm going to be a writer. Come and help me pack.

He disappears.

BRIAN: 500 francs! (*Turns and runs out.*)

CURTAIN FALLS

ACT II

Scene III

SCENE: *The same.*

TIME: *The next morning.*

> MARIANNE *is clearing away the breakfast,* JACQUELINE *helping her.* KENNETH *enters from window,* MAINGOT *following. They have evidently just finished a lesson.*

MAINGOT (*at window*): Dites a Monsieur Curtis que je l'attends. Il ne vaut pas la peine de continuer. Vous n'en saurez jamais rien.

KENNETH (*sadly*): Oui, Monsieur.

MAINGOT: Je serai dans le jardin. Oh, ma petite Jacqueline, que i'ai mal à la tete ce matin.

JACQUELINE: Pauvre, papa! Je suis bien fachée.

MAINGOT: Ça passera—ça passera. Heureusment le quatorze ne vient qu'une fois par an.

> *He goes back into garden.*

KENNETH (*calling*): Brian.

BRIAN (*off*): Yes, old boy?

KENNETH: Your lesson.

BRIAN (*off*): Won't be a second.

> KENNETH *closes the door and wanders mournfully over to the bookcase.*

JACQUELINE: Why so sad this morning, Kenneth?

KENNETH: You've heard the news about Alan.

JACQUELINE: Yes, my father told me.

KENNETH: Don't you think it's awful?

JACQUELINE: No. For one thing, I don't believe for a moment he's serious.

KENNETH: Oh, he's serious all right. What a damn fool! If I had half his chance of getting in the Diplomatic I wouldn't go and chuck it up.

> *Enter* BRIAN, *carrying a note-book.*

BRIAN: 'Morning all. Where's Maingot Père?

KENNETH: He's waiting for you in the garden.

BRIAN: Oh. (*Anxiously.*) Tell me, old boy, how is he this morning? Gay, happy—at peace with the world?

KENNETH: No. He's got a bad headache, and he's in a fiendish temper. (*He goes out.*)

BRIAN: Tut, tut. Couple of portos too many last night, I fear.

JACQUELINE: Why this tender anxiety for my father's health, Brian?

BRIAN: Well, Jack, I'm afraid I may have to deliver a rather rude shock to his nervous system. You see, I'm supposed to have done an essay on the Waterloo campaign, and what with one thing and another I don't seem to have got awfully far.

JACQUELINE: How far?

BRIAN (*reading*): La bataille de Waterloo était gagnée sur les champs d'Eton.

JACQUELINE: And that's the essay, is it?

    BRIAN *nods.*

Well, if I were you, I shouldn't show it to him. I'd tell him you did one of five pages and it got lost.

BRIAN (*doubtfully*): Yes, but something seems to tell me he won't altogether credit that story.

    Enter MAINGOT.

MAINGOT: Eh, bien, Monsieur Curtis, qu'est-ce qu'on attend? Vous êtes en retard.

BRIAN (*affably*): Ah, Monsieur, vous êtes bon—ce matin, J'espère?

MAINGOT: Non, j'ai affreusement mal à la tête.

BRIAN (*sympathetically*): Oh. C'est trop mauvais. A trifle hung-over, peutêtre? Un tout petit peu suspendu?

MAINGOT: Vous êtes fou ce matin?

    They go out together, MAINGOT *heard expostulating.*

BRIAN (*off, his voice coming faintly through the window*): Il est très triste, Monsieur. J'ai perdu mon essai . . .

    JACQUELINE *smiles. Having finished her clearing away, she takes off her apron and the handkerchief that covers her hair. She looks at herself in a pocket-mirror. The door at the back opens very slowly and* ALAN'S *head appears.*

ALAN (*whispering*): Jack!

JACQUELINE (*turning*): Hallo, Alan.

ALAN: Is Diana about?

JACQUELINE: She's in the garden. She wants to speak to you.

ALAN: I bet she does. But I'm taking good care she doesn't get a chance.

*He comes cautiously into the room. He is dressed in a lounge
suit preparatory for going away.*

I want to get my books together. (*He goes to bookcase.*)

JACQUELINE: Alan, you're not serious about this, are you?

ALAN: Never more serious in my life, Jack. (*He is collecting books
from the bookcase.*)

JACQUELINE: You're breaking Diana's heart, you know.

ALAN: Ha! Is that what she told you?

JACQUELINE: Oh, no. She wouldn't give herself away to me,
but I honestly think she is rather in love with you, Alan.

ALAN: Yes, that's just what I'm afraid of.

JACQUELINE: You know, you're the only man in the world who's
ever got away from Diana unscathed.

ALAN (*turning quickly*): Don't say that! It's unlucky. I'm
not out of the house yet.

He turns back to the bookcase as DIANA *comes quietly into the
room from the garden.*

JACQUELINE (*quickly*): Look out, Alan.

ALAN (*seeing Diana*): Oh, my God!

He darts out of the room, dropping all his books as he does so.
DIANA *follows him out purposefully, but is too late. After a
second she reappears.*

DIANA: It's no good, he's sure to have locked the door of his
room. (*She sits down mournfully.*) I'm afraid he's quite determined
to go. I feel dreadfully bad about it, because I'm responsible for
the whole thing. All this talk of writing is just nonsense. He's
only running away from me.

JACQUELINE: I don't altogether blame him.

DIANA: I suppose it's a wonderful compliment for a man to
throw up his career just for my sake, but I can't see it that way.
I'm really frightfully upset.

JACQUELINE: You don't look it.

DIANA: But I am, honestly I am. You see, I can't understand
why he should want to run away from me. I can't see what he's
got to be frightened of.

JACQUELINE: Can't you?

DIANA: If only I could get a chance to talk to him alone, I'm sure
I could persuade him not to go.

JACQUELINE: I'm sure you could, too. So is Alan. But I don't
think you'll get the chance.

Enter MARIANNE *from kitchen.*

MARIANNE (*to* JACQUELINE): S'il vous plaît, M'mselle, voulez vous venir voir la chambre de Lord Heybrook? Je l'ai preparée.

JACQUELINE: Bien, Marianne. Je viens tout de suite.

Exit MARIANNE, *and* JACQUELINE *follows her to the door.*

DIANA: Oh, does this Lord Heybrook arrive this morning?

She has turned back to the kitchen door as the other door opens and ALAN *comes in.* JACQUELINE *is momentarily alarmed for his safety, but sees* ROGERS, *who strolls in behind* ALAN, *and is reassured. She smiles and goes out.*

ALAN, *studiously avoiding looking at* DIANA, *goes over to the bookcase and picks up the books he has dropped.* ROGERS *takes a position between him and* DIANA, *nonchalantly looking up at the ceiling.*

DIANA (*quietly*): Bill, please go away. I want to talk with Alan alone.

ROGERS: Well, its . . .

DIANA (*shortly*): Bill, did you hear me? I asked you to go.

ROGERS (*firmly*): I'm sorry, I can't.

DIANA (*realising the situation, steps back with dignity*): Do you think it's necessary to behave like this?

ALAN: You can say anything you want to say in front of Bill.

DIANA: No, thank you. I'd rather not.

ALAN: Then you don't say it.

DIANA (*after a slight pause*): All right, if you're determined to be so childish. This is all I want to say. (*With great sincerity.*) Alan, you know your own mind. If you feel you must run away from me, go ahead. I won't try to stop you. I only hope you'll be happy without me. I know I shan't be happy without you.

ALAN (*beginning to fall*): You'll get over it.

DIANA: Oh, I expect so. You'll write to me occasionally, won't you?

ALAN: Oh, yes, every day, I expect.

DIANA: I'd like to know how you're getting on in your new career. I wish you the very, very best of luck.

ALAN: Thank you.

DIANA: I'll be thinking of you a lot.

ALAN: That's very kind of you.

DIANA: Well, that's really all I wanted to say, only . . . (*Falter-*

168

ingly.)   I would rather like to say good-bye, and that's a bit hard with Bill standing there like the Rock of Gibraltar.

There is a long pause.

ALAN (*suddenly*): Bill, get out.

ROGERS *doesn't budge.*

ALAN: Get out, Bill.

ROGERS *seems not to have heard.   ALAN approaches him menacingly.*

Get out, blast you!

ROGERS (*slowly*): Is that the voice of reason, my dear fellow?

ALAN *stares at him and suddenly collects himself.*

ALAN: Oh, thank you, Bill.   Come on, help me carry these books upstairs, and don't leave my side until I'm in that damned train.

They go towards the door.

DIANA: So you don't want to say good-bye?

ALAN (*at door*): Yes, I do.   Good-bye.

He goes out, followed by ROGERS.

DIANA, *in a sudden rage, hurls some books through the door after them.*

DIANA: You forgot some.

She goes to kitchen door.

(*Calling.*)   Marianne, à quelle heure arrive ce Lord Heybrook?

JACQUELINE (*calling from the kitchen*): Lord Heybrook's arriving at ten-fifteen.   (*She appears in the doorway.*)   He'll be here any moment now.

DIANA (*annoyed*): Oh, thank you very much.

JACQUELINE: Well, any luck with Alan?

DIANA (*shortly*): No.

JACQUELINE: He wouldn't listen to reason.

DIANA: Do you mind, Jacqueline?   I'm really too upset to talk about it.

JACQUELINE: Why don't you go to England with him, if you feel like that?

DIANA: How can I go chasing him across half a Continent? One has a little pride after all.

JACQUELINE: Yes, I suppose one has.

DIANA: Besides, if Alan really feels he'll be happier without me, there's nothing I can do about it.

JACQUELINE: No, I suppose there isn't.   (*Inconsequentially.*)   Poor Lord Heybrook!

DIANA: What's Lord Heybrook got to do with it?

JACQUELINE: Nothing. (*She wanders over to the window.*) It's a lovely morning for a bathe, don't you think? There's a cold wind and the sea is rough, but I shouldn't let that stop you.

DIANA: Really, Jacqueline, you're becoming quite nice and catty in your old age. (*Defiantly.*) As a matter of fact, I think I will have a bathe. Why don't you come with me?

JACQUELINE: Oh, no. My bathing dress isn't nearly attractive enough. Besides, I'm giving lessons all the morning. (*Looking at her watch.*) I'm supposed to be giving one now. Kit's late as usual.

DIANA: By the way, how are you getting on in that direction?

JACQUELINE: Not very well, I'm afraid.

DIANA: Oh, I'm sorry. I suppose Kit's terribly upset about me?

JACQUELINE: You needn't worry. I shall do my best to console him.

DIANA: I've been horribly unkind to him. After Alan's gone I shall have to be specially nice to him to make up for it.

JACQUELINE (*alarmed*): Oh, no.

    DIANA *raises her eyebrows.*

Oh, why don't you go to England with Alan? Heaven knows Alan's never done me any harm, but I can feel quite ruthless about anything that will get you out of this house.

DIANA: Excitable race, you French—I always say.

    Enter KIT.

KIT (*ignoring* DIANA): Sorry, Jack. I'm late.

JACQUELINE: All right, Kit.

DIANA: Well, I don't want to disturb you. (*Going to door.*) I'm going to have a bathe.

    DIANA *goes out.* KIT *stands shyly, holding a note-book.*

JACQUELINE (*adopting a schoolmistress manner*): Sit down, Kit. Have you done that stuff?

    They sit at table. KIT *hands her his note-book.*

Good. You must have worked quite hard.

    She bends her head over the note-book. KIT *gazes at her.*

KIT (*suddenly*): Jack, I want to say——

JACQUELINE (*hurriedly*): This is wrong. (*She underlines a word.*) You can't say that in French. You have to turn it. (*She writes something in the book.*) Do you see?

KIT (*looking over her shoulder*): Yes, I see.

JACQUELINE *continues to read.*

JACQUELINE: My dear Kit—— (*Reading.*) Une pipe remplie avec du tabac. What ought it to be?

KIT: Rekplie de tabac, of course.

JACQUELINE: Why didn't you write it, then? (*She underlines another word.*) Kit, this whole exercise is terrible. What on earth were you thinking of when you did it?

KIT: You.

JACQUELINE: Well, you'd better do it again.

KIT (*annoyed*): What! Do it all again?

JACQUELINE: Yes. (*Weakening.*)

KIT: Not the whole damn thing?

JACQUELINE: Certainly.

KIT (*with dignity*): Shall I translate you some "La Bruyère"?

JACQUELINE: All right.

KIT: Page one hundred and eight.

They take up their books in a dignified silence.

JACQUELINE: If I let you off, will you tell me?

KIT: I might.

JACQUELINE: Very well. You're let off. Only mind you, if you do another exercise as bad as that I'll make you do it again, and three more besides. Now, why were you thinking of me?

KIT: I was wondering whether I ought to tell you I was sorry for—for what happened last night, or whether I ought to pass it off with a gay laugh and a shrug of the shoulders.

JACQUELINE: Which did you decide?

KIT: I decided to leave it to you.

JACQUELINE: Well, we'll take the gay laugh, etcetera, for granted.

KIT: Very well. The incident is now closed, permanently and perpetually closed. (*He opens his book.*) Chapter four. Of love.

JACQUELINE (*puzzled at his attitude*): I don't know why you should have thought I wanted you to apologise. After all, what's a kiss between friends?

KIT: Alan told me this morning that you were in a steaming fury with me about it, so I thought——

JACQUELINE: Oh, I see. Alan's been talking to you about me this morning, has he? Come on, tell me, what's he been saying now?

KIT: I don't see why I shouldn't tell you. You see, last night, when Alan was a bit drunk, he played a stupid practical joke on me. He told me (*covering his face with his hands*)—this is a bit embarrassing, but it's a good laugh—he told me that you had been madly in love with me for two months. (*He uncovers his face and waits for the laugh, which doesn't come.*) Well, I, being also rather drunk, believed him, and so, as I was feeling rather sentimental, I —kissed you, as you remember; and of course I couldn't understand why you didn't fall into my arms and say, "At last, at last!" or some such rot. However, this morning Alan told me the whole thing had been a joke, and that you were really rather angry with me for—well—spoiling a beautiful friendship, and all that nonsense. So that's why I thought I'd better apologise.

JACQUELINE (*with sudden violence*): What a blasted fool Alan is!

KIT: Yes, it was a damn silly trick to play. Not at all like him.

JACQUELINE: Kit—supposing I—had fallen into your arms and said, "At last, at last!" or some such rot, what would you have done?

KIT: Oh, I should have kissed you again and said: "I've loved you all the time without knowing it," or some such idiocy.

JACQUELINE: Oh, Kit. You wouldn't.

KIT (*apologetically*): Well, I told you I was feeling sentimental last night, and what with seeing what a fool I'd been over Diana and trying to forget her, and suddenly hearing that you were in love with me, and being drunk——

JACQUELINE: You don't feel sentimental this morning, do you?

KIT: Lord, no. You don't have to worry any more. I'm quite all right now.

He takes up his book and tries to concentrate.

JACQUELINE: Isn't there any chance of your feeling sentimental again, sometime?

KIT: Oh, no. You're quite safe.

JACQUELINE: If I gave you a drink or two, and told you that what Alan said last night was the truth? And that I *have* been in love with you for two months and that I've been longing for you to kiss me every time I'm with you, would that make you feel sentimental?

KIT: There's no knowing what it mightn't make me feel.

Pause.

JACQUELINE: I haven't got any drink, Kit. Or must you have drink?

She stands up and KIT *embraces her.*

(*A little hysterically.*) At last! At last!

KIT: I've loved you all the time without knowing it.

JACQUELINE: Or some such idiocy.

KIT: I mean that, Jack.

JACQUELINE: Don't get serious, please, Kit. This is only a joke. It's only because we are both feeling a bit sentimental at the same time.

KIT: I've got a peculiar feeling in the stomach, and an odd buzzing noise in the head. I think that must mean I'm in love with you.

JACQUELINE: Oh, Kit, do you think there's a chance you may be feeling sentimental in two months' time?

KIT: I'll take ten to one.

JACQUELINE: Well, go on being beastly to me in the meanwhile, because I should hate it if you didn't.

KIT: I'll try, but it won't be easy.

ALAN *pokes his head cautiously round the door.*

ALAN: Is Diana about?

JACQUELINE: Come in, Alan. You're quite safe, and I've got some news.

ALAN *comes in, followed by* ROGERS.

ALAN: What news?

JACQUELINE: I don't want the Commander to hear it. (*To* ROGERS.) Do you mind awfully?

ROGERS: Oh, no. Not at all. Tell me when you're finished.

He goes out.

ALAN: Well, what's the news?

JACQUELINE: Kit says it's just possible that in two months' time he may feel quite sentimental about me.

ALAN: Well, well, well. You could knock me over with a feather.

KIT: You've got a lot to explain, Alan. What the hell do you mean by telling me a whole packet of lies?

ALAN: Is that the proper way to speak to one, who, by a series of tortuous ruses has at last brought you two love-birds together?

ROGERS (*appearing in doorway*): I can come in now, can't I?

JACQUELINE: How did you know?

ROGERS: Male intuition as opposed to female. I listened outside.

ALAN: Tell me, Jack, did Diana say anything about coming to England with me?

JACQUELINE: No, she's definitely staying here. She says your happiness comes first.

ALAN: For my happiness read Lord Heybrook. Thank God for His Lordship.

Enter KENNETH.

KENNETH: Alan, must you go?

ALAN: Yes, Babe, I must.

A car noise is heard outside. MAINGOT *appears at window.*

MAINGOT: Jacqueline! Jacqueline! Je crois que c'est Lord Heybrook qui arrive. Es-tu-prête?

JACQUELINE: Oui, Papa.

MAINGOT: Bien! (*He darts out again.*)

JACQUELINE (*excitedly*): Lord Heybrook! Oh, go and tell Diana, someone, or she'll miss her entrance.

KIT (*running to door*): Diana, Lord Heybrook!

JACQUELINE: What does he look like, Kenneth.

KENNETH: I can't see. Your father is in the light.

ALAN: Oh, sit down, all of you. Give the man a chance.

MAINGOT (*calling off*): Marianne! Les Bagages!

Enter DIANA, *in her bathing dress. She takes up a position of nonchalance, with her back to the garden door.*

MAINGOT (*off*): Par ici, Milord!

Enter LORD HEYBROOK *and* MAINGOT *from window.* LORD HEYBROOK *is a bright young schoolboy, about fifteen years old.* (*Escorting* LORD HEYBROOK *across the room.*) Alors vous êtes arrivé. J'espere que vous avez fait bon voyage . . . (*etc.*)

LORD HEYBROOK, *after smiling around shyly, goes out followed by* MAINGOT. JACQUELINE *collapses with laughter on* KIT's *chest. The others begin to laugh also.*

DIANA: Come and help me pack, someone. I'm going to catch that London train or die.

She disappears through door at back.

ALAN (*pursuing her despairingly*): No, no, oh, God, no! (*Turning at door.*) Stop laughing, you idiots. It isn't funny. It's a bloody tragedy.

But they only laugh the louder as the

CURTAIN FALLS

FLARE PATH

To
KEITH NEWMAN

THE CHARACTERS
(in the order of their appearance)

PETER KYLE

COUNTESS SKRICZEVINSKY (DORIS)

MRS. OAKES

SERGEANT MILLER (DUSTY)

PERCY

FLYING OFFICER COUNT SKRICZEVINSKY

FLIGHT LIEUTENANT GRAHAM (TEDDY)

PATRICIA GRAHAM

MRS. MILLER (MAUDIE)

SQUADRON LEADER SWANSON

The action passes in the Residents' Lounge of the Falcon Hotel at Milchester, Lincs.

ACT I
Saturday, about six p.m.

ACT II
SCENE I: *About three hours later.*
SCENE II: *Sunday morning, about five-thirty.*

ACT III
Sunday, about noon.

Flare Path was first produced at the Apollo Theatre, London, on August 13th, 1942, with the following cast:

COUNTESS SKRICZEVINSKY	Adrianne Allen
PETER KYLE	Martin Walker
MRS. OAKES	Dora Gregory
SERGEANT MILLER	Leslie Dwyer
PERCY	George Cole
COUNT SKRICZEVINSKY	Gerard Hinze
FLIGHT LIEUTENANT GRAHAM	Jack Watling
PATRICIA GRAHAM	Phyllis Calvert
MRS. MILLER	Kathleen Harrison
SQUADRON LEADER SWANSON	Ivan Samson
CORPORAL JONES	John Bradley

The play directed by Anthony Asquith

ACT I

SCENE: *The residents' lounge of The Falcon, at Milchester, Lincs.*

Downstage, left, a door marked "Lounge Bar." Upstage, left, a curved counter marked "Reception," behind which is a door bearing the label "Private." Back, left, swing doors leading on to road. Large bow windows at back, with window seats. Staircase, right, leading to a small landing at back and thence out of sight. Downstage, right, a door marked "Coffee Room." Centre, right, a fireplace with fire burning.

On the rise of the curtain the sole occupant of the room is DORIS SKRICZEVINSKY, a carelessly-dressed woman in the early thirties, inclined to fat. She has fallen asleep in a large arm-chair, a copy of Everybody's *open on her lap. A wireless at her side is emitting, at intervals, the trumpeted call sign of the B.B.C.*

PETER KYLE, a man of about thirty-five, dressed in correct country attire—too correct to be convincing—comes in from the road, carrying a suit-case. He looks round, then goes up to the reception desk and rings a small handbell. Nothing happens. He rings again. DORIS wakes up.

DORIS (*calling*): Mrs. Oakes!

MRS. OAKES comes in from the door marked "Private," her office. She is a tall, angular woman of middle age.

MRS. OAKES: Yes? (*Seeing PETER.*) Yes? What can I do for you?

PETER: I'd like a room, please.

MRS. OAKES: Single or double?

PETER: Single.

MRS. OAKES: Quite impossible. I'm sorry.

PETER: Oh.

There is a pause broken by the voice of the B.B.C. announcer.

ANNOUNCER: Hullo, Forces! Round the World in Eighty Days. A dramatisation of the novel——

DORIS switches it off. MRS. OAKES, paying no further attention to PETER, has come from behind her counter to collect a tea-tray.

DORIS (*derisively*): Round the world in eighty days! They do think up some queer ones, I must say.

MRS. OAKES: I never listen these days, except to the news. Finished with your tea, Countess?

DORIS: Yes, thank you, Mrs. Oakes.

MRS. OAKES *takes up the tray.* PETER *is watching her, exasperated.*

MRS. OAKES: Of course, I'm not saying it would be easy to think up new things all the time——

PETER (*loudly*): What about a double?

MRS. OAKES: You said you wanted a single.

PETER: Yes, but if you haven't got a single, I'd like a double.

MRS. OAKES: I'm sorry. We're full right up.

PETER: Then why did you give me the choice of asking for a single or a double?

MRS. OAKES: You might have been a married couple.

PETER: I might have been a sultan and full harem, but I don't see that makes any difference. If you haven't got a room, you haven't got a room, have you?

MRS. OAKES (*unmoved*): No. We haven't got a room. (*She goes into her office.*)

PETER *turns round.*

PETER: God, what a——

DORIS (*excitedly*): Why, it is!

PETER: I beg your pardon.

DORIS: You're Peter Kyle, aren't you?

PETER: Yes, I am. (*Politely.*) I'm afraid——

DORIS: Oh, no. You wouldn't know me. I saw *Light of Love* in Milchester only yesterday. Isn't that funny?

PETER (*abstractedly*): Yes, it is. (*He makes an obvious effort to be polite.*) It's over two years old now—*Light of Love.*

DORIS: Oh, we only get the old ones in Milchester. Well, I never—this is a thrill!

PETER: It wasn't a good picture either, I'm afraid.

DORIS: Oh, it was quite good, really. One or two bits were rather silly, I thought. You were ever so good, though.

PETER: Thank you very much.

DORIS: Not at all. I always think you're good.

PETER: I'm so glad.

She stares at him in wonder and awe. PETER *is evidently not unaccustomed to this. He walks forward and extends his hand graciously.*

How do you do?

DORIS: Oh, how do you do. My name's Doris. I won't tell you the other name, because you'd never be able to pronounce it. (*She hastily tidies her crumpled frock.*) You came over here to arrange about your new picture, didn't you. I read all about it in the *Express*.

PETER: Yes.

DORIS: And you're giving all your salary to the Red Cross. I do think that's fine. Of course, you're English, aren't you?

PETER: By birth, yes. But I've been an American citizen for the last seven years.

DORIS: Well, well, well! Peter Kyle! Would you believe it—drifting into the old Falcon—just like that—and asking for a room.

PETER: And not getting it.

DORIS: Oh, don't you worry about that. The idea! (*Calling.*) Mrs. Oakes!

MRS. OAKES *emerges from her office.*

MRS. OAKES: Yes? (*Glaring at* PETER.) I thought I told you——

DORIS (*excitedly*): Mrs. Oakes, don't you know who this gentleman is?

MRS. OAKES: No.

DORIS: Look at him carefully, and then tell me if you don't recognize him.

MRS. OAKES *stares at* PETER.

MRS. OAKES (*at length*): No, I can't say I do.

DORIS: Look again. Look at him side-view, then you'll see. (*To* PETER.) Turn round.

PETER (*embarrassed*): I think if you don't mind——

DORIS: There! You must know that smile. Who does it remind you of?

MRS. OAKES (*at length*): Mabel Smart's brother.

PETER: I think I'd better tell you my name straight away, otherwise this might go on all night. I'm Peter Kyle.

MRS. OAKES: Peter Kyle?

DORIS: Yes, you know. The film actor.

MRS. OAKES: An actor?

DORIS (*frenziedly*): You must have seen him, Mrs. Oakes. He's at The Palace this week in *Light of Love*.

MRS. OAKES: I don't go to The Palace. (*To* PETER.) Have you been at the Odeon in Skillingworth?

PETER: I've really no idea.

DORIS: Of course he has. He's very famous—so please, Mrs. Oakes, do try and fix him up if you can.

MRS. OAKES (*to* PETER): How long did you want to stay?

PETER: Just the one night.

MRS. OAKES: Just the one night. Well, Countess, seeing that the gentleman is a friend of yours I'll see what I can do.

PETER: That's terribly kind of you.

MRS. OAKES: Now, let me see. I could put up a bed for him in the attic—only I don't like to do that because of fire bombs.

PETER: I don't mind——

MRS. OAKES: No, but I do. I don't want my hotel burnt down.

PETER: But I'm not particularly inflammable.

MRS. OAKES: Possibly not—but the bed is. I know! There's Number Twelve. Wing Commander Taylor. He's Duty Defence Officer, so he'll be sleeping up at the Station to-night. You can go in there. (*She opens the register.*) Will you register, please? And fill in this form.

PETER: I'll fill it in and give it to you later.

MRS. OAKES: I can't send you up at once, because the Wing Commander might want to use his room before dinner.

PETER: That's quite all right.

MRS. OAKES: You must be careful not to touch any of the Wing Commander's things. He's most particular. Oh! (*She examines the printed form.*) I see you're an alien.

PETER (*nervously*): Er—yes, I am——

MRS. OAKES (*coldly*): Dinner is at half-past seven. (*She goes into her office.*)

PETER: Evidently she thinks I'm a spy.

DORIS: Oh, no, I'm sure she doesn't. It's only that we get so few civilians round here. There's only the aerodrome, you see, and nothing else at all. We're all Air Force here, you know. I suppose you came to see someone up at the station.

PETER: Well—I——

DORIS: I don't want to be inquisitive. I mean, curiosity killed the cat. But I just thought it was a funny place for a gentleman like you to come to, and I——

PETER (*deliberately*): I was on my way to town. I passed this place and thought it might be fun to stay the night. That's all.

DORIS: Fancy. Well, I'm glad you did, I must say.

PETER (*with automatic gallantry*): So am I.

DORIS (*simpering*): Silly.

PETER (*hastily*): When you say you're Air Force, does that mean you work up at the aerodrome?

DORIS: Oh, no. I'm no W.A.A.F. I haven't the figure for it. No—my husband's a pilot.

PETER: Fighter pilot?

DORIS (*shocked*): Oh, no, Bombers. Wellingtons. You must have seen them when you passed the aerodrome.

PETER: I'm not very good about aeroplanes——

DORIS: Aircraft. Yes, he's second pilot in a Wellington, is my Johnny. He's done quite a lot of raids. He's only got a few to go before they give him a rest. After a fixed number of operational trips they get given a rest, you know—put on to something safer— like teaching or groundwork. (*She delves in her bag.*) Have one of these. They're called Summer Crop. I should think they're pretty awful, but it's all they've got here.

PETER: You have one of these. They're Chesterfields.

DORIS: Oo, lovely! (*She takes one.*) However did you get them?

PETER: I smuggled over two thousand in with me from America.

DORIS: Naughty! Do tell me all about Hollywood. Do you know Carmen Miranda or Bing Crosby?

While she is speaking there is the sound of aircraft—heavy bombers —passing overhead. The noise is momentarily very loud. PETER *looks up.*

PETER: What are they?

DORIS (*casually*): Stirlings, I expect. They're four-engine aircraft, anyway. Probably from Shepley. Been a day raid most likely. The boys'll know. Tell me, did you meet Carmen Miranda or Bing Crosby?

PETER: I've never met Carmen Miranda, but I know Bing Crosby fairly well.

DORIS: Fancy! Whatever's he like?

Another aircraft can be heard passing overhead. This time it is DORIS *who looks up.*

PETER: He's very nice. As a matter of fact, our houses are quite near each other and——

DORIS (*sharply*): Sh! (*She jumps up and listens intently.*) There's something wrong with that one. (*She runs to the window, opens it and sticks her head out.* PETER *follows her.*) There she is! See?

PETER (*looking out*): Yes. God, what an enormous thing. It looks all right to me.

DORIS: She's flying on three engines. Been shot up, I expect (*The sound passes into the distance. Suddenly.*) Oh, lor!

PETER: What's the matter?

DORIS: She's landing. Look! They've put the undercarriage down. She's going to land on our aerodrome.

PETER: My God, so it is. It's coming in.

> *There is a pause, while* DORIS *and* PETER *stare intently out of the window. The sound of the aircraft engines fades suddenly as they are throttled back.* DORIS *turns quickly away from the window.* PETER *continues watching.*

DORIS: Is she down?

PETER: Yes, I think so. It's gone out of sight behind those hangars. (*He turns round from the window and moves as if to close it.* DORIS *stops him with a quick gesture. She is still listening intently. There comes the sound of the aircraft engines.*)

DORIS: It's all right. She's taxi-ing back. (*She nods to* PETER *to close the window.*)

PETER: It was in trouble all right. It was flying all lop-sided.

DORIS: Probably flown, by the famous Chinese pilot—Wun Wing Low. (*She titters expectantly. but* PETER *does not laugh.*) Not my joke, Teddy Graham's. He's a flight loot up at the Station. Ooo!—I've suddenly thought—you must know Mrs. Graham, Teddy Graham's wife—Patricia Warren, the actress, you know. She was in a play of yours in New York. The part was only a—cough and a spit, she says, but you might remember her. She's staying here.

PETER: Really?

DORIS: Do you remember her?

PETER: Yes, I do.

DORIS: She's ever so nice, I think. Don't you?

PETER: Yes. Charming.

DORIS: She won't half be surprised when she sees you. She went up for a nap. Shall I call her down?

PETER: No, please don't. I'll see her later, anyway.

DORIS: She's only been here since yesterday morning. It's the first chance she's had of coming to see her hubby, as the play she was acting in in London only came off last week. He's just been made captain of a Wellington, too—she's as proud as proud of him. It's a treat to see them together—it is really.

PETER (*abruptly*): I feel it's time for a drink.   Can I get you one?

DORIS: Thank you, Mr. Kyle.   I'll have a gin and lime.   There's the bell by the door.

> PETER *presses a bell.   A man in the uniform of a Sergeant Air Gunner comes in from the road.   He is about 35, small, dark and insignificant.   His name is* DAVID MILLER, *and he is known, naturally as Dusty.*

DUSTY: Evening, Countess.

DORIS: Hullo, Dusty.

DUSTY: Spotted my wife anywhere?

DORIS: I don't think she's come yet, Dusty.   She was coming by bus, wasn't she?

DUSTY: Four-twenty-five from Lincoln—so she should 'ave been 'ere twenty minutes ago.   She's a proper mucker-upper, though —she'll go and catch the wrong bus, you see—end up in Grimsby, and then blame me.   (*While he is speaking he is taking off his overcoat. He now turns and sees* PETER.)   Oh, excuse me——

PETER: We were just going to have a drink.   Will you join us?

DUSTY: Thank you, sir.   I don't mind.

PETER: I've rung the bell, but nothing seems to happen.   (*To* DUSTY.)   What does A.G. stand for?

DUSTY }
DORIS } (*simultaneously*): Air gunner.

DORIS: Didn't you know that?   You are ignorant.

PETER: Yes, I am, I'm afraid.   So you're the man who sits in the rear turret?

DUSTY: That's right.   Tail-end stooge—that's me.

PETER: What's it like being a tail-end stooge?

DUSTY: Oh, not so bad.   Gets a bit cold sometimes.

PETER: A bit cold is an understatement, isn't it?

DUSTY: Don't know.   Depends, really.   Some nights it's all right.   Other nights you come down and you got to get a bloke with a 'ammer and chisel to get you off of the seat.

> · A boy of about fifteen, PERCY, wearing an apron, comes through the door marked "Lounge."

PERCY: Anybody ring?

PETER: Yes, I rang.   I want a gin and lime—— (*To* DUSTY.) What's yours?

DUSTY: Beer, please, sir.

PETER: A beer and a whisky and soda.

PERCY (*with a broad smile*): There's no whisky.

PETER: Then I'll have a gin and tonic.

PERCY (*with a broader smile*): There's no tonic.

PETER: Then bring me a pink gin.

PERCY (*disappointed*): Yes, you can have that. (*To* DUSTY.) Was that a Stirling come down 'bout ten minutes ago, Sergeant?

DUSTY: That's none of your business what it was, Nosey.

PERCY: Garn, I knows a Stirling when I seen one. Anyone hurt inside?

DUSTY (*with dignity*): I've no idea, I'm sure.

PERCY (*with relish*): Bet there was. I saw an ambulance driving out. (*He goes out.*)

DORIS: Was anyone hurt?

    DUSTY *nods.*

Bad?

DUSTY: Two bumped off—tail gunner and wireless op. Cannon shells. Other gunner caught it—not bad, though.

DORIS: Been a daylight do, has there?

DUSTY: Big one. (*With a glance at* PETER.) Talk about careless talk!

DORIS: Oh, don't mind him. You don't know who he is, do you?

DUSTY: No. Can't say I do.

DORIS: It's Peter Kyle.

DUSTY (*after a pause*): Cor! (*He gazes awestruck at* PETER.)

PETER: What's *your* name, Sergeant?

DUSTY: Miller, sir.

PETER: I'm glad to meet you. (*He shakes hands.*)

DUSTY: Peter Kyle. Well, I'm a—— Do you know Dorothy Lamour?

PETER: No. I can't say I do.

DUSTY (*plainly disappointed*): Oh!

    PERCY *comes in with the drinks.*

PERCY: It *was* a Stirling come down. Fred in the bar seen 'er, too.

DUSTY: Fred in the bar can be wrong sometimes, I presume, or is he omnificent?

PERCY: I don't know what he is, but 'e knows it was a Stirling. Shot up something terrible it was, 'e says.

    PETER *pays him.*

PETER: Keep the change.

PERCY (*surprised*): Thank you, sir. Thank you. (*At door.*) Where's it to-night, Sergeant? Berlin?

DUSTY: It'll be a clip on the ear-'ole for you, my lad, if I 'ave any more of your lip. Beat it?

> PERCY *goes. His voice can be heard in the lounge before the door closes behind him.*

PERCY (*off*): Sergeant says it's Berlin to-night.

DUSTY: Cor! Did you hear that?

DORIS: Needs a good spanking. (*To* DUSTY *in a low voice.*) Nothing on to-night, is there, dear?

DUSTY: Not so far as I know.

DORIS (*cheerfully*): Tinkerty-tonk, Mr. Kyle!

PETER: Good health!

> *They drink. There is the sound of a car drawing up in the road outside, and a Flying Officer (*COUNT SKRICZEVINSKI*) comes in. He wears the Polish Air Force eagle over the left breast, and the word "Poland" on his shoulders. He is over forty, tall and thin, with a permanent and slightly bewildered smile.*

DORIS: Hullo, Johnny Ducks, you're early. (*She comes forward, kisses him lightly on the cheek, and brings him forward to* DUSTY *and* PETER.) Is Teddy with you?

COUNT: 'E—poots—car—garage. (*He speaks English with the greatest difficulty, always retaining his bewildered expression.*)

DUSTY: Evening, sir.

COUNT: Good—evening.

DORIS: Johnny, I want you to meet a very famous man.

COUNT: Pardon?

DORIS (*pointing to* PETER): Very—famous—man. Film star. Understand? Peter Kyle.

COUNT (*not having understood*): Oh, yes—please.

PETER: How do you do? (*He shakes hands. The* COUNT *clicks his heels slightly.*

DORIS: Isn't he sweet when he does that? First time I met him he kissed my hand. Of course, I had to fall for him after that, didn't I, Johnny ducks?

> *The* COUNT *smiles at her vaguely and she squeezes his hand.*

You must excuse his English, Mr. Kyle. It's not up to much, but it's getting better. He's having English lessons up at the Station— aren't you, Johnny ducks?

COUNT: Please?

DUSTY: English—lessons, sir. Your wife says you are having English lessons.

COUNT (*with a sudden burst of loquacity*): Oh, yes. English lessons. I learn much. 'Ow are you to-day, Mrs. Brown, please? Se Eiffel Tower is se towellest beelding in se vurruld.

DORIS: World, Johnny, world. Not vurruld.

COUNT: World. World.

MRS. OAKES *appears at the office door.*

MRS. OAKES: Good evening, Count.

COUNT: Good evening, Missus.

MRS. OAKES: You'll be in to dinner, I presume?

COUNT: Oh, yes, sank you, please.

MRS. OAKES: And you'll be staying the night? No early breakfasts or late suppers? (*She winks heavily.*)

COUNT: No, please. To-night I stye wiss my vife.

MRS. OAKES *nods and goes out.*

DORIS (*to* COUNT): Not stye. Stay. To-night I stay with my wife.

DUSTY (*calling*): Oh, Mrs. Oakes!

MRS. OAKES' *head reappears.*

MRS. OAKES: Yes?

DUSTY: It's all right about that double room for to-night, isn't it?

MRS. OAKES: Yes. You've got Number 2. Do you want to go up now?

DUSTY: No, thanks. The wife's not come yet. Should've been 'ere near an hour ago. (*Gloomily.*) Just like her, I will say.

MRS. OAKES: She'll turn up—you'll find.

Her head disappears as TEDDY GRAHAM *comes in through the front door. He is a Flight Lieutenant, and wears the D.F.C. His age is 24.*

TEDDY: Hullo, Doris, my beautiful. How's every little thing? Evening, Sergeant. Where's the wife?

DUSTY: Don't know, sir. Gone off course a bit—looks like.

TEDDY You told me her navigation was pretty ropey.

DUSTY: It's lousy. If she don't come soon I'll post her as missing —believed got in the wrong bus.

TEDDY: I should. Johnny, you clot? What about that beer you were going to get me?

COUNT: I not forget. (*He rings bell.* TEDDY *suddenly sees* PETER *and approaches him cautiously.*)

TEDDY: Good God! It's—not—Peter Kyle—is it?

DORIS: Yes, it is, Teddy. It really is. Isn't it wonderful?

TEDDY: Pukka gen?

DUSTY: Pukka gen, sir.

TEDDY: Good Lord! I say—I mean—Good Lord! I say, I'm most awfully glad to meet you, sir, and all that.

PETER: Must you call me "Sir"?

TEDDY: No, I suppose not—I mean—Peter Kyle! Well, well, well! (*He shake's Peter's hand energetically*.) This calls for a party, don't you think, boys and girls? (*Calling*.) Percy!

COUNT: Please—I wish——

TEDDY: All right, Johnny—these are mine. (*Pointing at* PETER.) Very famous bloke here, Johnny.

COUNT: Oh, yes, sank you.

> PERCY *appears promptly, his manner, when he speaks to* TEDDY, *surprisingly deferential*.

PERCY: Yes, Flight Lieutenant Graham, sir?

TEDDY: Where have *you* been? We've been ringing for half an hour.

PERCY: Sorry, sir. Didn't know it was you, Flight Lieutenant Graham.

TEDDY: Another round for these people, whatever they're having, Percy, and pints for the Count and me.

PERCY: Yes, sir. Berlin to-night, Flight Lieutenant Graham?

TEDDY: What? No, Percy. Home, Sweet Home, to-night.

> PERCY'S *face falls. He goes out.*

TEDDY: I say, this has rather shaken me—you know—I mean your being here, in the old Falcon—just like—I mean—a commercial traveller or something. No offence, or anything——

PETER: That's all right.

TEDDY: Good Lord, you must know Pat. That's my wife. Patricia Warren. She was—still is—I mean she still uses the name and all that. (*Calling*.) Pat! Pat! Are you upstairs?

PATRICIA (*her voice coming from upstairs*): Hullo, Teddy. I heard you come in.

TEDDY: Come on down. There's something down here that's going to shake you considerably.

PATRICIA: Oh? Just coming.

TEDDY: I say, I suppose you do know her. I mean, she was in a play of yours, you know—tiny part, but she shoots a line about your having been very kind to her an all that——

PETER: Does she? Yes, I remember her well.

TEDDY: Look—you go there—(*he points to a place directly beneath the stairs*)—so she won't see you as she comes down——

PETER (*protestingly*): No, I think——

DORIS (*pushing him*): Go on, silly! Look out!

PATRICIA GRAHAM *comes down the stairs. She is about* TEDDY'S *age, perhaps a year or two older.*

PATRICIA: What's all this about my being shaken?

TEDDY: Nothing, darling. Just to get you to come down.

PATRICIA: Hullo, Johnny. Good evening, Doris.

TEDDY: This is Sergeant Miller—my tail gunner. A very bad type——

PATRICIA: He doesn't look it. How do you do? (*Brightly.*) It's funny the loose way you Air Force people use your slang. For instance, to shake someone or to be shaken seems to cover anything from crashing in flames to seeing a caterpillar or something.

PETER *emerges from the recess under the stairs.* PATRICIA *is facing him. She stands quite still.* PETER *smiles, but she does not smile in return. She turns her head quickly to look at* TEDDY, *who is gazing at her, smiling expectantly. Then she looks back at* PETER.

PETER: Hullo.

PATRICIA: Hullo. (*They shake hands.*)

TEDDY: Well, darling, are you shaken, or are you shaken? Now, be honest.

PATRICIA: I'll be honest. I'm shaken.

PERCY *comes in, staggering under the weight of a loaded tray.* Which of these is for me?

TEDDY: Well—as a matter of fact——

PATRICIA: Teddy, you don't mean to tell me you've left me out? I'll have a pink gin.

TEDDY: Another pink gin, Percy.

PERCY: Yes, sir.

TEDDY: Come on, everybody.

PERCY *goes out.*

PATRICIA (*to* PETER): When did you arrive?

DORIS: Only a few minutes ago. Just fancy—Peter Kyle blowing into the old Falcon—just like that. Happened to be passing and thought it would be fine to stay the night. You should have seen my face.

PATRICIA (*brightly*): Yes. What's the news from the aerodrome, Teddy?

TEDDY: Nothing much. (*Raising his glass.*) Cheers, everybody!

PATRICIA: There must be some news, or are you going all careless talk on me?

TEDDY: First time I've ever known you take an interest in what's going on at the aerodrome. As a matter of fact, it's been a quiet day, hasn't it, Sarge?

DUSTY: Pretty quiet, sir.

TEDDY: A Stirling force-landed a few minutes ago. You probably saw it.

PETER: The Countess and I saw it.

DORIS: Don't call me Countess, please, Mr. Kyle. Or, if you do, give me my full name, which is Countess Skriczevinsky. (*She screws her face up in a mock effort to pronounce the name.*)

COUNT (*correcting her gently*): Please Countess. Skriczevinsky.

DORIS: Get Johnny correcting me for a change!

> *There is a general laugh. The* COUNT *looks slightly more bewildered.*

Sorry, ducks. I can say it. I was only fooling. (*Correctly.*) Countess Skriczevinsky.

> *The* COUNT *smiles.*

PATRICIA: What was the matter with the Stirling that force-landed?

TEDDY: Been shot up in a raid. Big raid, too, I believe. I can't tell you where, of course.

> PERCY *comes in with* PATRICIA's *pink gin.*

PERCY: 'Ell of a do on Kiel this afternoon.

TEDDY (*startled*): Come here, Percy. (*Regarding him sternly.*) Who told you that?

PERCY: Just come through on the six o'clock.

TEDDY: Oh, the laugh's on me.

PERCY: 'Ell of a do it must 'ave been. Blenheims, Wimpeys, 'Alifaxes and Stirlings. We lost seventeen. Shot down twenty-two of theirs, though. (*He goes out.*)

TEDDY: Seventeen? Not too good. (*He meets* DUSTY's *eye.*) I reckon the squadron's done pretty well up to now to keep out of these daylight dos, don't you?

DUSTY (*fervently*): You're telling me.

COUNT (*suddenly*): I—have—wish to go on sese daylight dos.

TEDDY: You mean you don't have wish.

COUNT: No, no. I *do* have wish. I have wish to see my bombs to fall——

There is a slight pause.

TEDDY: I see what you mean, Johnny old boy.

PATRICIA: I want another drink.

TEDDY: Good Lord! You haven't finished that one already?

PATRICIA: Yes.

PETER (*calling*): Percy!

PERCY appears at the door.

(*Politely.*) What were you drinking, Mrs. Graham?

PATRICIA: Thank you, Mr. Kyle. It was a pink gin.

PETER: A pink gin for Mrs. Graham—and the same again for the others.

PERCY goes out.

DORIS: My Johnny'll be getting tinky-boo. He can't stand more than a couple, can you, ducks?

COUNT: Yes, please.

DORIS: You mean, no, thank you.

COUNT: No, sank you.

DORIS: Thank you, Johnny. Thank. Th-ank.

COUNT: Sank you. Sank you.

TEDDY: Good old Johnny. Keep cracking—it'll come.

PERCY comes in with new drinks.

PERCY (*off*): Hurry up with those pints, Fred.

TEDDY: Just as well we've got to-night at home, eh, Dusty?

DUSTY (*gloomily*): I wouldn't put it past 'em to send us out now. They done it before.

TEDDY: Dusty's the world's prize moaner. He even moaned to me over the intercomm. because he'd shot down a Messerschmitt. Tell them about it, Dusty.

DUSTY (*alarmed*): No, Mr. Graham, sir, please. Not now.

PATRICIA (*politely*): Do tell us, Sergeant.

DUSTY: It's nothing, Mum, really. Mr. Graham's told you it's only I shot down a Messerschmitt, I think.

TEDDY: What do you mean, you think? It was at night, Patricia. Nothing else in the sky for miles around except us and this 110, and he still thinks someone else might have shot it down. Tell 'em, Dusty.

DUSTY: They'll think it's a line, sir.

PATRICIA: Why don't *you* tell the story, Teddy?

TEDDY: I didn't see it. We were stooging along over the Dutch coast somewhere, and suddenly I heard Dusty's voice over the inter-comm. saying: (*Imitating* DUSTY's *gloomy voice*) "'Ullo, skipper. Tail calling. Me. 110's just been at us. Sod's gone into the drink on fire. Over."

There is a general laugh. DUSTY *looks acutely uncomfortable.* "Gone" *is the operative word.*

PATRICIA (*to* DUSTY): You did shoot at it, though, didn't you?

DUSTY: Oh, yes, Mum. I shot at it all right. Bright moon there was. Saw it as clear as I'm seeing you. He opens up 'bout five 'undred yards with 'is cannons, and I've got 'im in my sights, and 'e's getting bigger all the time, and I press the triggers and there's a ruddy great glow all of a sudden and down 'e goes into the drink turning and twisting. I thought——

There is a pause. Everyone, including the COUNT, *is listening intently.*

DUSTY: Crikey!

PATRICIA: That's not what I'd have thought.

DUSTY: First time I'd ever seen a Messerschmitt, and down he goes—just like that. (*He clicks his teeth unbelievingly.*)

TEDDY: Good show, Dusty. You get another beer for that.

A small woman, much muffled up, enters from the road and comes down right. DUSTY *puts his beer down and walks forward.*

DUSTY: 'Ullo, Maudie.

MAUDIE: Hullo, Dave.

They do not kiss. The others have politely turned their backs.

DUSTY: Got on the wrong bus, did you, Maudie?

MAUDIE (*accusingly*): You said the Skillingworth bus, Dave.

DUSTY: Yes, that's right. Four-twenty-five from Lincoln.

MAUDIE: Well, I went to Skillingworth and you weren't there.

DUSTY: Lor, Maudie, I didn't tell you to go to Skillingworth. You should 'ave got off at Milchester.

MAUDIE (*still accusingly*): You said the Skillingworth bus, Dave.

DUSTY: Yes, but the Skillingworth bus goes through Milchester; you should 'ave got off at Milchester.

MAUDIE: You never said nothing about Milchester. You don't look very well, Dave. Have you been getting those backaches?

DUSTY *looks round hurriedly at the others.*

DUSTY (*hastily*): Here, Maudie! You sign your name here.

MAUDIE (*not to be put off*): Because if you have, I've brought that medicine you left behind last leave—the one your doctor gave you——

DUSTY: All right, Maudie. Here's where you sign. Here.

TEDDY *detaches himself from the other group.*

TEDDY: So she got in to base at last, Dusty.

DUSTY: Yes, sir. Brought her in on the beam.

TEDDY: How do you do, Mrs. Miller?

DUSTY: This is Flight Lieutenant Graham, Maudie—you know—the one I was telling you about. He's my skipper.

MAUDIE: Pleased to meet you.

TEDDY: How do you think he's looking?

MAUDIE: A bit peaky, I told him. I think he must have been getting those backaches of his——

DUSTY (*hastily*): If you'll excuse us, sir, we'll be nipping up-stairs——

TEDDY: See you both later.

DUSTY *shepherds* MAUDIE *across the room to the stairs, carrying her small suit-case.*

MAUDIE (*on the stairs*): The man at Skillingworth said I should have caught the four-forty-five from Lincoln.

DUSTY (*heatedly*): He doesn't know what he's talking about. Four-twenty-five's all right, if you done what I told you.

MAUDIE: He said the four-forty-five doesn't go through Skilling-worth at all, and all I had to do was to change into a Milchester bus at Windowbrook—you did say the Skillingworth bus, Dave. (*They pass out of sight.*)

PETER: The henpecked hero.

DORIS: Dusty's not henpecked, believe me. I bet he gives as good as he gets. Shall *we* go upstairs, Johnny ducks? I must tidy up a bit and dinner's quite soon, and you'll want a shave.

COUNT: Please?

DORIS: Shave, dear. (*She strokes his chin.*)

COUNT: Oh, yes. Not—shave—sis—morning. Very—pricky.

DORIS: Prickly, duckie.

PATRICIA: Perhaps he meant pretty.

DORIS: He meant prickly—and he's right. I don't like my beautiful going about looking like an old porcupine. Come on, Johnny. Upstairs.

COUNT (*with a great effort*): Yes. Excuse, please. I must go up to my room where I will shave.

TEDDY: Terrific, Johnny! Well done!

COUNT (*delighted*): That was good how I am saying him?

DORIS: Yes, my precious, but that wasn't. That was bloody awful how you were saying him. (*They pass out of sight.*)

TEDDY: Talk about henpecking—Doris rules her old Count with a rod of iron.

> There is a pause. Neither PATRICIA nor PETER answer him. PATRICIA is occupied in not looking at PETER.

PETER: What's that? I'm sorry.

TEDDY: I said Doris rules her old Count with a rod of iron.

PETER: Yes. I feel awfully sorry for him.

TEDDY: Why? Doris is all right.

PETER: Yes. She seems charming. Only—well, of course, it may just be that he doesn't speak any English.

TEDDY: Even if he didn't speak a word of English, I don't think he'd run any risk of mistaking Doris for the Duchess of Dillwater.

PETER: No, I suppose not. How long have they been married?

TEDDY: I don't know. He was married to her when they formed the Polish Squadron on the Station. He's good value, old Johnny. (*He finishes his beer.*) I'm going to have a bath before dinner. (*He strolls to the stairs.*) I'm sure you two are longing to get down to a nice theatrical gossip match.

PETER: We'll have quite a lot to talk about, I expect.

TEDDY (*on the stairs*): I bet you will. All about Angel Fanny and Sweetie-pie Cyril. Darling, can I borrow your eau-de-Cologne?

PATRICIA: Yes, but don't take too much—it's absolutely priceless.

TEDDY: I'm going to pour it on with a bucket. If I can't look like the screen's great lover, I can at least smell like a glamour boy. So long. (*He goes out of sight, whistling. There is a pause.*)

PETER: He's nice, but what a baby!

> PATRICIA looks angrily at him.

Darling, don't be angry, please.

PATRICIA: Angry? (*Wearily.*) Oh, Lord, what an idiot you are!

PETER: I don't see that I've done anything so wrong in coming down to face the music.

PATRICIA: Face the music? How beautifully Hollywood! What was your idea? To get Teddy alone and say "I love your wife"?

PETER: If you must know, yes.

PATRICIA (*bitterly*): How did you visualise the scene after that?

Was it like your last film, when you let Spencer Tracy knock you down, and saved each other's lives just before the fade-out? (*She turns away from him.*)   And you call Teddy a baby!

PETER (*stubbornly*): I'm sorry, but I've never been able to see why you should have to do the telling alone.

PATRICIA: Because this isn't a film, and there's no need for you to worry about whether you're playing a sympathetic part.

PETER: You're being rather brutal.

PATRICIA (*near tears*): I'm trying to be.

PETER (*approaching her*): Pat, darling.

> PATRICIA *turns quickly away*, PETER *staring at her, bewildered.*

PETER: This hasn't made any difference, has it?

PATRICIA: Of course it hasn't made any difference.

PETER (*after a pause*): I'll go away to-night.

PATRICIA: What's the use?   He's seen you and spoken to you. He's heard us calling each other Mr. Kyle and Mrs. Graham.   You've quite quietly reduced the whole thing to the level of a rather nasty little intrigue.

PETER (*obstinately*): You'd much better let me tell him.   I can explain——

PATRICIA (*violently*): I'm the one to tell him—the only one, Pete.

> PETER *looks at her in silence, then shrugs his shoulders and turns away.   There is a pause.   Then* PATRICIA *follows him and puts her hand on his arm.*

PATRICIA (*with a change of tone*): Sorry, Pete. Oh, darling. (*Kisses him.*)   I am hating all this, you see.

PETER: I know.   Are you sure I can't help?

PATRICIA: I'm afraid you can't.   Nobody can.

PETER: What are you going to tell him?

PATRICIA: Everything.

PETER: Starting way back?

PATRICIA: Way back.   It *is* way back, I suppose?

PETER: April twenty-seventh, nineteen thirty-eight.

PATRICIA: You always did have a date complex.

PETER: So did you.   What about our celebrations on the twenty-seventh of every month.   You can't have forgotten them?

PATRICIA (*nodding*): Fifteen altogether.

PETER: I wish you'd told him that part of it when you married him.   Then this wouldn't be so difficult now.

PATRICIA: In films the wife always tells her husband about her past affairs—doesn't she?

PETER: Shut up about films, darling. Why didn't you tell him? Funk?

PATRICIA: No, I didn't see why I should,

PETER: Yes, but I still think it would have been better——

PATRICIA: Pete, don't be so dense. If I'd told him anything about you at all, I'd have had to admit that I was still in love with you when I married him—and that was something I didn't want to admit even to myself.

Pause.

PETER: You *were* a fool to run out on me, weren't you?

PATRICIA: You *were* a fool to let me go.

PETER: Well, I couldn't very well have stopped you, could I?

PATRICIA: You could have come over here a bit sooner than you did. I couldn't go to you after the war—or a letter would have been rather nice.

PETER: I was making a big experiment, darling, you know that —trying to live without you. It wasn't a success.

PATRICIA: Nor was mine.

Pause. PETER looks at her for a moment, then turns away.

PETER (*in a deliberately casual voice*): When you married Teddy, how much did you feel for him?

PATRICIA: I don't know, Pete; he didn't give me much chance. He was on a week's leave, and we were married before he went back to his squadron. What the papers would call a whirlwind war-time romance.

PETER: But now you do know, don't you?

PATRICIA: Yes, I know now.

PETER turns to her.

PETER: Tell me, then, how much do you feel for him now?

PATRICIA smiles.

I'm horribly jealous of him. You know that.

PATRICIA: I'd be angry if you weren't. You can't know anyone as well as that without feeling something, and something rather strong.

PETER: Is there much to know?

PATRICIA: Not much—but what there is, is—well—just terribly nice. (*After a slight pause.*) But in the sense which you mean, I don't feel anything for him at all.

PETER: That's true, isn't it, Pat?

PATRICIA: Yes, it's true. I'd have given quite a lot to have said to you the other day, "Go back to America, Mr. Kyle. I'm married and in love, and I don't want you." It's a pity I couldn't, isn't it?

PETER: I suppose you might say it's a pity for both of us, but somehow I don't think so. (*They embrace.*) You won't run out on me again, will you?

PATRICIA: You know why I did, don't you?

PETER: Because of the row——

PATRICIA: Not because of the row. If it hadn't been over that, it would have been over something else. I ran out purely and simply because I couldn't bear not being married to you.

PETER (*laughing*): Considering we'd been living—as you might say—in sin—for well over a year——

PATRICIA: I know. I hated Rita for not giving you a divorce, but you see even after we'd been living together for months and months people still behaved to me as the latest Peter Kyle girl friend. In the end it made me so frightened of losing you that I ran away from you. D'you understand that?

PETER: No.

PATRICIA (*smiling*): Of course you don't. It's mad, isn't it?

PETER: Absolutely batty—anyway, now that Rita has given in——

PATRICIA: Don't worry. All the Ritas in the world wouldn't get me to make the same mistake again—or any mistake again. (*After a pause.*) I'll tell Teddy to-night. Ring the bell; I want another drink.

PETER *does so.*

PETER: Why didn't you last night?

PATRICIA: There was a party. They were all very sweet, and they all had gallons of beer, and they all sang songs, very bawdy most of them—and finally two or three of them passed out like logs.

PETER: What about Teddy. Did he pass out too?

PATRICIA: Yes. I had to put him to bed, poor lamb.

PETER: Charming for you.

PATRICIA: No, it wasn't—I mean it was, rather.

PETER: It couldn't have been.

PATRICIA: I don't know. I quite enjoyed it. Perhaps because I was so relieved that I hadn't got to tell him.

Enter PERCY.

PERCY: You rang.

PETER: Yes, Percy.   I want a pink gin for Mrs. Graham.

PERCY: Coo! That's the third, isn't it?

PETER: Yes, Percy.   That's the third.

PERCY: Coo! (*He turns to go.*)

> TEDDY *appears on the landing.*

TEDDY: Hey, Percy! (*To the others.*)   You've ordered, haven't you?

PETER: Yes, we have.

PERCY: Yes, sir?

TEDDY: Get me a beer.

PERCY: O.K., Flight Lieutenant Graham, sir.   (PERCY *goes out.*)

PATRICIA: You've been very quick.

TEDDY: As far as a bath went, I've had it.

PETER: You had a bath?

TEDDY: No.   The water was cold.

PETER: But you said you had it.

TEDDY: I had it—meaning I didn't have it.

PETER: How can you have had it when you didn't have it?   I don't understand.

PATRICIA: You're being very dense.   It's Air Force slang.

PETER: Oh, I see.   So you're still unbathed?

TEDDY: Yes, but I smell gorgeous.   Smell!

PETER: Gorgeous.

TEDDY (*to* PATRICIA): Smell!

PATRICIA: Gorgeous, Teddy.

PETER: How long have we got before dinner?

TEDDY: About half an hour, if it's not out on its E T A.

PETER: E T A?

TEDDY: Estimated time of arrival.

PETER: Oh, I see.   Well, I think *I'll* go up now.   I haven't even seen my room yet.   (*He walks up the stairs.*)

TEDDY: Did you have a nice bee, you two?

PETER (*on the stairs*): Yes, thank you, Teddy.   (*He leans over the banisters.*)   Do you mind me calling you Teddy?

TEDDY: Good Lord, no!   It's an honour.

PETER: An honour?   Thank you, Teddy.   (*He goes out.*)

TEDDY: Nice bloke, considering.

PATRICIA: Considering what?

TEDDY: He's an actor.

PATRICIA: Thank you for the comment on my profession.

TEDDY: Darling, don't be a clot. I didn't mean you. You're the old exception that proves the old rule, if you see what I mean.

PATRICIA: What old rule is that?

TEDDY: Well, actors are funny blokes. They never seem to be themselves. They only worry about what sort of effect they're having on other people.

PATRICIA: They act—in other words?

PERCY *comes in with the drinks.*

TEDDY: Yes, I suppose that's it. They never seem to do or say anything naturally. They're always thinking of an invisible audience. I bet they even act in the bathroom. (*He takes a beer from* PERCY, *who goes out giggling.*)

PERCY (*off, in the lounge*): Do you know what Flight Lieutenant Graham just said? He said——

The door closes.

TEDDY: Percy'll get me a bad reputation. Don't you agree, though, darling?

PATRICIA (*lightly*): Not altogether. I think they feel things like other people, you know—although, I admit, they're inclined to act what they feel rather than just—feel.

TEDDY: Oh, well. Perhaps you're right. Don't let's argue, anyway. We never have and we never will. (*He raises his glass.*) Cheers, darling!

PATRICIA: Cheers! (*She gulps her drink, and makes a wry face.*)

TEDDY: I say. That went down the old hatch pretty quick, didn't it?

PATRICIA: Teddy——

TEDDY: Darling, I've just thought. Talking about actors acting and all that. We all act, in a way. At least, I know I do.

PATRICIA (*smiling*): Do you, Teddy?

TEDDY (*seriously*): Yes, I do. I don't mean with you so much. Up in the mess, with the blokes. They call me P O Prune—he's a character in The Training Manual—sort of crazy, good-tempered, half-witted sort of bloke—you know the type—and I—well, I kind of act P O Prune for them. Yesterday, for instance, I was up on an air test, and I saw the C.O.'s car pulling out of the gate, so I put the old Wimpey into a dive and beat him up—you know, pulled out only a few feet above his head and stooged round him. I didn't particularly like doing it, and I had the hell of a strip torn off about it afterwards—but—well—I was being P O Prune, you see, and the blokes had a good laugh.

PATRICIA *is staring at him. When he finishes she turns her head away quickly.* TEDDY *notices the movement.*

Sorry. I'm being a bore.

PATRICIA (*uncertainly*): No, you're not. Go on.

TEDDY: I say, Pat, is anything the matter?

PATRICIA (*wipes her eyes quickly*): Nothing. I'm being an actress, that's all.

TEDDY (*puzzled*): Did I say anything?

PATRICIA: No. I'm a bit tight, I think. When I'm tight I get weepy. I'm all right now.

TEDDY: Lesson to me not to talk about myself. I'm ashamed of you, Graham, making a woman cry. (*There is an awkward pause.*) Oh, by the way. Have you any plans for to-morrow evening?

PATRICIA (*uncertainly*): No—I—that's to say, I don't think so.

TEDDY: Let's go over to Lincoln and beat up The Saracen's Head a trifle, shall we?

PATRICIA: If you like.

TEDDY: We might take old Johnny and Doris along with us, too. I've got an idea this hole is getting you down a bit. We'll make a night of it to-morrow.

PATRICIA (*impulsively*): Teddy——

TEDDY: Yes?

PATRICIA: I've got something I must tell you.

TEDDY: All right. Don't look so serious about it. What is it?

PATRICIA: Not here. Shall we go upstairs?

TEDDY: This sounds awful. You look like our C.O. at his worst. Are you going to tear me off a strip?

PATRICIA *is already walking up the stairs.*

PATRICIA: Don't talk, Teddy, please.

TEDDY: I know. You want me to pay a dress bill.

PATRICIA (*violently*): Don't talk!

An Air Force officer, SQUADRON LEADER SWANSON, *comes in quickly. He is about fifty-five, and wears last war medals, but no wings.*

SWANSON: Teddy—thank the Lord I've found you.

TEDDY: Hullo, Gloria.

SWANSON: Come here, quick. (*Seeing* PATRICIA.) Oh, excuse me.

TEDDY: This is my wife. Squadron Leader Swanson—our adjutant—a shocking type.

SWANSON: Good evening, Mrs. Graham. Can you spare me your husband for a moment?

TEDDY: Is it anything important? We were just——

SWANSON: Yes, it is. Damned important.

Pause. TEDDY *nods.*

TEDDY: Oh. Oh, I see. (*To* PATRICIA.) You'll have to excuse me, darling. Go along to our room.

PATRICIA *looks from one to the other. Then without a word she goes along the passage.*

SWANSON (sternly): What's the idea of marrying a glamour girl? She's far too good-looking for a type like you.

TEDDY: I could marry Garbo if I tried. What's the trouble, Gloria?

SWANSON: You know.

TEDDY (*simply*): Damn!

SWANSON: Just come through from Group.

TEDDY: What time take-off?

SWANSON: 22.00 hours. Briefing 19.45.

TEDDY: This is a hell of a time to let us know. Who's going? Everyone?

SWANSON: No. A apple, L London, U uncle. And a kite from the Polish squadron—S sugar.

TEDDY: Johnny's. What's the job?

SWANSON: Special. Very hush-hush. Not exactly a piece of cake, I believe. What in hell was the idea of pooping off the Station like that? They told you this morning something might still come through.

TEDDY: They knew where to find me. I went up to ops. at five-thirty. There was nothing on then—and, Christ, if Group can't make up their minds by five-thirty——

SWANSON: I wouldn't have put it past you, P O Prune, to have gone roaring off to Brighton or somewhere for the week-end, and then we'd have had a pretty little court martial on our hands.

TEDDY: You'd have got me out of it, Gloria.

SWANSON: I bloody well wouldn't. What have you done with your crew?

TEDDY: They're all up at the station except Miller, the gunner. He's here. His wife's come down, poor blighter. I suppose we can't find a relief for him, can we?

SWANSON: No, it's too late. I gather you brought old Count Kiss-me-Quick down with you?

TEDDY: Yes. He's here.

SWANSON: Then you'd all better get cracking. You can use my car.

TEDDY: I'll use my own. (*He goes to foot of stairs. Calling.*) Johnny! Sergeant Miller! What's the met. report like?

SWANSON: All right, I think.

COUNT *appears, followed by* DORIS.

COUNT: What is, please?

TEDDY: Come on down. Sorry, Doris. No wives.

DORIS: Oh, I get you. O.K., ducks. (*She goes back up the stairs, meeting* DUSTY *on the landing.*) You're wanted, Dusty. (*She goes out.*)

DUSTY *looks down at the group below, then frames an inaudible but obvious expletive.*

DUSTY (*calling*): Stay there, Maudie. I'll be back in a tick. (*He comes downstairs*).

TEDDY (*in a low voice*): We've got some nice cheerful news for you boys. It's going to make your evening.

DUSTY: Didn't I tell you this'd happen?

TEDDY: You did, Dusty.

COUNT: We—go out to-night?

TEDDY: Yes, Johnny. Take-off 22.00 Briefing 19.45.

DUSTY: 'Ell of a time to tell us, I must say. Caught us bending proper this time. Group must be fair busting their stays with laughter.

TEDDY: I bet they are. Are you all ready, Johnny?

COUNT: I go upstairs. One minute only.

TEDDY: Go and say good-bye to your wife, Dusty. I'm sorry this had to happen. I'll drive you both up. I'll just go and get the car out.

SWANSON: I'll follow you later. I'm not going away from here without a drink.

SWANSON *goes into lounge.* TEDDY *goes out at back.* MAUDIE *has come quietly down the stairs.*

DUSTY: Maudie, I told you to stay in the room.

MAUDIE: What's up, Dave?

DUSTY: Bit of bad luck, Maudie. I got to leave you to-night.

MAUDIE: I only got one night. Don't go out to-night, Dave.

DUSTY: It's not my doing, old girl.   Been a bit of a muck-up at Group.

MAUDIE: What's Group?

DUSTY: Group Headquarters.   Where the orders come from.

MAUDIE: Why don't you tell them your wife's come down, and she's only got the one night?   They might send one of the other boys instead.

DUSTY: No go, Maudie.

MAUDIE: Oh, Dave.

DUSTY: I tell you what.   After you've had your supper—good supper they give you 'ere, too—you go up to bed, see, and get some sleep.   I'll be back 'bout four or maybe five, and we'll still have some time together.   Your bus don't go till one to-morrow.

MAUDIE: All right, Dave.   If they tell you you've got to do it, you've got to do it, I suppose.   Try and get back soon.

DUSTY: 'Course, I will.   I'll be back before you know I'm gone. I got the best skipper in England, and I'll tell him to step on it to-night.

> TEDDY *has come in quickly in time to hear the last sentence.   He waits a second, then walks forward.*

TEDDY: Oh, Mrs. Miller, I'm terribly sorry about this—it's the cruellest bad luck.

MAUDIE: I was asking Dave, Mr. Graham, if it wouldn't do no good to tell this Group that his wife's come down.

TEDDY (*gently*): I'm afraid not.   You see, there wouldn't be time.

MAUDIE: Oh, I see.   (*To* DUSTY.)   You going now?

DUSTY: This minute, Maudie.

MAUDIE: Good-bye, Dave.

DUSTY: Good-bye, old girl.   You do what I told you, now.   Get some sleep.

TEDDY: If there's anything you want, Mrs. Miller, I know my wife would be only too glad——

MAUDIE: No, thank you, Mr. Graham.   There won't be nothing. (*She goes up the stairs.*)

> DUSTY *blows a kiss to* MAUDIE, *and goes out quickly.*

(*On the stairs.*)   Take care of him, sir.   Don't let him go doing none of those silly tricks like he was telling me about—shooting at searchlights and such.

TEDDY: No, I won't.   I promise you.

MAUDIE *goes out, passing the* COUNT, *who comes running down the stairs.*

COUNT: I am most happy.   It is two weeks we have not go out.

TEDDY: You're a glutton for trouble, aren't you?

COUNT: Please?

TEDDY: Doesn't matter.   Jump in the car, Johnny.   I'll follow you.

COUNT *goes out.*

(*Calling.*)   Pat!

PATRICIA *appears on landing.*

PATRICIA (*descending the stairs*): You're going up to the Station, aren't you?

TEDDY: Yes.   I've got to rush.   I just want to say good-bye. I hoped this wasn't going to happen while you were here.   I'm awfully sorry.

PATRICIA: It's a raid, I suppose.

TEDDY: It's not exactly a practice stooge-around.

PATRICIA (*helplessly*): Teddy, I don't know what to say.

TEDDY: Happy landing—or just—come back.

PATRICIA: Come back.

He kisses her.

TEDDY: Good-bye, darling.   God willing, I'll be waking you up at the hellish hour of five or so to-morrow morning.   (*He goes abruptly to the door.*)   Oh, by the way, whatever it was you had to tell me will have to wait till I get back.   I suppose that's all right with you?

PATRICIA: Yes.   That's all right with me.

He smiles at her and goes out.

DORIS *is on the stairs, coming down.   She passes* PATRICIA *and pats her arm comfortingly, without saying anything.   Behind her* MAUDIE *appears and quietly descends the stairs.*

The sound of a car moving away breaks the silence.

CURTAIN

ACT II

Scene I

SCENE: *The same, about three hours later.*

> PETER *is sitting on the fender, and* PATRICIA *is sitting by the fire.* MAUDIE *is in a chair, right, apart from them. Coffee things are on the table, right. The wireless is going.*

ANNOUNCER: . . . at the controlled price of two and ten a pound, and will shortly be obtainable throughout the United Kingdom. (*Pause.*) That is the end of the nine o'clock news. To-night's talk is by a sergeant wireless operator from one of the Stirlings which took part in this afternoon's strikingly successful raid on the harbour and docks of Kiel.

PATRICIA: Turn it off. (PETER *does so.*)
You don't mind, do you, Mrs. Miller?

MAUDIE: No, thank you. I wasn't listening, anyway.

> *The lounge door opens and* DORIS *appears, accompanied by a rattle and hum of voices. She has a drink in her hand and a set of darts.*

DORIS: Anyone hear the nine o'clock? I clean forgot the time.

PATRICIA: We've just turned it off.

DORIS: There wasn't anything fresh, I suppose. No pincers on anything anywhere?

> *An R.A.F. corporal appears at the door.*

CORPORAL: Come on, Countess. We still want a double-two.

> PATRICIA *shakes her head.*

DORIS (*to* CORPORAL): Take my turn, Wiggy. I'll be back in a minute. (CORPORAL *goes out.*) Why don't you all come in here? We're having a slap-up do.

PATRICIA: I don't think so, if you don't mind.

DORIS: Perhaps you're right. The boys are a bit noisy.

PATRICIA (*hastily*): It's not that.

DORIS: I know, ducks. You don't have to tell me. Do you remember the old joke about wives waiting up for their husbands at five in the morning with a rolling-pin? Makes me laugh some-

206

times when I think of it, it does, really.　　There's a full moon to-night.
I think I'll just go and have a look.

　　She goes out of the front door.

PETER: I've rather taken to the Countess.　What's going to
happen to her after the war, I wonder?

PATRICIA: Oh, she'll go to Poland with her Johnny, and find herself
mistress of an enormous estate, with thousands of serfs, or moujiks,
or whatever they are.　She'll probably make a big success of it.

PETER: Supposing there is an after the war.

PATRICIA: Or supposing there's a Johnny.

　　DORIS *re-enters and stands by inside door.*

PETER (*slowly*): Or supposing he wants to take her.

PATRICIA: Yes, that's rather a point, I admit.

PETER: I'm afraid it's *the* point.　Our Countess has a personal
interest in the war continuing.

DORIS: The sirens have just gone in Skillingworth.

CORPORAL (*off*): What's yours, Countess?

DORIS (*over her shoulder*): Gin and ginger.　(*To* PATRICIA.)　It's
on Hull, I believe, but they may drop a couple on the aerodrome.
They do sometimes.　Tinkerty-tonk, Mrs. Miller!

MAUDIE: Tinkerty-tonk!

　　DORIS *disappears into lounge.*

PETER: Purely as a matter of idle interest—is there a shelter here?

PATRICIA: I don't know.　If there is I don't suppose anyone
would bother to use it.

PETER: I suppose if I'd been in England longer than a mere three
months, I might become as blasé about raids as you are.　(*Sharply.*)
Listen!　Those ours?

MAUDIE (*breaking a long pause*): Theirs.

PETER: Oh, are they?　How do you know?

MAUDIE: I lived in London till we were bombed out.

PATRICIA: I live in London, too, but I can never tell the difference.

MAUDIE: Perhaps you don't listen for it like what I do.

　　There are three muffled explosions.

PETER: Bombs?

PATRICIA (*smiling*): No—guns.　You've got a lot to learn.

PETER: Superior beast.　(*He touches her hand, and both look round
at* MAUDIE.)

PATRICIA (*she gets up and goes over to* MAUDIE): Is there anything
you'd like, Mrs. Miller?　Some coffee or something?

MAUDIE *looks up.*

MAUDIE: No, thank you, Mrs. Graham.

PATRICIA: That's not a very comfortable chair you've chosen. Wouldn't you like to come over by the fire?

MAUDIE: I'm quite comfy here, thank you.

PATRICIA: It's rotten luck, your having only the one night.

MAUDIE: I'll have a bit of to-morrow before the bus goes.

PETER: Do you have to go far?

MAUDIE: Only to St. Albans.

PATRICIA: Can't you possibly stay another night?

MAUDIE: No, I must be to work seven o'clock Monday. It's a laundry, you see.

PETER: Couldn't you ring your people up and explain? I'll ring them up for you, if you like.

MAUDIE: Oh, no, please. You mustn't.

PETER: Why not?

MAUDIE: They wouldn't like it. I'd be losing my job, and that'd never do—not now it wouldn't. Besides, I must be to work Monday morning. There's a lot to be done Mondays.

PATRICIA: I'm sure if you'd let Mr, Kyle explain——

MAUDIE (*firmly*): No, Mrs. Graham. Thank you all the same.

Pause.

PETER: How do you like your work in the laundry, Mrs. Miller?

MAUDIE: Oh, it's not so bad. I'm new to it, of course.

PETER: You haven't always done that kind of work?

MAUDIE: Oh, no. Not peace time, I didn't. I didn't have to work peace time. Dave had a good job, you see, and we had our own home in Eccleston Bridge Road—nice place it was. Of course, it's down now. Dave worked in London Transport—conductor—might have been inspector quite soon.

PATRICIA: And now he's a rear gunner in a Wellington bomber, shooting down Messerschmitts. (*To* MAUDIE.) Don't you ever find it unreal, what's happened to your husband and yourself?

MAUDIE: Unreal? No, I don't see it's unreal. It's happened, hasn't it?

PATRICIA: Yes, it has.

MAUDIE: Mind you, I'm not saying I like him being a gunner; it's not good for him in those turret things. They're wickedly cold. He told me so himself—and he gets horrible backaches. He used to get them when he was working on the buses. Besides, it's no good saying they always get back from these raids, beacuse they don't—not all of them. Then I'm not saying I liked being bombed out and going to live in St. Albans with Dave's Aunt Ella, who I've never got on with and never will—and working at the Snowflake—but what I say is, there's a war on, and things have got to be a bit different, and we've just got to get used to it—that's all.

PETER: Yes, I see. Very sensible.

    There is a sudden burst of voices as the lounge door opens and DORIS *comes in. From the lounge we can hear the* BARMAN'S *voice shouting:* Time, gentlemen, please. It's gone half-past nine. Time, gentlemen, please.

DORIS (*humming to herself*):
    I don't want to join the Air Force
    I don't want to go to war.

Phew! The Countess Skriczevinsky is a teeny bit tippy-o. (*Seeing* MAUDIE.) Hullo, Mrs. Miller, dear. Everything O.K.?

MAUDIE (*with dignity*): Yes, thank you for asking.

DORIS: Nothing you'd like me to get you? A little dinky, or anything?

MAUDIE (*cuttingly*): It's very kind of you, I'm sure, but I won't have a little—dinky. (*She sniffs contemptuously and gets up from her chair.*) Good night, Mrs. Graham.

PATRICIA: Good night, Mrs. Miller.

MAUDIE: Good night, Mr. Kyle.

PETER: Good night.

    Without saying good night to DORIS *she begins to mount the stairs.*

MAUDIE (*on the stairs*): Oh, by the way, Mrs. Graham, on account of my Dave is rather funny about me not mentioning his backaches to nobody, please don't say nothing to him about me having told you about them.

PATRICIA: All right, Mrs. Miller. I won't say a word.

DORIS (*calling*): Good night, Mrs. Miller, ducks. Sleep tight.

MAUDIE: I'd say you were more likely to do that than what I am, Countess. (*She goes out.*)

DORIS: Oo, did you hear that? I bought that properly, didn't I? Sleep tight! I'll give her sleep tight!

PATRICIA: I shouldn't brood on it, Doris.

DORIS: I suppose she thinks it's common for a Countess to have a few drinks with the boys.

PATRICIA (*soothingly*): I'm sure she doesn't.

PETER: As a matter of fact, I know lots of countesses who don't stop at having a few drinks with the boys.

DORIS *turns slowly in his direction.   She glares at him.*

DORIS: Now you're making fun of me, Mr. Peter Kyle, and I don't like it.

PETER (*contrite*): I'm sorry.

DORIS: Now, don't blame me for being a countess. It's not my fault. I didn't want it. I'd much rather be plain Mrs.—but Johnny likes people to call me Countess, so I've got to let them, see. But don't you be funny about me just because of that.

PATRICIA (*hastily*): He wasn't being funny about you, Doris.

PETER: Of course I wasn't——

DORIS: And another thing—I overheard everything you said about me and my Johnny just now. How I had a personal interest in the war going on.

PETER *and* PATRICIA *start.   There is a pause.*

PETER: I think you misheard me.

DORIS: Misheard my eye. That's what you said all right.

PETER: If I did, I've no idea what I meant.

DORIS: I know what you meant. You meant my Johnny's going to leave me flat the minute the war's over. That's what you meant. I'm only all right for him as long as the war goes on, and as soon as it's over and he gets back home he'll realise he's made an awful muck-up in marrying me and he'll—he'll—— (*She chokes and turns her back quickly.*   PATRICIA *goes up to her.*)

PATRICIA: Doris, my dear, don't be so idiotic. Even if Mr. Kyle did say that—and he didn't—it doesn't matter, because you know perfectly well it isn't true.

DORIS: I don't know it isn't true. I wish I did. I think it *is* true. (*She turns round.   Defiantly.*) But I don't want the war to go on—just because of that.

PETER (*simply*): Please believe me. I never said you did.

Pause.

DORIS: Oh, dear. I've gone and made a fool of myself again. Sorry, dear. Sorry, Mr. Kyle. Oh, dear—Peter Kyle! I've been longing to meet him all my life! Then, when I do, I go and snap his head off.

PETER: I really *am* most terribly sorry if I said anything to make you think——

DORIS: Oh, for heaven's sake! I'd no business to listen, anyway. Forget it. Wonder if it's clouding over at all. (*She goes to the window.*) Turn out the light for a sec, will you, ducks?

PETER *turns the light out.* DORIS *sticks her head out of the window.*

No, it's a lovely night, I'm afraid.

PATRICIA: Why afraid?

DORIS: If the weather was dud they might call it off. They won't, though. There's a lovely moon. What's the time?

PETER: A quarter to ten.

DORIS: They haven't lit the flare path yet.

PATRICIA: What's the flare path?

DORIS: Lights in a line—so that they can see when they're taking off. You ought to know that, married to a flight loot.

MRS. OAKES *comes in from her office and turns on the light.*

MRS. OAKES (*with a scream*): My black-out! (*She turns off the lights again.*)

DORIS: All right. We'll do it, Mrs. Oakes.

PETER *turns on the lights.*

MRS. OAKES: Have they gone yet?

DORIS: You shouldn't know they were going at all.

MRS. OAKES: Well, something made them all go back to the aerodrome in an awful hurry. (*With a heavy wink.*) I suppose it could have been an ENSA show. What time are they going to be back? That's all that concerns me.

DORIS (*returning the wink*): My guess is the ENSA show will be over about five in the morning.

MRS. OAKES: Your guess is as good as anyone's, Countess. Will the last one up please turn off the lights. I'm going to bed. Breakfast is at eight-thirty, Mr. Kyle—to-morrow being Sunday, we don't serve it in the bedrooms, as we are so shockingly understaffed.

PETER: That's quite all right. I don't have breakfast.

MRS. OAKES, *on her way to the stairs, stops dead.*

MRS. OAKES (*appalled*): You don't have breakfast?

PETER (*nervously*): No. I—er—just a cup of tea, I mean—but as a general rule I—er—well—(*defiantly*) I don't have breakfast.

DORIS: He's an actor, you see, Mrs. Oakes. He has to keep his figure.

MRS. OAKES: His figure. I see. I'm afraid I can make no reduction in the price of the room.

PETER: That's quite all right.

MRS. OAKES (*severely*): It's not all right at all, Mr. Kyle. I'm sure I don't like to charge people for what they don't have. But, you see, there *is* a war on, and if you don't have breakfast you must just take the consequences, that's all. Good night. (*She goes out.*)

PETER: What consequences? Duodenal ulcer?

PATRICIA (*laughing*): No, darling. Paying for it.

There is a slightly awkward moment following this slip.

DORIS: Wonderful the way you stage people darling each other. To hear you sometimes, you'd think you were passionately in love. (*Suddenly*). There's the All Clear—can you hear it?

PATRICIA (*after listening*): Yes, I can—just. Good.

DORIS (*almost simultaneously*): Damn! (*Answering* PATRICIA'S *unspoken enquiry.*) They wouldn't take off with Jerry overhead. They couldn't light the flare path, you see. Of course, sometimes old Jerry hangs about over the aerodrome for hours, and they don't know he's there. Then, just when they've lit the flare path and the boys are taking off—or coming in, more likely—he'll swoop down on them and shoot them up. You're a sitting target when you're coming in—so Teddy says—and you're dead beat probably and thanking God you've got back, and then suddenly—— (*She stops.*) Filthy trick, I think. Of course, we do the same over on their aerodromes. What's the time, Mr. Kyle? Sorry to keep troubling you.

PETER: Twelves minutes to ten.

DORIS: I'll go and watch the take-off from my room. You see better from up there. It won't be for a bit yet, of course. Good night. (*She goes to the stairs.* PATRICIA *and* PETER *say good night.*)

DORIS (*to* PETER): Sorry, ducks.

PETER (*imploringly*): Please!

DORIS (*laughing*): Please! You sound like my Johnny. (*On the stairs.*) If there's anything you want in the middle of the night, Pat dearie, can't sleep, or anything—don't worry about waking me up. I'll be quite glad to have company. Nighty night. (*She goes out.*)

There is a silence between PETER *and* PATRICIA *for a moment.*

PETER (*with a sudden explosion*): God damn it!

PATRICIA *goes to him, but says nothing.*

What right has she to go listening at doors? It wouldn't have been so bad if she didn't know it was true.

PATRICIA *puts her hand out and touches his. He takes it and looks down at it, examining a ring on her finger.*

I had rather a good taste for a film star in those days, hadn't I?

PATRICIA: It was very good taste.

PETER: Dripping with the wages of sin.

PATRICIA: I suppose I should have sent them all back to you. That's what a nice girl would have done.

PETER: A nice girl wouldn't have had anything to do with me in the first place.

PATRICIA: Oh, I think she would, Pete. (*As an afterthought.*) Not that I'm claiming to be a nice girl.

PETER: Why did you have anything to do with me?

PATRICIA: I had my reasons.

PETER: What were they? The reasons.

PATRICIA: You do like to be told, don't you?

PETER: I've had to do without being told for over a year now.

PATRICIA: And whose fault was that?

PETER (*promptly*): Mine.

PATRICIA: That's a surprise.

PETER (*invitingly*): So now.

PATRICIA: All right. I loved you first for being kind to a shy and imported small-part actress in your play.

PETER: I had my reasons.

PATRICIA: I know you did. I loved you for that too—because when the reason was removed you went on being kind.

PETER: Perhaps I still had hope.

PATRICIA: Perhaps. You certainly had cause for it, hadn't you?

    PETER *nods smilingly.*

I'm not going on with a long catalogue of your virtues.

PETER: I'm glad to know that it would be long.

PATRICIA: Only long because what are virtues to me are perhaps vices to other people. No, Pete, I don't suppose other people think you're very nice. They see through your act quite easily, I think—it's not awfully difficult to see through.

PETER: That's what you've always said, but I think it's a very good act.

PATRICIA: The modest, shy, quiet, cultured, self-possessed film star? It never has made sense, Pete. People see through it at once, and they take it for granted that what's underneath must be nasty because what's on top is so nice. Whereas I know what's underneath and I love it because it's simple and childish and—I don't know— just rather helpless.

PETER: Do you remember that awful row we had in Jack and Charlie's when you first said that?

PATRICIA: It wasn't a row—not one of our real ones—just a sulk.

PETER: We were both extremely dignified with each other for about a week, I remember that.

PATRICIA: Very hoity-toity until we met each other under a bed playing sardines in that awful woman's house in Long Island.

PETER: My God, yes, I remember. (*They laugh—gravely.*) What fools we were to miss a whole damned year.

PATRICIA *nods without speaking.*

Pat, don't bully me if I say something to you, will you?

PATRICIA: No, darling.

PETER: Well, I'm getting old, Pat.

PATRICIA: Old? You're thirty-nine.

PETER: Thirty-nine when you left me, forty-one now. Not old, really; just a nice, ripe, fruity middle-age. Perfectly all right if I were a good enough actor to play middle-aged parts.

PATRICIA: But you are.

PETER: The Studio doesn't think so. After my next picture I'm out. Oh, well, it's not only that, Pat, and this will sound (*he smiles at her shamefacedly*) funny, I suppose, if you happen to look at it like that. It's the war, you see. I don't understand it, Pat—you know that—democracy—freedom—rights of man—and all that—I can talk quite glibly about them, but they don't mean anything, not to me. All I know is that my own little private world is going—well, it's gone really—and the rest of the world—the real world—has turned its back on me and left me out, and though I want to get into the circle, I can't. I hate that, Pat—I hate being left out in the cold. I know it's a selfish way of looking at it, but I don't care. So you see—I do—what with one thing and another—I do happen to need you. (*His voice trails away into an embarrassed silence.*)

PATRICIA (*uncertainly*): Yes, you do, Pete. I'm glad that you do.

PETER: All very shy-making. I'm sorry.

PATRICIA, *saying nothing, puts an arm round his shoulder.*

It's only that I worry sometimes.

PATRICIA: You don't need to. You should know that by now.

PETER: Things can happen.

PATRICIA: Not to me.

PETER (*lightly*): You're a faithful type?

PATRICIA *winces slightly*.

PETER (*quickly*): Damn! I'm awfully sorry.

PATRICIA: It's all right. It's only that I'd forgotten him for the moment.

PETER: After to-morrow——

> *There is a noise at the front door.* SWANSON *comes in.*

SWANSON (*jovially*): Hullo—'ullo. Mrs. Graham, eh? Thought I'd find you up. (*He looks at* PETER.)

PATRICIA: Good evening, Squadron Leader. This is Peter Kyle—Squadron Leader Swanson.

SWANSON: Oh, yes. You're the actor type, aren't you? I heard all about you from Teddy. He's been burbling about meeting you all the evening. Shooting a terrific line.

> PETER *smiles politely.*

I say, I suppose you wouldn't like to come up to the Station to-morrow? Say a few words or something. Give the blokes a hell of a thrill—something to write to their girl friends about, instead of official secrets.

PETER: I'd love to, but as a matter of fact I'm leaving for London to-morrow.

SWANSON (*hangs up his coat*): Oh, pity. Well, perhaps some other time. Waiting up for the take-off, eh? Won't be long now. After they've gone take my advice—toddle off to bed and get some sleep. Won't seem any time before he's back again. As a matter of fact, old Teddy asked me to come along and see if you were all right and all that.

PATRICIA: It's very kind of you.

SWANSON: Not at all. (*Apologetically.*) As a matter of fact, I'm not much good as a comforter on these occasions. I get so damned nervous myself.

PETER (*making conversation*): You're not flying to-night yourself?

SWANSON: Good Lord—I don't fly. Look. Nothing up here. (*He flicks his breast.*) Just an old wingless wonder. Adjutant. Combination nurse and maid of all work to the Squadron. No business in the Air Force at all, really. Ought to be in the Army, like I was in the last war. (*He is piling up cushions to form a pillow.*) My bed for to-night.

PETER: My God! It isn't *your* room I've taken, is it?

SWANSON: Lord, no. I sleep up at the station as a rule. But when the boys are out on a job I like to be up when they come in, and I can't trust that damn fool of a batman to wake me.   It's warmer down here, too.

PATRICIA: Let me help.

SWANSON: Oh, please don't bother.

PATRICIA: It's not an awfully good fire.

SWANSON: It'll burn up.   Teddy calls me Gloria, you know. No respect for senior rank.   Shocking.

PETER: Mrs. Graham.   Are you going to take the Squadron Leader's advice, or are you going to wait up?   If you are, I'd be very happy to——

PATRICIA: I'll go to bed.   I think it's better.

PETER: I see.   Well, good night.

PATRICIA: Good night.

PETER (on the stairs): Good night, sir.

SWANSON, who has been blowing away at the fire, straightens himself.

SWANSON: What's that?   Oh, are you off to bed?   Good night. Oh, I say.

PETER: Yes?

SWANSON: Have you met Alice Faye?

PETER: Yes.   Once.

SWANSON: Good Lord!   (He returns to the fire.)

PETER: Good night, Mrs. Graham.

PATRICIA: Good night, Mr. Kyle.

PETER goes out.

PATRICIA is still kneeling beside SWANSON, who is puffing away at the fire without effect.

PATRICIA: You'll never get it to go like that.   Here, let me. (She takes a sheet of newspaper and uses it to draw the fire.)

SWANSON: Takes a woman to think of that.   (He looks at his watch.   Pause.)

PATRICIA: You're very fond of Teddy—Squadron Leader?

SWANSON: Who isn't?   Look out.   That'll burn.   (He pulls the paper away.   The fire is glowing.)

PATRICIA: Who isn't?

SWANSON: Of course, I'm fond of 'em all, if it comes to that, but I don't know the others as well as I know old P O Prune.   We call him that, you know.

PATRICIA: Yes, he told me.

SWANSON: He's not quite so prunish as he lets on. I've seen him sometimes—— (*He breaks off.*) Dammit, you're his wife. You must know him better than I do.

PATRICIA: Yes, of course.

SWANSON: I hate all this patriotic bilge in the newspapers, but, my God, we do owe these boys something you know.

PATRICIA: Yes.

SWANSON: It's going pretty well now. Thank you. (*He stands up.*) You've been married a year or so now, haven't you?

PATRICIA: Just under a year.

SWANSON: He's damned lucky, if I may say so. I was scared stiff when I heard he'd married an actress. He's the type who might have fallen for some awful bottle-party floosie who'd have let him down with a wallop. (*He fumbles in his pocket and produces a slip of paper.*) Oh, by the way, I knew I had something to show you. Some joker put this in the Mess Suggestion Book. I copied it out. Thought it might amuse you. (*He hands it to her.*) Read it out.

PATRICIA (*reading*): Suggested that Flight Lieutenant Graham shall in future be permitted to mention his wife's name not more than ten times per diem; and that on each subsequent mention of the said wife's said name—to wit, Patricia, or Pat, Paddy, Paddykins, and other such nauseating diminutives—over and above the allotted ten times per diem, Flight Lieutenant Graham shall forfeit to all officers within hearing a pint of beer. (*She finishes reading.* SWANSON *chuckles delightedly.* PATRICIA *continues staring at the slip of paper.*)

SWANSON: You see. Practically everyone in the mess has signed it—even little Tinker Bell, the Signals Officer—who dies of fright if you speak to him.

    PATRICIA *hands it back.*

SWANSON: Go on, keep it. I thought it might be fun for you to have—with all the names on it——

    An aircraft's engines can be heard. SWANSON *turns abruptly to the window.*

Turn off the light.

    PATRICIA *turns out the lights.* SWANSON *pulls back the curtains, allowing the moonlight to illumine the room.* PATRICIA *joins him at the window.*

There's the flare path—do you see? Those little points of light. There's one taking off now.

    The noise of the aircraft's engines increases.

They're making their run from the far side of the field, across this way.   There's one off, thank God!

The noise passes directly overhead and fades.

It's a hellish tricky business, taking off on a night like this, with no wind and a full load of bombs. Hellish tricky. Worse than landing.   Here's the next just starting his run.

PATRICIA: Which is Teddy's?

SWANSON: Can't tell.   They don't take off in any particular order.   There are only four aircraft flying to-night—A Apple, L London, U Uncle—that's Teddy—and S Sugar from the Polish Squadron.   (*Sharply.*)   God!

PATRICIA: What's the matter?

SWANSON: It's all right.   He's off.   I thought he wasn't going to make it.   He must have cleared that fence by inches.

The noise passes overhead and fades.

Next one's coming up. (*Sharply.*) Hullo! What's that? The first one seems to be circling round up there.   Can you hear him?

PATRICIA: No.   Do you think it might be a German?

SWANSON: I hope to God it's not.   There is one circling round up there.   Ah, there he goes, the next one—do you see?   You can just pick him up.   That dark shape.

PATRICIA (*in alarm*): His engines are on fire.

SWANSON (*laughing*): No.   That's the exhaust.   It always looks like that.   You can see it miles away.   Useful to night fighters. Good boy!   Nice take-off.   One more to go.   (*He listens intently again.*)   Ah, here he comes.   Here's the last one starting his run. See him?

PATRICIA: Yes, I see him.

SWANSON: God!

PATRICIA (*almost simultaneously*): Why have they turned out the flares?

There is a sudden rattle of machine-gun fire, followed by three loud but dull-sounding explosions.

They're bombing the aerodrome.   It was a German.

SWANSON (*shouting*): Brakes, you idiot, brakes!   Don't take off.

There is another rattle of machine-gun fire, followed by another explosion, sharper than the bomb bursts and with a tearing, rending sound, following it.   PATRICIA stifles a scream.   A dull red glow appears at the window.   SWANSON pulls the curtains to violently.

(*Quietly.*)   Put the lights on.

PATRICIA (*in a panic*): I can't find the switch. I can't find the switch. I can't——

DORIS (*in matter-of-fact tones*): It's on the left of the door, by the hall.

> *The room is suddenly flooded with light.* PATRICIA *is standing by the switch.* DORIS *is at the foot of the stairs, fully dressed. She is standing quite still.*
>
> SWANSON *goes over to telephone and lifts receiver.*

SWANSON: Milchester 23.

> PETER *appears in a dressing-gown. He runs downstairs.*

PETER: What happened?

SWANSON: An aircraft crashed or was shot down, taking off.

> PETER *walks across to* PATRICIA *and takes her hand.* MAUDIE *has come down the stairs behind him in time to hear* SWANSON'S *last line.*

MAUDIE: It's not Dave, is it?

DORIS: We don't know who it is, dear. The Squadron Leader's finding out for us. (*She puts an arm round* MAUDIE.)

SWANSON (*at telephone*): Hullo. Put me through to Controller— Squadron Leader Swanson . . . Hullo, Manning! Swanson here . . . Yes, I saw it. What happened? . . . No, no, of course not, but at least you know which aircraft it was . . . Yes . . . I see . . . All right. (*He rings off and turns round.*) The crashed aircraft is A Apple.

MAUDIE: Dave.

DORIS: No, dear. We're all right.

SWANSON: L London, U Uncle—that's Teddy's—and S Sugar are all airborne, and are now on their way——

> *There is a pause. Nobody moves.* SWANSON *turns abruptly and goes out.*

CURTAIN

NOTE: *While the curtain is lowered, denoting the passing of time, the sound of an aircraft's engines in flight continues to be audible until some seconds after the raising of the curtain on Scene II.*

ACT II

SCENE II

SCENE: *The same, about five-thirty the following morning.*

The sound of an aircraft's engines can be heard. SWANSON *and* DORIS *are at the window, outlined against the faint light of early dawn. The sound of the engines ceases as they are throttled back.*

SWANSON (*at length*): He's down all right.

DORIS: It's Johnny's, I'm almost sure. I recognised the engines.

SWANSON: That's absurd, my dear Countess, if you don't mind my saying so. All Wellingtons sound alike.

DORIS: Not to me they don't.

PATRICIA *appears on the stairs.*

PATRICIA: Is that one of them back?

SWANSON: Morning, Mrs. Graham. Yes, it's the second to come in. The first one landed about twenty minutes ago.

PATRICIA: I must have been asleep. Are either of them Teddy's?

SWANSON: Don't know yet. Don't like to keep on ringing Ops.

DORIS (*cheerfully*): We'll know soon enough, anyway.

MRS. OAKES *comes out of the coffee-room with a loaded tray. She is in a rather elaborate deshabille.*

MRS. OAKES: May I have the curtains drawn please? I want to switch on the lights.

SWANSON: It's still black-out, I suppose.

He pulls the curtains to, blacking out the room. DORIS *switches on the lights.*

MRS. OAKES: It's black-out until five fifty-two. Will you give me a hand with this table?

SWANSON: Of course. What's the time now?

MRS. OAKES: Just gone half-past. I thought I'd lay a table in here. It's warmer with that fire. (*She puts the tray on a table. Acidly.*) I must say I can't quite understand how it has kept in all this time. I usually have to relight it.

SWANSON (*embarrassed*): Well, as a matter of fact——

MRS. OAKES: Quite, Squadron Leader. I see. (*To* PATRICIA.)

Shall I lay a place for you, Mrs. Graham? I expect you'll want to have breakfast with your husband, won't you—now that you're up?

PATRICIA: I won't want much to eat.

MRS. OAKES: There isn't much to eat. Now let me see—Flight Lieutenant Graham, Flying Officer Count Skriczevinsky, Sergeant Miller—that'll be five with you, Countess, I'm afraid I can't provide for casuals like you, Squadron Leader.

SWANSON: That's all right. I'm going home, anyway, as soon as they come.

MRS. OAKES: I won't wake Mrs. Miller up. I peeped into her room as I came past, and she was sound asleep. (*She is laying the table.*)

PATRICIA: Can I help you?

MRS. OAKES: No, thank you, Mrs. Graham. I can manage very well.

PATRICIA: Do you always do this yourself?

MRS. OAKES: Well, I haven't got five hundred servants, Mrs. Graham, and the ones I have got wouldn't stay long if I made them work at this time in the morning. (*She elbows* PATRICIA *out of the way and goes out into the coffee-room.*)

PATRICIA: There's one more to come in yet, isn't there?

DORIS: Yes, ducky.

PATRICIA *looks down at the neatly-laid table.*

PATRICIA: Five places! How horribly smug and complacent it looks.

DORIS (*soothingly*): After flying all night they've got to have something to eat when they come back.

PATRICIA: Supposing they don't come back?

Pause.

DORIS: Poor dearie. This is the first time you've been here for a do, isn't it?

PATRICIA: A do. Oh, God, how I hate all this polite Air Force understatement. Isn't there a more dignified word for it than a do?

SWANSON: Come and sit over here, Mrs. Graham. Quite a good fire, you know—thanks to me.

PATRICIA *looks from* DORIS *to* SWANSON.

PATRICIA: I think I will. (*She sits down by the fire.*) I'm sorry. I didn't sleep much. (*She looks up at* DORIS, *who is fully dressed.*) You didn't sleep at all—either of you.

DORIS: Oh, I went off now and then. Didn't I, Squadron Leader?

SWANSON: You snored once.

DORIS: Oh, I didn't. You fibber! (*She giggles.*) I'm sure I don't know what Johnny would say—the Squadron Leader and me down here together all night and no chaperon.

SWANSON: Probably challenge me to a duel or something. Rapiers at dawn behind the Admin. Block.

DORIS: Serve you right for smirching my honour. Snored! I never snored in my life.

PATRICIA (*staring at* DORIS): I wish I understood. (*She stops.*) You're very brave.

> *There is the sound of a car in the road outside.* DORIS, PATRICIA *and* SWANSON *all rise abruptly and face the front door. The car draws up outside the hotel. A door bangs and the car moves on. There is a pause. Then* DUSTY *enters. He wears Air Force battle-dress and a high-necked jumper.*

DUSTY: Morning all.

PATRICIA (*quickly*): Teddy——?

DUSTY: Putting the car away, Mum. (*Seeing the fire.*) Cor! Give me a piece of that. (*He walks to the fire, passing* SWANSON *on the way.*) Morning, sir.

SWANSON: Morning, Sergeant. Good trip?

DUSTY (*gloomily*): Proper muck-up from beginning to end.

DORIS: S Sugar back yet?

DUSTY: Not yet, Countess.

SWANSON: You and L London are back, then. You were the first to land, I suppose?

DUSTY: Yes, sir. About half an hour ago. (*Exclamatorily.*) What about A Apple? Shook us considerable, that did.

SWANSON: You saw the crash?

DUSTY: Yes, I was in the tail, you see, sir. I called up the skipper and we circled round her for a bit. Cor! what a blaze. Nobody got out, did they, sir?

SWANSON (*shortly*): One man was thrown clear. The navigator.

DUSTY: Old Ginger Walsh, that is. Good old Ginger! Is he hurt bad?

SWANSON: They think he'll recover.

DUSTY: I'll trot along and see him to-morrow. How's the wife been behaving herself, Countess? O.K.?

DORIS: O.K., Dusty. She went up to bed early, and she's still asleep.

DUSTY: This fire don't half feel good on my behind.

TEDDY *enters. His wrist has been bound up with a handkerchief. He is similarly dressed to* DUSTY.

SWANSON: Hullo, Prune. Trust you to get down first. What did you do—drop your bombs on Bognor and dash for home?

TEDDY: That's about it—only it wasn't Bognor, it was Little-hampton—wasn't it, Sarge?

DUSTY: That's right, sir. All our bombs fell in the target area.

TEDDY (*turns to* PATRICIA): Hullo, darling.

PATRICIA: Hullo, Teddy.

TEDDY: You shouldn't have got up.

SWANSON: What have you done to your wrist, Teddy?

TEDDY: What? Oh, that. It's nothing at all. It got into the way of a flame float I was throwing out.

SWANSON: Let's have a look. (*He undoes the handkerchief*). You ought to have it seen to.

TEDDY (*crosses to fire*): I'll take it along to the M.O. to-morrow. Hullo, Doris.

DORIS: Hullo, Ted.

SWANSON: What sort of a trip did you have? Sergeant's just said it was a proper muck-up.

TEDDY: He's prejudiced. I wouldn't let him shoot up a train he'd taken a dislike to.

DUSTY: It looked so blooming pleased with itself, puffing along down there.

TEDDY: Wonderful moon. You could see everything. Not even our navigator could go wrong.

SWANSON: Any incidents?

TEDDY: Turned intelligence officer on me, have you, Gloria?

SWANSON: If you don't want to tell me——

TEDDY: No incidents, Gloria, if you exclude the fact that we had half our tail-plane shot away.

DUSTY: Wallowing about we were, coming home, like a fat old woman learning to swim. Fair turned me stomach.

TEDDY: Catted—did you, Dusty?

DUSTY: Wasn't so bad for you, sir, up front.

TEDDY: It's never so bad for the driver, they say.

MRS. OAKES *comes in with a loaded tray.*

MRS. OAKES (*politely*): Good morning, gentlemen.

TEDDY: Morning, Mrs. Oakes. What have you got there for us? (*He lifts the cover off the dish. Joyfully.*) Eggs and bacon!

MRS. OAKES: I'd be glad if you wouldn't shout it to the entire hotel. I'm infringing regulations.

TEDDY: Mrs. Oakes, I could kiss you from head to foot.

MRS. OAKES: I trust you'll do nothing of the sort.

TEDDY: Eggs, Dusty. Eggs! You know what eggs are, don't you, or have you forgotten?

DUSTY: You mean those round things that used to come out of hens in peace time?

TEDDY: That's right. Come and sit down, Pat. I could eat a house. I could eat you, Mrs. Oakes.

DORIS (*sharply*): Sh! Quiet! (*She listens intently.*) Sorry. Thought I heard a Wimpey.

MRS. OAKES: Is the Count not in yet?

DORIS: No, not yet. I think if you don't mind, duckies, I'll go up to my room. I can hear better from up there. (*She goes up the stairs. An uncomfortable silence has fallen on the room. From the landing.*) Save Johnny and me one of those eggs, won't you, dear?

TEDDY: You bet.

DORIS *goes out.*

SWANSON: Any news of S Sugar?

TEDDY: No. They're worried at Ops. They were over the target twelve minutes before us—but they've heard nothing from them since.

Pause.

MRS. OAKES: I'll put this over here, by the fire. . . . If he comes in very late, knock on my door and I'll come down and make him some more. (*She puts a covered dish by the fire—she goes up the stairs.*)

TEDDY: As usual, I can't thank you enough.

MRS. OAKES: Don't be ridiculous. I dare say some people would be glad to have the chance of doing it. I'm going to bed now. Good morning.

TEDDY: Good morning, Mrs. Oakes.

MRS. OAKES *goes out.*

SWANSON: Me for bed, too. Good show, Prune. Glad to see you back. Good night.

TEDDY: Good night, Gloria. (*Severely.*) I take an extremely poor view of your waiting up like this. Don't let it occur again.

SWANSON: God, you don't think I waited up for you, do you? Keeping the women company, that's all.

TEDDY: Then you're a dirty old man.

SWANSON (*to* PATRICIA): What did I tell you? No respect. Shocking. (*He goes out.*)

TEDDY: Come and sit down, boys and girls.

PATRICIA *sits between* TEDDY *and* DUSTY.

Did you see the take-off?

PATRICIA: Yes.

TEDDY: That crash was a bit of bad luck. It doesn't happen very often, you know. Plate, darling?

PATRICIA: I don't want anything to eat, thanks awfully.

TEDDY: On the level?

PATRICIA: On the level. I couldn't, really.

TEDDY: All the more for us, eh, Dusty?

DUSTY: Well, sir, between you and me, I don't feel any too peckish myself.

TEDDY (*quickly*): Anything wrong?

DUSTY: No, sir. Just that ride home. Cor, I still feel it down in the old darby kel. If you don't mind, sir, I think I'll go up and have a bit of shut-eye.

TEDDY: Poor old Dusty! I'm awfully sorry. I *did* try and keep her steady, you know, but——

DUSTY (*strenuously*): Cor, stuff me! Going to say it's your fault now, I suppose?

TEDDY: Well, it is, in a way.

DUSTY: Cor, stone me up an apple. (*To* PATRICIA.) Isn't a skipper in the world would've brought us 'ome safe to-night, bar 'im, and he goes and apologises for giving me stummick trouble. Cor, stuff me sideways, what a man?

TEDDY: Good night, Dusty.

DUSTY: Good night, sir. (DUSTY *goes out.*)

TEDDY *is standing at the foot of the stairs.* PATRICIA *is still sitting at the table, her back to him.*

TEDDY (*murmuring*): Good old Dusty! Don't you like old Dusty, darling?

PATRICIA: Yes, Teddy. Very much.

TEDDY: Darling!

PATRICIA: Yes, Teddy?

TEDDY: I said, didn't you like old Dusty?

PATRICIA: Yes, I said I did very much.

TEDDY: Did you? Darling——

PATRICIA: Yes?

TEDDY: Where are you?

    PATRICIA *turns her head sharply and looks at him for the first time.*

PATRICIA: Here, Teddy.

TEDDY: Where? I can't see. Pat, come here. I want you.

PATRICIA: I'm here, Teddy. (*She kneels down beside him and tries to support him.*) I'm here, beside you. (*She looks round for help.*) Oh, God!

TEDDY: It's funny. I couldn't see you. I don't think I feel very well. It's nothing. Just a bit tired, that's all. (*He fumbles at his breast pocket and pulls out a flask. He tries to open it, but fails.* PATRICIA *takes it from him. It twists sideways.*)

    PATRICIA *opens it. He tries to take the flask from her, but she restrains him. She holds it while he drinks. He coughs and splutters.*

TEDDY: Cherry brandy. Filthy stuff. Keeps you warm, though. (*He shakes his head.*) What are we doing—kneeling down? We look as if we were praying or something. (*He struggles to his feet, supported by* PATRICIA.) God, what an exhibition! I'm sorry.

PATRICIA: Do you feel well enough to go up to bed?

TEDDY: I feel well enough, but I'm not going to. With eggs and bacon on the old menu—what an idea?

PATRICIA: You're ill. You're not just tired. You're ill. I'm going to ring up a doctor.

TEDDY: I'll murder you if you do. Come on. (*He crosses to the table—his hands are still shaking.*) You watch me make a pig of myself. (*He picks up a knife and fork. Then he suddenly puts them down with a clatter and pushes the dish away.*) No good.

PATRICIA *walks towards telephone.*

    What are you doing?

PATRICIA: I'm going to get a doctor.

TEDDY: No, you don't. (*He grasps her hand.*)

PATRICIA: I'm sorry, Teddy. I must. (*She shakes her hand free and walks towards the telephone.*)

TEDDY (*imploringly*): Don't, Pat, please.

PATRICIA: It's much better, Teddy. (*She lifts the receiver.*) Hullo . . . hullo . . .

TEDDY (*in a hard voice*): Do you want to get me chucked out of the Air Force.

PATRICIA: What do you mean?

TEDDY: Put that receiver down.

    PATRICIA *replaces receiver.*

Come here.

PATRICIA *walks slowly up to him. He puts his hand on her shoulder.*
They always say a man should have no secrets from his wife, don't
they?

PATRICIA: Yes.   Tell me.

TEDDY: All right.   Do you know what's the matter with me?
Funk.   Just ordinary, common or garden, plain bloody funk.

PATRICIA: Don't be absurd.

TEDDY: If a doctor examined me now, his diag—whatever it is—
would be simply this.   Here's a bloke who doesn't like flying.

PATRICIA (*stares at him, then smiles*): What about this? (*She
touches his D.F.C. ribbon.*)

TEDDY: The doctor would say to himself—bloke's got the D.F.C.
Must have been all right once.   Then he'd ask me—how many
ops. have you done, my lad?   Seventeen, sir.   Doc says to himself
—bloke packs up after only seventeen trips, eh?   Just couldn't take
it, I suppose.

PATRICIA: Don't talk like that, Teddy.   It's sheer nonsense.   The
doctor would say—this man's ill.   Probably nothing to do with
flying at all.   He ought to have a rest.

TEDDY (*bitterly*): A rest?

PATRICIA: What's wrong with that?

TEDDY: There's nothing wrong with it.   It's very nice—for
some people.   Ground job.   Promotion probably.   I'd have a fine
time as a Squadron Leader admin. at a training school—flaunting
a D.F.C. and shooting a line with the pupils.   The only thing is,
some of the pupils might wonder why I'd only done seventeen trips
before being grounded, and a few of them might guess.

PATRICIA: In a case like this nobody would dare say a thing.

TEDDY: Only my friends.   They'd say: Oh, yes—Teddy Graham
—not a bad bloke.   Didn't like flying, that's all.   And on my
confidential report they'd put—grounded.   Lack of moral fibre.
That's the official phrase for—no guts.

PATRICIA (*angrily*): Listen, Teddy.   There's no sense in all this.
If you're too ill to fly——

TEDDY: I'm not too ill to fly.   I fly all right.   You heard what
Dusty said.

PATRICIA: Yes, but it may not always be like that.

TEDDY: It will always be like that.

PATRICIA: What about your crew?   Is it fair to them?

TEDDY (*clenching his fists*): What's fair on my crew is my business.

PATRICIA: It's their lives you're risking as well as yours.

TEDDY: I'm their captain. Their captain. I wouldn't risk their lives.

PATRICIA: You are.

TEDDY: Don't, Pat, don't. You don't know—I can't bear it——

PATRICIA: I'm sorry, Teddy. (*She puts her hand on his arm. He falls at her feet. He lays his head on her lap and sobs.*)

PATRICIA: Oh, my dear, my dear.

TEDDY (*his voice muffled by sobs*): A bloody Messerschmitt put a cannon shell in our tail-plane—we went straight down in a dive— I heard Dusty on the intercomm. He said—I thought I'd bought it, Skipper, but I'm all right—we were in a vertical dive and I couldn't pull out—I couldn't pull out, and Dusty said he was all right. (*He is shaken by a further outburst of sobbing.* PATRICIA *strokes his head, saying nothing.*) All the way back I had to fight to keep her on course—every one of them must have known it was odds against our getting home—but they trusted me—they trusted me—I heard the wireless op.—say to the navigator—he's only just come on the crew—he said—don't worry, windy. Skipper'll get us home. Oh, my God! Skipper'll get us home. . . .

PATRICIA: You got them home.

TEDDY: You don't know what it's like to feel frightened. You get a beastly, bitter taste in the mouth, and your tongue goes dry and you feel sick, and all the time you're saying—This isn't happening—it can't be happening—I'll wake up. But you know you won't wake up. You know it is happening, and the sea's below you, and you're responsible for the lives of six people. And you have to pretend you're not afraid, that's what's so awful. Oh, God, I was afraid to-night. When we took off and saw that kite on fire, I didn't think: There are friends of mine in that. I thought (*slowly*): That might happen to us. Not very—pretty, is it? (*He recovers himself slowly,* PATRICIA *watching him in silence. Then he turns away from her.*)

TEDDY: Now you know it. Lack of moral fibre. I'm glad I told you.

PATRICIA: I'm glad, too.

TEDDY: Lend me a handkerchief.

    PATRICIA *gives him one from her pocket.* TEDDY *takes it, turns his back on her, and wipes his eyes. Sits on the sofa.*

God, what you must think of me!

PATRICIA (*sits next to him*): Teddy, look at me.

> *He turns reluctantly to face her.*

Why didn't you tell me all this before?

TEDDY: I didn't want you to know you'd married a twirp.

PATRICIA: You damned little fool! (*She snatches the handkerchief back from him.*)

TEDDY: Now, don't *you* start. One exhibition's enough for to-night.

PATRICIA (*fiercely*): I'm all right.

TEDDY: Thank God I've had the courage to tell you. I couldn't tell anyone else in the world. I couldn't. But you help me, you see, so much.

PATRICIA (*angrily*): I don't help you at all. I've never tried to. How could I, when you keep these things from me?

TEDDY: You do help me—just by being—well—you—and, incidentally, by being my wife. It was you who got us home to-night. Not me.

PATRICIA (*desperately*): That's not true, Teddy. You're just saying that because you think I like to hear it. But it's not true.

TEDDY: Try leaving me and see what happens. (*Pause.*) I admit you've got every reason to now. You must think you've got married under false pretences.

PATRICIA (*quietly*): No. I don't think that.

TEDDY: Thank you, Pat. (*Pause.*)

PATRICIA (*gently*): I still think you should see a doctor. Someone who'll understand and try and help you.

TEDDY: I don't need any help. Except yours. I do need that.

PATRICIA (*after a pause*): Why go on with it, Teddy? You've done your share. More than your share.

TEDDY (*slowly*): I have got quite a few more trips to do before I get given a rest.

PATRICIA: But there's no magic in any particular number. It may be more for some and less for others.

TEDDY: It may be more for me. It's not going to be less. We've got to win this war somehow, you know. God, how *Daily Mail*! I'm glad nobody heard it but you. (*He gets up.*) You know, I feel better now than I've felt for months. I feel almost well enough to cope with Mrs. Oakes' bacon and eggs. (*He raises cover and looks.*) No. I spoke too soon.

PATRICIA (*dully*): They must be cold by now.

TEDDY: They are. I say, darling.

PATRICIA: Yes?

TEDDY: Poor old Mrs. Oakes is going to be rather upset when she comes down in the morning and finds her precious eggs haven't been touched. (*He brings the dish over to her.*) I'd hate to hurt the old thing's feelings. (*He looks round.*) I know. The coal shovel. (*He is staring at the dish by the fire.*) I'd forgotten about old Johnny. (*He looks at his watch.*) If anything has happened to him, be kind to old Doris, won't you? I'm not much good at saying the right things on these occasions. We'd better leave it there, just in case. (*He takes the shovel from* PATRICIA.) I won't be long. I'm just going to have a look at the garden. (*He goes out with the shovel and the covered dish.* PATRICIA *sits, without moving, her chin resting on her hands.* PETER *comes down the stairs in a dressing-gown.*)

PETER: I heard his voice. He got back all right, then?

PATRICIA: Yes.

PETER: I'm glad. Poor Pat! You must have had a rough night. (*He takes her hand. She withdraws it sharply. He stares at her, surprised. She stands up. There is a pause. Then* TEDDY *comes in with the dish in his hands.*)

TEDDY: Hullo!

PETER: Hullo! I'm glad to see you back.

TEDDY: Thanks.

PETER (*indicating dish*): What are you doing with that?

TEDDY: I've been burying six fried eggs and twelve rashers of bacon in a flower-bed. Crazy type, you see, old Graham. By the way, it's broad daylight. Look. (*He pulls back the window curtains, admitting the morning sun.*) Come on, darling. Time we were in bed. (*He takes her hand and leads her up the stairs.* PETER *watches them from below.*)

CURTAIN

END OF ACT II

●

230

ACT III

SCENE: *The same, about twelve noon the same morning.*

DORIS is on the window-seat, a Sunday paper on her lap, gazing out of the window. PERCY comes in from the lounge.

PERCY: Twelve o'clock, Countess. Bar's open.

DORIS (*abstractedly*): What? Oh, thank you, Percy.

PERCY: Fun and games last night, eh? That Wiggy Jones. He's a one, eh? That song: I don't want to join the Air Force. That's a song, eh? Been trying to remember it all morning.

DORIS: You'd better forget it, Percy. It's not a song for little boys.

PERCY: Garn with your little boys! Bit of a do up at the aerodrome last night, eh? Did you 'ear 'bout it? One got shot down taking off.

DORIS: I saw it.

PERCY: Did you? Coo, wish I 'ad. Saw the wreckage this morning, though. Burnt right out, it was. 'Orrible! (*In a confidential whisper.*) Where was it last night, do you know?

DORIS: Eight o'clock news said it was the Rhineland.

PERCY: Rhineland, eh? It was Rhineland last time they went. I knew something was up when they didn't come down to dinner. Flight Lieutenant Graham, 'e tried to fox me. Nothing on to-night, Percy, 'e said. 'Ome, sweet 'ome to-night. I knew 'e was keeping something up 'is sleeve. Count went too, didn't 'e?

DORIS: Yes. He went.

PERCY: 'Ow is 'e this morning? All right?

DORIS: He hasn't come back yet.

There is a pause. PERCY stares at her unbelievingly.

PERCY: Not come back?

DORIS: Of course, they may have force-landed somewhere.

PERCY: That's what's 'appened, you mark my words. Count's not one to get 'imself shot down by those dirty 'uns.

DORIS: I'm afraid though, Percy, if they had force-landed, they'd have let Milchester know.

There is another pause.

PERCY: Coo, I'm sorry, Countess.

DORIS: That's all right, Percy.

PERCY: I seen 'em go off night after night, and they always got back. Never thought they wouldn't, some'ow. Course you'd 'ear it on the wireless: "Some of our aircraft failed to return." Never thought it'd 'appen to us, though. Coo! Makes yer think, don't it? (*He stands uncertainly at the door.*) Anything I can get you, Countess? Gin and lime or anything?

DORIS: No, thanks.

PERCY: I'll see it's on the 'ouse.

DORIS: No, Percy. Ta, all the same.

    MRS. OAKES *comes in from the coffee-room.* PERCY, *seeing her, darts out into the lounge.*

MRS. OAKES: Any news, Countess?

DORIS: No, not yet. The Squadron Leader is going to let me know as soon as he hears anything.

MRS. OAKES: I expect he'll come back all right. Do you feel it cold in here, Countess? Would you like a fire?

DORIS: No, thanks. It's a lovely day, really. Like summer.

    PETER *comes in through the front door.*

MRS. OAKES: I saw you admiring our garden, Mr. Kyle. How do you like it?

PETER (*perfunctorily*): Very much. Is Mrs. Graham still not down?

MRS. OAKES: I don't think so. I haven't seen her.

PETER: But it's nearly lunch-time.

MRS. OAKES: Just gone twelve.

PETER: I suppose you couldn't—— (*He stops.*)

MRS. OAKES: Couldn't what, Mr. Kyle?

PETER: It doesn't matter. I'll wait. (*He sits down.*)

    MRS. OAKES *goes to the door of her office.*
(*Brusquely.*) Get me a whisky and soda, please.

MRS. OAKES: That's hardly my province. (*She goes to lounge door. Calling.*) Percy!

PERCY (*appearing at lounge door*): Yes, mum?

MRS. OAKES: A whisky and soda for Mr. Kyle.

PERCY: Yes, mum. There's no whisky, mum.

MRS. OAKES (*to* PETER): There's no whisky.

PETER: Is there any brandy?

MRS. OAKES (*to* PERCY): Is there any brandy?

PERCY: Yes, mum.

PETER: Brandy and soda, then.

MRS. OAKES: Brandy and soda, Percy.

PERCY: Yes, mum.

> PERCY's *head disappears.*
>
> MRS. OAKES *walks to the door of her office.*

MRS. OAKES: The next time you're requiring a drink, will you be good enough to press the bell marked "Waiter"?

> PETER *does not answer.*
>
> MRS. OAKES *goes out.*
>
> PETER *is engaged in reading some pencilled sheets of paper, which look as if they had been torn from a pocket-book.* PERCY *comes in with a brandy and soda.*

PERCY: Brandy and soda, sir. Two and ten.

PETER (*looking up*): What? Oh, all right. (*He throws two coins on to the tray with a clatter.*) Keep the change.

PERCY: Thank you, sir. Thank you. (*He goes up to* DORIS *and puts something into her hand.*)

PERCY: Countess.

DORIS: What's this, Percy?

PERCY: Bele. An Indian god. Bought 'im at a fair. You hold 'im in your right 'and, and whatever you wish comes true.

DORIS: Oh. (*She puts it in her right hand, holds it a second and returns it to him.*) Thanks, Percy.

PERCY: No. You keep 'im. It don't work if it's not yours.

DORIS: Don't you want him?

PERCY: No. You keep him. Just been thinking. Count might 'ave baled out over the other side, then 'e'd be a prisoner of war.

DORIS: I'd rather anything than that.

PERCY: Why? It's not so bad.

DORIS: The Germans don't treat Poles as prisoners of war.

PERCY (*after a pause*): Cor! They're proper swine, aren't they?

> PERCY *goes out.*
>
> PETER *stuffs the sheets of paper into his pocket and stands up. He looks up at the stairs, and then impatiently at his watch. He appears suddenly to notice* DORIS *for the first time. He clears his throat.*

PETER: I heard about your husband from Mrs. Oakes. I'm most terribly sorry——

DORIS: Thank you, Mr. Kyle, but I've not given up yet. What I always say is, while there's life there's—hope.

> SWANSON *has come in quickly, and* DORIS *speaks the last word looking straight at him over* PETER's *shoulder. Her voice falters.* PETER *turns round.*

SWANSON: Morning, Kyle.   Do you mind if I see the Countess alone for a moment?

PETER: No.   Not at all.   (*He goes to lounge door.*)   If Mrs. Graham comes down will you tell her that I want to see her—most urgently. It's very important.

SWANSON: Right.   I'll tell her.

   PETER *goes into lounge.*

   SWANSON *does not look at* DORIS, *who has not taken her eyes off his face.*

DORIS (*at length*): Come on, dear.   Tell us.

SWANSON: Well, I'm afraid it may be rather a shock——

DORIS: That's all right.   I've had the shock.   Tell us.

SWANSON: Your husband's aircraft did send out a signal this morning, at approximately 04.25.   It said simply: Am force-landing on the sea.   Then they sent out call signs for about ten minutes, and the D.F. stations got a pretty accurate fix on them.   Then nothing more was heard.   Since daylight this morning aircraft and power boats—the Air Sea Rescue chaps—have been out looking for them, and about half an hour ago they signalled us that the wreckage of a Wellington bomber had been found—within three miles of the spot fixed by the D.F. people.   So I'm afraid it looks—— (*He stops.*)   They're continuing the search: they had a rubber dinghy on board, and it's just possible they might have been picked up by some vessel which hadn't a wireless or any way of letting us know.

   DORIS *shakes her head.*

DORIS: It's better not to think of loopholes.   I'm quite ready to face it.   Johnny's dead.

SWANSON (*automatically*): You're very brave.

DORIS: That's the second time that's been said to me since last night.   It isn't true.   I'm just—ready, that's all.

   PATRICIA *comes down the stairs.*

Thanks for taking all this trouble, Squadron Leader.   I know what a bind it must be, breaking bad news to people.

   She turns towards the stairs and come face to face with PATRICIA. Hullo, ducks.

PATRICIA: I overheard what you said.   Is it—Johnny?

DORIS: Yes, dear.   They found bits of poor old S Sugar floating in the drink.   It looks as if he's bought it all right.

PATRICIA: I'm terribly sorry——

DORIS: I know you are.

PATRICIA: Is there anything I can do.

DORIS: No, dear. Thanks all the same.

DORIS *goes up the stairs and out.*

PATRICIA: Isn't it awful how hopelessly inadequate the ordinary social phrases are at a moment like this? (*Bitterly.*) I'm terribly sorry.

SWANSON: That's all one can say, I think.

PATRICIA: Is there no hope?

SWANSON: Officially, yes. Unofficially—— (*He shakes his head.*) She prefers to take the unofficial view, and I dare say it's better she should. (*Pause.*) Well, I must be going. Sunday papers haven't come, and I've volunteered to go down to the village to collect them.

PATRICIA: Is there a chemist in the village that's open on Sunday?

SWANSON: We can beat one up for you, if you like—why?

PATRICIA: I want to get some stuff for Teddy's wrist. Are you driving in? Will you give me a lift?

SWANSON: Yes, but do you mind waiting five minutes? I've got to dash up to the station first.

PATRICIA: That's all right. Whenever you're going.

SWANSON: I'll get cracking. (*At door.*) How is his wrist?

PATRICIA: Oh, it's all right, but it looks as if he might have got some dirt in it.

SWANSON: How is he apart from that this morning?

PATRICIA: A bit tired, I think. They had rather a shaky do last night.

SWANSON: Shaky do? Learning the old vernacular, eh? Well, I'll dash. Oh, by the way, Kyle's waiting for you in there. (*He points to the lounge.*) Says it's most important.

PATRICIA: Oh, thank you.

SWANSON: Won't keep you long.

SWANSON *goes out.*

PATRICIA *looks, undecided, at the lounge door. Then she turns quickly to go back upstairs. The lounge door opens and* PETER *comes out.* PATRICIA, *half-way up the stairs, turns slowly.*

PATRICIA: Peter—please—I don't want to see you. I told you——

PETER: You're going to see me.

PATRICIA: Not now. I'll come up to London. I'll see you there. I'll explain——

PETER: Explain what?

PATRICIA *slowly nods towards the letter in his hand.*

Five little bits of paper dumped on my bed with my morning tea, and you expected me to jump on the first train up to London and fade quietly out of your life muttering, "It's a far, far better thing" —— (*Bitterly.*) Who's living in a film world, you or me?

PATRICIA: I was coming to see you in London. I had to write it down because it helped me to think. I couldn't have said it. I can't say it now. I'm sorry I wrote it though. Pete, it wasn't awfully brave.

PETER: You really want me to take this letter seriously?

PATRICIA: Yes, Pete.

PETER: This is how seriously I take it. (*He tears the letter up into small pieces.*) Never play this sort of trick on me again as long as you live. If you have any more of these bouts of conscience, or— whatever it is—come and tell me—but for the love of God don't send me any more notes by any more chambermaids. I've had the worst morning of my life. (*He turns his back on her and lights his cigarette with unsteady fingers.*)

PATRICIA: Try and understand, Pete, I'm not doing this for fun.

    PETER *turns.*

PETER: Doing what?

PATRICIA: Leaving you.

    There is a pause. PETER *stares at her unbelievingly.*

PETER: Shut up, Pat, don't talk nonsense.

PATRICIA: I'm leaving you, Pete.

    PETER *puts his cigarette out and takes a step towards her.*

PETER: Why?

PATRICIA: I've told you. Teddy needs me.

PETER: Do you think I don't?

PATRICIA: He's my husband.

PETER (*bitterly*): That's very good. (*He turns away, obviously trying hard to control himself. When he turns back to face her, he tries to smile.*) In your letter you say that it's your duty to stay with your husband. You did say duty, didn't you?

PATRICIA: I don't know, I can't remember.

PETER: You did say duty. Your duty to him, or to me, or to yourself, or to your country, or to what—what does duty mean anyway? I'm sorry, Pat, I don't understand, really I don't.

PATRICIA: I didn't think you would, Pete.

PETER: I know you don't feel anything for him, you've told me so.

PATRICIA: Did I?

PETER (*he looks at her startled, then walks up to her*): What was it you found out last night?

PATRICIA: I can't tell you. It wasn't only about Teddy, it was something about myself, too, something I didn't know before. (*Desperately*.) I can't explain myself, Pete, I told you I wouldn't be able to.

PETER (*urgently*): You've got to try.

PATRICIA: I can't—I can't.

She turns to go. PETER goes quickly up to her and turns her round to face him.

PETER: You must explain yourself. You're leaving me. Why?

PATRICIA *says nothing.*

You're leaving me. Do you understand what that's going to mean to me? This isn't some ordinary little intrigue that can be smashed in a second, this is something that's vitally important.

PATRICIA: No!

PETER: What?

PATRICIA: This isn't important. We thought it was, but it isn't, not now anyway. That's one of the things I found out last night. (*She stops uncertainly*.)

PETER (*quietly*): Go on.

PATRICIA: I was awfully sure about things until last night. I had made a fool of myself once before, that time I ran away from you, because of conventions and what other people said and thought. I made up my mind, never again. You know that. I used to think that our private happiness was something far too important to be affected by outside things, like the war or marriage vows.

PETER: Yes it is, Pat, far too important.

PATRICIA: No, it isn't, Pete, beside what's happening out there (*she points to the window*); it's just tiny and rather—cheap—I'm afraid. I don't want to believe that. I'm an awful coward. It may be just my bad luck, but I've suddenly found that I'm in that battle, and I can't——

PETER: Desert?

PATRICIA: Yes, desert.

PETER: Very heroic.

PATRICIA: I'm sorry if it sounded like that. Heaven knows it's far from the truth.

PETER (*after a pause*): Pat, listen to me. You say you love me. I know that's true. I love you too, but more than that, I need you so much that if you go away from me now I just don't know what I'm going to do. That's not a line, Pat, the sort of thing one says at a moment like *this*, it's true—I just don't know what I'm going to do.

PATRICIA: Oh, Pete—— (*She takes his shoulders.*)

PETER: Come with me, Pat, we'll go away, we'll forget about Teddy——

PATRICIA (*moves away*): No.

> *There is a long pause.*

PETER (*at length*): Haven't you forgotten something?

PATRICIA: What?

PETER: I'm desperate, Pat. I'll do anything in the world to stop you leaving me.

PATRICIA (*stating a fact*): No, Pete, you wouldn't do that.

PETER: Where's Teddy?

PATRICIA: Upstairs.

PETER: Will you go up now and tell him that you're coming away with me? (*Calling.*) Percy!

> *PERCY appears.*

PERCY: Sir?

PETER: Go and tell Flight Lieutenant Graham that I'd like to see him.

PERCY: Yes, sir. (*He goes to the stairs.*)

PETER: Tell him that it's important.

PERCY: Yes, sir, I'll tell him.

> *PERCY goes out.*

PATRICIA (*quietly*): I could deny it, you know.

PETER: It won't be difficult to prove.

PATRICIA: Whatever you tell him won't force me to leave Teddy.

PETER: Won't it? I think that's for Teddy to say.

> *There is a pause.*

PATRICIA: You won't do it, Pete.

> *SWANSON comes in through the front door.*

SWANSON: All ready, Mrs. Graham? Haven't been long, have I?

> *PATRICIA, staring at PETER, turns her head slowly.*

PATRICIA: What? No, you've been very quick.

> *PERCY runs down the stairs.*

PERCY: Flight Lieutenant Graham's in his bath, sir. Says he'll be down directly.

PETER: Right. Thank you. (*He throws him half a crown.*)

PERCY: Thank you, sir. Thank you.

> *PERCY goes out.*

SWANSON: Well, we'd better get weaving, or we'll find this chemist feller has gone to lunch.

PETER: I don't think Mrs. Graham's going with you, after all. Are you, Mrs. Graham? Didn't you say you had to stay in?

> Pause. PATRICIA *reaches for her coat.*

PATRICIA: No, I'm not staying in. I must get that stuff for Teddy.

> SWANSON, *a little puzzled, holds the door open for her.*

SWANSON: I can get it for you, quite easily, you know— if you'd rather stay behind.

PATRICIA: Thank you, but I'd rather come with you.

> PETER *is staring at her.* *She meets his eyes for a brief instant, then turns and goes out quickly.* SWANSON *follows her.*
>
> PETER, *left alone, lights a cigarette.* DUSTY's *and* MAUDIE's *voices can be heard outside.* PETER *goes to the window-seat.* DUSTY *and* MAUDIE *come in.*

DUSTY: Aunt Ella's all right if you treat 'er all right. There's nothing wrong with Aunt Ella.

MAUDIE: *You* don't have to live with her, Dave.

DUSTY: You need tact, Maudie, that's all, just a bit of tact.

MAUDIE (*firmly*): You need a frying-pan—that's what you need.

DUSTY: That's the wrong attitude. What I say is—— (*He catches sight of* PETER *in the corner.*) Oh, good morning, sir.

PETER (*shortly*): Good morning.

DUSTY: Nice day, isn't it?

> MAUDIE *has walked across the stage towards the stairs, which she is now mounting.*

Where you going, Maudie?

MAUDIE: Up to our room. I've got my packing to do.

DUSTY: Heavens, Maudie, you don't want to pack yet. You've got loads of time. Bus doesn't go till one.

MAUDIE: I don't want to miss it, Dave.

> DUSTY *chases her up the stairs.*

DUSTY: You won't miss it, Maudie, that I promise.

MAUDIE: If I don't get packed I will miss it.

DUSTY: But you 'aven't got nothing to pack, bar one nighty and a toothbrush——

> MAUDIE *disappears.*

(*To* PETER.) Women?

> DUSTY *goes out.*
>
> PETER *gets up and walks across to the lounge door.* DORIS *appears on the landing.*

DORIS: Mr. Kyle?

PETER *turns.*

PETER: Yes?

DORIS: Are you good at languages?

PETER: I know French and Spanish and some German.   Why?

DORIS: Can you tell me what language this is written in? (*She hands him a letter.*)   It isn't Polish, that's all I know.

PETER (*glancing at letter*): It's French.   (*He hands the letter back.*)

DORIS: Yes, of course.   He spoke French like he spoke Polish.   I suppose he thought it'd be easier for me to get translated.

PETER: It's from your husband?

DORIS: He left it with me.   I was only to read it if something happened to him.   Funny—it's the only letter I've ever had from him.   (*She looks at letter, knitting her brows.*)   You know French. Will you read it for me?

PETER: Do you mind?   I'd rather not.

DORIS: Oh, don't worry.   I'll get someone else.

PETER *takes the letter from her.*

PETER: Sorry.

DORIS: Thanks, Mr. Kyle, dear.   Sorry if it's a bother. If there's anything in it that's—well—you know—you won't tell anyone, will you?

PETER: No.

DORIS: Of course you wouldn't.   O.K., dear.   Go ahead.

PETER: It begins: "It will be necessary for you——"

DORIS: Doesn't he start with dear Doris, or anything?

PETER: No.

DORIS: The French for dear is chère, isn't it?   That's the only French word I know.· All right, go on.

PETER (*translating slowly*): "It will be necessary for you to translate"—no—"to have this letter translated.   I do not yet express myself in your language well enough to say what I wish to say to you.   I am not able to leave you without telling you what your kindness and devotion have meant to me——"

DORIS: Silly.

PETER: —"Since the murder of my wife and boy in Varsovie"— that's Warsaw.

DORIS: The Nazis machine-gunned them on the road, just as they were leaving——

PETER: "I did not think to feel"—it's rather difficult this.   I think he means: "I did not think I would feel any human emotion again"—that's not quite right, I'm afraid.

DORIS: I know what he means.   Go on.

PETER: "I came to your country with only one thought, to continue to fight against the Germans until I myself found the death in battle which I—have—sought—for a long time.   It is not always easy, living in a strange country whose manners—whose customs and language and humour I could not understand.   At first it seemed intolerable—and would have been so if I had not had the—blessed—good fortune to meet you, my beloved wife——"

DORIS: Chère?

PETER: No.   Bien-aimée—well-loved.

DORIS: I see.   Go on.

PETER: "I found in you what I had lost in Warsaw—I had thought for ever—an—understanding and a sympathy"—sympathie means something a little different to sympathy.   It's rather hard to translate.

DORIS: I think I know what it means.

PETER: "—an understanding and a sympathy so strong"—powerful—"that the words we neither of us could speak did not need to be spoken.   I can only thank you with a full heart—and it is with real sorrow that I take my leave of you now.   I would have so much wished to have repaid you for the sacrifice you made for my sake, in giving up your career—as hotel-keeper——"

DORIS: Hotel-keeper?

PETER: Hotelière.

DORIS: I was a barmaid, dear.   I was behind the bar when I first met him.   The Crown at Pulborough.   He came into the public bar one night and said he was lost, only nobody could understand him.   I walked with him as far as where he was going.   When he said good night he kissed my hand.   He came into the Crown a lot after that—always the public bar, I don't know why.   Hotel-keeper.   That's Johnny all over.   Sorry, dear.   Go on.

PETER: "I would have so much wished to have repaid you for your sacrifice—by taking you with me, after the war, to Poland, where I might, in some very small measure, have been able to make a return to you of the material debt I owe you: the other debt I can never repay.   Good-bye, my dear, dear wife.   I love you for ever."

PETER *finishes translating, folds the letter up, puts it back into the envelope and returns it to* DORIS.

DORIS: Ta.   (*She puts the letter in her bag and gets up.   She blows her nose furtively, and walks to the stairs.*   PETER *lights another cigarette, purposely not looking at her.*

DORIS: I shan't forget the way you did that. You made it sound very nice. (*She reaches the landing.*) You didn't make up that last bit, did you?

PETER: No. It's in the letter. You can get anyone to translate it for you.

DORIS: Thanks, dear. Just so long as I know.

DORIS *goes out.*

MRS. OAKES *enters from coffee-room, some sheets over her arm. She bends down at the foot of the stairs and picks up the scraps of paper which* PETER *had torn up in his scene with* PATRICIA.

MRS. OAKES (*clicking her teeth disapprovingly*): What's this? A paper-chase?

PETER: They're mine. (*He takes the scraps of paper from her and stuffs them in his pocket.*)

MRS. OAKES: Waste paper receptacles are provided, Mr. Kyle. Besides, there's such a thing as salvage, you know.

PETER: I'm sorry. It was very untidy of me.

MRS. OAKES *goes up the stairs, meeting* TEDDY, *who comes running down, dressed in ordinary uniform—not battle-dress.*

TEDDY: Hullo, you old dusky enchantress. We made rather a hole in your bacon and eggs last night, eh?

MRS. OAKES *glances round hurriedly at* PETER.

MRS. OAKES: By which you mean the sausages, I suppose.

TEDDY: That's right. The sausages. Delicious.

MRS. OAKES: I'm glad you liked them, I'm sure.

MRS. OAKES *goes up the stairs and out.*

TEDDY (*to* PETER): You wanted to see me about something, didn't you?

PETER: Yes, I did.

TEDDY: Any objection if I order a beer first. I've got a thirst on.

PETER: Go ahead.

TEDDY: Anything for you?

PETER: No, thank you.

TEDDY *goes to lounge door.*

TEDDY: A somewhat boozy type, old Graham, I'm afraid. (*Calling.*) Hey, Percy. Bring me a beer, and jump to it!

PERCY (*off*): Yes. Mr. Graham, sir.

TEDDY (*to* PETER): Bad show about Johnny, isn't it?

PETER: Yes. I'm very sorry.

TEDDY: He was good value, old Johnny. One of the very best.

(*Pause.*) They're a bit different from us, these Poles, you know. Crazy types, most of them.   They're only really happy when they're having a crack at Jerry.

PETER: The same doesn't apply to you?

TEDDY: Not exactly.   I'm quite ready to admit we sometimes find it a bit of a bind.

PERCY *comes in with a half-pint of beer.*

Well, bung-ho!   (*He takes a gulp of beer.*)   Chalk it up, Percy.

PERCY: Yes, sir.

PERCY *goes out.*

TEDDY: O.K., Kyle.   Shoot.   Give us the five-second burst.

PETER *does not reply.*

Go ahead.   What have you got to say to me?

PETER: Nothing.

TEDDY: What do you mean—nothing?

PETER: Nothing.   Just good-bye.   I'm leaving this morning.

TEDDY: Oh, sorry to hear it.   Percy told me it was something important.

PETER: He must have got it wrong.   It's quite unimportant.

TEDDY (*contrite*): I say, I'm most frightfully sorry.   I didn't mean that, you know.   I mean, you'll be coming down again, won't you?

PETER: No.   I'm leaving on the Clipper within a few days. You won't see me again.

TEDDY: Wish I was a film star.

PETER: Do you?

TEDDY: Dashing madly about all over the world, pursued by fans, making pots of money, glamorous females hurling themselves at you wherever you go.

PETER: It's not so much fun as it sounds.

TEDDY: Not exactly a bind, though.   I say, I nearly forgot. (*He fumbles in his pockets and produces a note-book.*)   You've got to write something in my book.

PETER: I'd rather not, if you don't mind.

TEDDY. What do you mean, you'd rather not?   I'll take it as a personal affront.

PETER: It's only that I don't know what to say.

TEDDY: Say anything—preferably something I can shoot a line about.   You know—to my life-long buddy—or—to the whitest man I ever knew—no, what about—to Teddy Graham, dauntless eagle of the skies, from his humble admirer and friend——

PETER (*suddenly losing control*): For God's sake, shut up!

> TEDDY *starts. There is a pause.*

TEDDY: Sorry. Only my warped sense of humour, you know.

> PETER *snatches the book, scribbles something in it hurriedly and returns it to* TEDDY.

TEDDY: Thanks a lot. (*He reads it.*) Oh, thanks. Between you and me I never know what that means, although it's the Air Force motto.

PETER: I don't know what it means. either.

> TEDDY *puts the note-book away.*

Sorry for the outburst. I don't feel too well this morning.

TEDDY (*sympathetically*): You don't look any too well. Hardly the smooth, glamorous lover of the screen. (*He puts a hand over his mouth.*) Sorry. Is that a brick?

PETER: Yes. I'm getting old, you see, Teddy, and that's something I don't care to be reminded of.

> *A car door slams outside, and* PATRICIA *comes in. She stands just inside the door.*

TEDDY: Hullo, darling. Did you get that stuff?

PATRICIA: Yes. It wasn't what you asked for, but the chemist said it was just as good. (*She hands him a packet.*)

TEDDY: Thanks most awfully. Kyle's leaving us this morning. Did you know?

> PATRICIA *looks at* PETER.

PATRICIA: Yes. He told me.

TEDDY: He's off on the Clipper in a couple of days. Lucky type, isn't he?

PATRICIA: Yes.

> TEDDY *occupies himself with his beer. There is a pause.* PETER *turns abruptly and makes for the stairs.* MRS. OAKES *comes down simultaneously.*

PETER (*to* MRS. OAKES): Can you get me a car?

MRS. OAKES: Yes, Mr. Kyle. When do you want it?

PETER: As soon as possible.

MRS. OAKES: I'll do my best.

> PETER *goes out.*

He looks ill—Mr. Kyle. Is anything the matter with him?

TEDDY: It's that dinner you gave him last night, I expect.

MRS. OAKES: Indeed it isn't. I had the rissoles myself, and there's nothing wrong with me.

TEDDY: We haven't all got your cast-iron stomach.

MRS. OAKES: Flight Lieutenant Graham! (MRS. OAKES *goes out.*)
    TEDDY *kisses* PATRICIA *on the cheek.*

TEDDY: You don't look any too well yourself this morning.
Do you feel all right?

PATRICIA: Oh, I'm all right. When will you be flying again?

TEDDY: Don't know. Not for two or three days, anyway.
They'll be working on that tail-plane of ours. Next time I go on a
trip, I suppose you'll be back in London.

PATRICIA: No, I won't.

TEDDY (*spluttering into his beer*): Don't give me heart failure.
You mean you're going to stay down here?

PATRICIA: Yes, Teddy, if you want me to.

TEDDY: Don't be an utter clot, darling! If I want you to!
God, how marvellous! How long will you stay?

PATRICIA: For good.

TEDDY: For good—but what about your new play? Aren't you
starting rehearsals next week?

PATRICIA: No, I'm not going to do it. I'm turning it down.

TEDDY: You'll give up the flat?

PATRICIA: Yes.

TEDDY: Oh, boy! Yippee! (*He vaults into the sofa.* PATRICIA
watches him, unsmiling. TEDDY *pulls himself up short, a trifle crest-
fallen.*) I say, Pat—you're not doing this because of—because of——

PATRICIA: No, Teddy. I want to stay with you. (PATRICIA *has
been unwrapping the parcel from the chemist. She approaches* TEDDY *now
with a bandage and a bottle of iodine.*) I think I'd better do this now.

TEDDY: All right, nurse. (*He bares his wrist.*) I warn you I shall
scream.

    PATRICIA *dabs iodine on his wrist.*

PATRICIA: Sorry.

TEDDY: It doesn't hurt at all. (*Suddenly.*) Ow! D.A.

PATRICIA: D.A.?

TEDDY: Delayed action.

    PATRICIA *begins to bandage the wrist.*

PATRICIA: I'm not very good at this, I'm afraid.

TEDDY: You're much too beautiful to be good at bandaging.

PATRICIA: Teddy?

TEDDY: Yes, darling?

PATRICIA: You have been rather a fool, you know.

TEDDY: Have I?

PATRICIA: We've been married nearly a year now.

TEDDY: You're telling me.

PATRICIA: We don't know each other awfully well, do we?

TEDDY: No, I suppose we don't—at least I know you all right—every little bit of you—but I admit I have been a bit of a dark horse with you. But now, after last night——

PATRICIA: Last night isn't enough. It's not enough unless you go on telling me things—unless you——

TEDDY: What?

PATRICIA: Unless you treat me more like a wife and less like a show-piece.

TEDDY (*shocked*): Show-piece?

PATRICIA (*slowly*): Suggested that Flight Lieutenant Graham shall in future be permitted to mention his wife's name not more than —how many times—per diem—ten—was it?

TEDDY: Oh, Gawd! How did you hear about that?

PATRICIA: It doesn't matter.

TEDDY: I'll kill Gloria.

PATRICIA. No, don't. He thought—I'd be pleased. I was too —in a way—but—well, you see what I mean, don't you?

TEDDY: God! Tear me off a strip, I deserve it.

PATRICIA: No, you don't. It's not really been your fault; at least it's been much more mine than yours.

TEDDY: Oh, darling, what utter bilge! It's not been your fault at all.

PATRICIA: It doesn't much matter whose fault it's been, Teddy, does it, providing we both make a bit of an effort from now on? There—— (*She finishes bandaging and stands up.*)

TEDDY: Thanks awfully. Darling, talking about show-piece. Well, when I first asked you to marry me, I never thought you'd say yes, and when you did I could never quite believe there hadn't been a mistake somewhere. And so I've always been a bit scared of you. And when we've been together, I've always been afraid of boring you—and so I tried awfully hard not to bore, and so, of course, I always did bore you—and that is why show-piece is just about right, I suppose. But now, after last night, well——

PATRICIA: Go on, Teddy.

TEDDY: Well, it's just that I do love you—and I don't know—somehow, I'm not scared of you any more.

Dusty and Maudie come down the stairs, Dusty carrying Maudie's suit-case.

TEDDY: Morning, Sergeant. How's the old tum?

DUSTY: Not so bad, sir. Feels 'ellish empty, though.

TEDDY: Needs refuelling, I expect. Hullo, Mrs. Miller. How are you this morning?

MAUDIE: Very well, thank you, Mr. Graham. Dave and I went for a walk, and he showed me your Wellington.

TEDDY (*startled*): What? How did you get her past the guards?

DUSTY: She only saw it from the road, sir. It's still out at dispersal.

MAUDIE (*accusingly*): Did you know that it's got a big hole in its tail?

DUSTY (*hastily*): 'Course he knew, Maudie. He's only the jolly old skipper.

MAUDIE (*firmly*): Yes, but you told me that he sits up there in front. He might not have known what was going on at the back.

TEDDY: I don't usually, Mrs. Miller, but as a matter of fact I did know about the hole.

MAUDIE: I thought you ought to know, Mr. Graham; that's why I told you. It looks very dangerous—a great big hole like that.

TEDDY: Thank you, Mrs. Miller. You were quite right to tell me. We're going to have it seen to.

MAUDIE: I'm very glad to hear it.

DUSTY: You must forgive my wife, sir. I'm afraid she don't know much about aircraft.

TEDDY: That's all right, Dusty. My wife doesn't either.

MAUDIE: I do know about aircraft—I know which are ours—which are theirs.

TEDDY: I wish Dusty—Dave—were as hot on aircraft recognition.

During the last few lines the front door has opened quietly and the COUNT *has been standing just inside the door, taking off his flying jacket. He is in full flying kit, dishevelled, dirty and damp. He waits patiently for a lull in the conversation before launching himself into speech.*

COUNT: Is—please—my wife—in home?

TEDDY (*with a shout*): Johnny!

They all move towards him.

Johnny, you old sod! Is it really you? Are you all right?

COUNT: Yes—please—sank you.

DUSTY (*shaking his hand*): Good show, Count, old cock, old cock!
Good show, sir!

TEDDY (*calling*): Doris——

PATRICIA (*stopping him quickly*): Don't! I'll go and tell her.
It's better. (*She runs up the stairs.*)

TEDDY (*deliriously*): Johnny, you wicked old Pole! What in
hell have you been up to? Tell us what happened, Johnny. Where
have you been?

COUNT: Please—we fall in se drink.

TEDDY: Yes, I know you fall in the drink. How did you get out
of the drink? That's what I want to know.

COUNT: Please—I tell you——

SWANSON *comes bursting in through the front door.*

SWANSON (*shouting*): Johnny, you old bastard! Are you all
right? What happened? (*To* TEDDY.) The whole of his ruddy
crew are just piling off a lorry at the guard-room—all jabbering like
monkeys—and the only thing we can get out of any of them is—
"Please we fall in se drink."

TEDDY: That's all we can get out of Johnny up to now.

DUSTY: We haven't given him much of a chance yet, sir.

TEDDY: Quite right. Quiet, everyone! Come on, Johnny.
The floor is yours. You fall in the drink. What happened then?

COUNT: We—land—pumkek.

TEDDY: Pancake. Yes——

COUNT: We—not hurt—not much. We go pouf——

SWANSON: You go pouf?

COUNT (*helplessly*): We go pouf.

TEDDY: I've got it. They inflate their rubber dinghy.

COUNT: Dinghy—yes. We—— (*He makes gesture of rowing.*)

TEDDY: Spot a ship?

COUNT: No.

DUSTY.: Swim.

COUNT (*repeating gesture*): No, we——

SWANSON: Ah, row.

COUNT: Yes, sank you—we raow sree hour—see Lysander—far
—far—make hola!—No good.

TEDDY: Pilot was having his lunch.

COUNT: We raow—anosser two hour—sen—get out——

SWANSON: Get out? Out of the dinghy? Why?

COUNT: We walk please.

SWANSON: You can't ruddy well walk. You're in the ruddy water.

COUNT: Yes, please. We walk in se ruddy water.

DUSTY: They wade ashore, sir.

COUNT: We see—a pheasant.

SWANSON: What's a pheasant got to do with it? You saw a pheasant on the beach?

COUNT: Not—on—beach. By—gottage.

SWANSON: I still don't see——

TEDDY: He means peasant.

COUNT: Yes, please—in gottage—no telephone. At first—pheasant—peasant—not—understand—'e sink we 'ave parachutes—se enemy—but when 'e see Poland (*he points to the lettering on his arm*) 'e find anosser peasant——

SWANSON: Pheasant.

COUNT: —anosser pheasant wiss big motor. 'E drive us. I see telephone near road. I make to stop and try telephone se aerodrome. I say—please Milchester 23. Zey say—please, sree hour delay, Winchester. I say—Milchester, please. Zey say—yes, please, Winchester. I say—bloody nuts and we go on.

TEDDY: And here you are, please?

COUNT: Yes, sank you.

TEDDY: Good old Johnny!

> DORIS *comes down the stairs.* The COUNT *walks across to her and kisses her.*

DORIS: Hullo, ducky. So you've come back to me.

COUNT (*kisses her hand*). You worry, no?

DORIS (*smiling*): Oh, no. Where have you been?

COUNT: Please—I fall in se drink.

DORIS: Yes, I know, but what happened then?

TEDDY (*imploringly*): Doris—have a heart. He's only just finished telling us the story.

SWANSON: Yes. They all went pouf, and were picked up by pheasants. All sorts of fun and games.

DORIS: I'll make him tell me the story later. Only it had better be good Johnny ducks, after all you've done to me.

> *There is a sudden shriek from* MAUDIE.

MAUDIE: My bus!! I missed it.

DUSTY: Cor! So you 'ave.

SWANSON: Doesn't matter, Mrs. Miller. We can't bother about buses at a moment like this.

MAUDIE: But I have to bother——

SWANSON: I'll drive you into Lincoln this afternoon.

MAUDIE: That's very kind of you, I'm sure, but I'm going to St. Albans.

SWANSON: Or, better still, Grantham.   Plenty of trains from there.

TEDDY: Don't worry, Mrs. Miller.   We'll get you to St. Albans, if we have to fly you there and drop you by parachute.

MAUDIE (*doubtfully*): I'd rather have gone by bus.

TEDDY: This calls for the party of the century.   Percy!

> PERCY *enters.*

PERCY: Cripes, the old Count!   (*Rushes to him.*)   Coo, I'm glad you're back.   Where have you been?

COUNT: Please, I fall——

TEDDY
SWANSON } He fall in se drink.

TEDDY: Percy!   Pints for everyone.   We'll come and help you. Come on, Dusty.   Come on, Gloria.

> SWANSON, TEDDY *and* DUSTY *make for the bar.*

DUSTY (*going*): I won't be a tick, dear.

MAUDIE: But, Dave, my bus!

DUSTY: As far as your bus goes, you've had it. (DUSTY *goes into bar.*)

> DORIS *and the* COUNT *go towards bar.   They stop to kiss.*   MRS.
> OAKES *comes out of her office.*

MRS. OAKES: Good gracious, the Count!   Well, this is a nice surprise.   We'd quite given you up.

> *They shake hands.*

TEDDY (*coming out*): Gin and lime for you, Doris?

DORIS: Yes, please.

> (*They move to the bar.*)

COUNT: Please, I am dirty to go in there.

DORIS: You're filthy, to go anywhere, Johnny.   But I shouldn't worry just this once.

> PERCY *has come out with two pints.   He puts them on table, right.*

PERCY: Countess, what about Bele now?

DORIS: Of course it was Bele.   Thank you ever so much.   (*She hugs* PERCY *and cries on his shoulder.*)   Silly, crying when he's come back.

PERCY: 'Course not, it's only natural.

DORIS: Well, here he is.

PETER *appears on the landing and begins to come downstairs.*

PERCY: No, you keep him.   Never did me any good.

DORIS: Thanks, Percy.   I think I will.   You never know.

They go into bar.

DUSTY *and* SWANSON *come from bar, each carrying a pint, and* DUSTY *has a port for* MAUDIE.   PETER *has got to the desk.* MRS. OAKES *appears.*

MAUDIE: Dave, I don't think I should.

DUSTY: Go on, Maudie.   You'll need a few ports if you're going to be dropped by parachute.   Won't she, sir?

SWANSON: Well, Mrs. Miller, here's fluff in your latchkey!

MAUDIE: Fluff in yours!

TEDDY *runs in from bar to foot of stairs.*

TEDDY: Pat!   Pat!   Come on down.   You don't know what you're missing.   Come on, Kyle!   (*He runs back to bar.*)

DUSTY *and* SWANSON *are whispering together.*

MRS. OAKES (*to* KYLE): You'll notice I haven't charged you for the breakfast after all.

PETER: Yes, I see.   Thank you very much.   (*Pays bill.*)

MRS. OAKES: By the way, I trust you left the Wing Commander's things just as they were?

PETER: Yes, I was very careful.

PATRICIA *appears on landing.*

MRS. OAKES: You could have had No. 2 for to-night.   I'm sorry you're leaving us so soon.

PETER I'm afraid.   (*Pauses as he sees* PATRICIA.)   I had no choice. (*He gets his hat off stand.*)

MRS. OAKES: Good-bye and thank you.

PETER: Thank you.

MRS. OAKES *goes into office.*

PATRICIA (*from stair*): Good-bye.

PETER: Good-bye, Mrs. Graham.   (PETER *goes out.*)

SWANSON *whispers to* MAUDIE.   *She giggles.* PERCY *enters with another port for* MAUDIE.   *Singing is heard in the bar.*

PERCY: Talk about George Formby!

MAUDIE (*taking port*): Tinkerty-tonk.

SWANSON: Tinkerty-tonk!

TEDDY (*enters from bar*): We're making old Johnny sing.   Come on, Johnny!

DORIS *pushes him into room.*

TEDDY: Go on, Johnny.   Try again.

COUNT: Oh, no, please.   I sing so bad.

DORIS (*calls out*): Come on, Percy!   Come on, Fred!   Come and hear Johnny sing.

ALL *come on, carrying pints.*

SWANSON: Go on, you old clot.

DUSTY: Go on, sir.

TEDDY *makes* JOHNNY *get up on centre table.*

COUNT (*Sings, helped for the first line by the others*):

> I don't want to join the Air Force,
> I don't want to go to war.
> I'd razzer hang around.
> Piccadilly Underground,
> Living on ze earning of a 'igh-born lady . . .

MRS. OAKES *comes in.* JOHNNY *fades on* "'igh-born lady."

MRS. OAKES (*severely*): Quite, Count!

COUNT (*gets off the table*): Beg pardon, please.   Sey make me sing.

TEDDY: Where's old Kyle?   Let's make him join the party.

PATRICIA (*from the window*): He's gone.

TEDDY: Gone?   Oh, pity!   Still, we can do all right without him.   Come on, darling. (*He holds out his arm to her to join the circle.*)

SWANSON: Now, then, boys and girls!   All together.   Never mind Mrs. Oakes.   She's heard it before.

> We don't want to join the Air Force,
> We don't want to go to war . . .

They sing in unison. PATRICIA *stands still for a moment, watching.   Then she walks forward to join the group.* TEDDY, *singing lustily, puts an arm around her.*

CURTAIN

An Invitation to You!

If you are not already among the many thousands of readers on our mailing list we invite you to send us your name and address. We will then post to you immediately PAN RECORD, our Magazine and Descriptive List of all PAN titles available; and thereafter you will regularly receive future issues and news of PAN Books. Please note that PAN Books should be ordered from any bookseller.

In case of difficulty, write to us.

PAN BOOKS LTD
8 HEADFORT PLACE, LONDON, S.W.1

Famous Plays Series

J. B. PRIESTLEY

Three Time-Plays

(*Dangerous Corner, Time and the Conways*
and *I Have Been Here Before*)

Mr. Priestley, who is acknowledged internationally to be among the best playwrights of our time, explains in a Foreword specially written for this volume that the three plays here included are linked together by interest in the problem of Time: "Each play deals with Time in an unusual way, but not in the same way. Each rejects the ordinary conception of Time, but each offers its own particular solution of the problem."

In *Dangerous Corner* the author assumes the possibility of a split in the time-process, so that from a given moment two alternative series of events are open to his group of people who face a parting of the ways. *Time and the Conways* was inspired by the theory of 'repetitive' Time put forward by J. W. Dunne and called by him 'Serialism.' Finally, *I have Been Here Before* is based on an idea of a 'circular Time' recurring in human existence, although those concerned may with great effort divert the curve of repeated disaster.

Even readers who have little interest in the philosophical aspect of these plays will be enthralled by their dramatic qualities. The characters are such as we meet in our everyday life; the situations are tense and exciting; and the plays, like Mr. Priestley's novels from *The Good Companions* onward, are exceptionally 'readable.' These dramas have been produced with enormous success in many different countries.
(2s.)

THIS IS A PAN BOOK

EMLYN WILLIAMS

The Corn is Green

(with *The Wind of Heaven* and *The Druid's Rest*)

This volume contains three of Emlyn Williams's best-known plays. All have been broadcast several times, and *The Corn is Green* was filmed with Bette Davis starring. There is an autobiographical and sharply Welsh flavour in the plays that adds to their intrinsic interest. The schoolmistress in *The Corn is Green* is based on Emlyn Williams's own teacher at Holywell County School. The landlord of the village inn and his wife in *The Druid's Rest* (the only light comedy Mr. Williams has so far written) are modelled on his own parents, who kept the White Lion Inn, Glanrafon, Flintshire, when he was the same age as the little boy in the play (who is a bookworm obsessed by murder stories). The setting of *The Wind of Heaven*—a retelling, as a sort of nineteenth-century parable, of the story of the young Christ as seen through the eyes of both believers and unbelievers—is again the Welsh countryside of his childhood, which, as he realised on visiting Palestine during the 1939-1945 war, bears a strong resemblance to the New Testament scene.

Emlyn Williams has served the British theatre for twenty years with conspicuous success as actor, playwright and producer. On leaving Oxford University, where he took parts in the productions of the Dramatic Society, he became an actor; in 1930 his performance in an Edgar Wallace play and his staging of his own play *A Murder Has Been Arranged* set him firmly on his three-sided career. He has acted chiefly in his own plays, and also in several well-known films, including his own *The Last Days of Dolwyn*.   (2s.).

THIS IS A PAN BOOK

OSCAR WILDE
Lady Windermere's Fan
(with *The Importance of Being Earnest* and *An Ideal Husband*)

These three brilliant light comedies illustrate all that was best in Oscar Wilde's literary work—they are still unsurpassed for wit, dexterity and 'finish.' Not only were the original productions received with tremendous enthusiasm, but later revivals have met with similar success. *An Ideal Husband* has also been filmed in colour.

(For publication January 1951.)

JOHN GALSWORTHY
Escape
(with *The Eldest Son* and *The Skin Game*)

These three impressive plays display everyday aspects of English social life and ways of thought during, roughly, the first quarter of the present century. In *Escape* Captain Denant, serving a sentence for what was only a serious crime through bad luck, escapes from Dartmoor and asks aid of various people, each of whom reacts differently to the situation. *The Eldest Son* deals with the problem of conventional sex-morality and class tradition. *The Skin Game* shows a quarrel between an old-fashioned and financially hard-pressed landowner and an aggressive *parvenu* manufacturer, leading to tragedy through lack of a spirit of understanding. All three plays finely exemplify Galsworthy's dramatic power, his breadth of sympathy and his gentle humour as a social philosopher.

(Temporarily out of print. Reprint ready Spring 1951. 2s.)

THESE ARE PAN BOOKS